Career Options for Biomedical Scientists

Career Options for Biomedical Scientists

EDITED BY

Kaaren Janssen
Richard Sever

Cold Spring Harbor Laboratory Press

COLD SPRING HARBOR LABORATORY PRESS
Cold Spring Harbor, New York • www.cshlpress.org

CAREER OPTIONS FOR BIOMEDICAL SCIENTISTS

Publisher	John Inglis
Director of Editorial Development	Jan Argentine
Project Manager	Inez Sialiano
Production Editor	Rena Springer
Production Manager	Denise Weiss
Cover Designer	Pete Jeffs

Library of Congress Cataloging-in-Publication Data

Career options for biomedical scientists / edited by Kaaren Janssen, Cold Spring Harbor Laboratory Press, Richard Sever, Cold Spring Harbor Laboratory Press.
       pages cm
   Includes bibliographical references and index.
   ISBN 978-1-936113-72-9 (hardcover : alk. paper)
1. Medical scientists--Vocational guidance. 2. Pathologists--Vocational guidance.
I.   Janssen, Kaaren A., editor of compilation. II. Sever, Richard, editor of compilation.

   R852.C37 2014
   610.28023--dc23
                              2014004892

Contents

1 Introduction, 1
Richard Sever and Kaaren Janssen

2 A Career at a Small Liberal Arts College, 5
Jennifer Punt

3 Core Facility Management, 23
Claire M. Brown

4 Academic Administration, 43
Lydia Villa-Komaroff

5 Careers in Science and Grant Administration: View from the National Institutes of Health, 59
Marion Zatz and Sherry Dupere

6 At the Crossroads of Science and Society: Careers in Science Policy, 77
Amy P. Patterson, Mary E. Groesch, Allan C. Shipp, and Christopher J. Viggiani

7 Working for a Scientific Society, 93
Martin Frank

8 Leaving the Bench and Finding Your Foundation, 109
John E. Spiro

9 Patent Law: At the Cutting Edge of Science, but Not at the Bench, 121
Salim Mamajiwalla

10 Biotech Start-Ups and Entrepreneurship, 135
Susan Froshauer

11 A Career for Life Scientists in Management Consulting, 147
Rodney W. Zemmel

12 Medical Communications: The "Write" Career Path for You?, 159
Yfke Hager

13 Science Journalism and Writing, 177
Helen Pearson

14 Careers in Science Publishing, 197
John R. Inglis

Index, 215

1

Introduction

Richard Sever and Kaaren Janssen

Cold Spring Harbor Laboratory, Cold Spring Harbor, New York 11724

A PhD and postdoctoral work were once considered to be a training route to a permanent academic position, a journey that would culminate in a tenure-track position and, ultimately, stability as a principal investigator at a university or research institute. Some might falter along the way or rethink their career, but most scientists expected to tread the same path that their predecessors trod to tenure.

This is no longer the reality for most science graduates. Universities are awarding more PhDs than ever before, and more than half of these individuals will become postdocs (Cyranoski et al. 2011). However, there has been no equivalent increase in the number of tenured faculty positions at universities and research institutes (Fig. 1). In the 1960s, most scientists who obtained a PhD could expect a permanent academic position. In contrast, only approximately one in four PhDs in the U.S. now translate to a tenure-track position, and even fewer will ultimately result in tenure (National Institutes of Health 2012). In other words, the majority of PhD students will never obtain the tenured post for which many initially believed they were being trained.

Fortunately, there is now increasing recognition within academia that career options once labeled as "alternative" are not in fact the alternative but the norm. Most mentors now also accept that many of their scientific progeny will pursue such options—not because they fail on the road to tenure but because they actively choose careers that offer a different experience and the chance to develop other skills. A PhD is still training for a scientific career but not one as narrowly defined as a research faculty position.

Turning off the track to tenure remains a daunting prospect, however, and there are few ways of finding out about the many other career options available. Scientific societies and institutions occasionally organize career

1

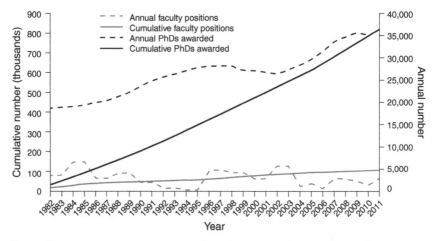

Figure 1. (Black) The increase in the number of PhDs awarded in science and engineering in the U.S. compared with (gray) changes in the number of faculty positions over the same period. (Reproduced from Schillebeeckx et al. 2013, with permission from Macmillan Publishers Ltd.)

discussion sessions or host speakers who have made the transition, but in this book, we comprehensively examine the career options available to biomedical scientists, gathering the perspectives of a group of scientifically trained individuals who have had great success in numerous different professions.

The experiences of the contributors range from jobs that in some respects resemble traditional scientific positions, such as teaching, grant administration, and core facility management, to jobs that require additional formal training, such as patent law, or, in cases such as management consultancy, can take one away from science entirely. In all of the professions featured in the book, individuals who hold PhDs in biomedical sciences are common and, in many of the careers discussed, a PhD and postdoctoral experience are advantageous if not essential qualifications. Nevertheless, it is worth paying close attention to the specifics of each case. Staying on for a postdoc could be an advantage if you wish to work as a journal editor, for example, and it keeps your options open, but it will put you 3–8 years behind many of your new peers if ultimately what you want to be is a journalist.

The first chapters of this book—teaching in liberal arts colleges, core facility management, and academic administration—describe careers that resemble and are related to traditional academic careers in many respects but have a different primary emphasis: the interests of students, a facility, or a department or educational institute as a whole. Those who work for foundations or scientific societies or in science policy or grant administration, the subject of the four subsequent chapters, share some overlap in their activities, but because the missions and constituencies of these organizations differ, the work required does as well. In patent law and management consulting, these interests are clients; in start-ups, they are customers and investors. As the chapters on these subjects make clear, this changes the nature of the work significantly. The last three chapters of this book deal with careers in communication, covering medical communications, science journalism, and scientific publishing. Superficially similar, these all involve writing about science, but the purpose and audience are different in each case; so too are the skills required.

Despite the differences among these professions, however, several common themes emerge. Perhaps most importantly, it is clear that the skills developed in the course of a PhD/postdoc are not wasted: They are directly applicable to these other careers. Critical thinking, problem solving, and the ability to sift through and make sense of a variety of data are as essential to a patent lawyer or a management consultant as they are to a principal investigator. Digesting complex scientific concepts, identifying flaws in the logic of a study, and communicating them effectively are as critical a part of the job of a journal editor as a research professor. And rigorous evaluation of proposed lines of scientific enquiry is just as important to a grant-giving organization as it is to the head of a lab. Job candidates should always remember these parallels. In most cases, when you leave the bench and apply for your first job in a new profession, you will have little or no demonstrable direct experience. But if you can convince an interviewer that your skills are transferable, you will have a foot in the door.

Another common theme throughout the book is that these careers are neither second rate nor second choice. Teaching science at a liberal arts college, for example, is not a consolation for lack of success in research (a strong research program is often essential) but a choice for people who wish to put more time into teaching. Working for a journal or scientific society requires you to increase the breadth of your scientific knowledge, not reduce it. And no one should imagine that mastering the law in addition to molecular biology and genomics makes being a patent attorney an easy way out. All of the professions represented here are extremely competitive, with tens to hundreds of applicants for every entry-level position. Those charged with selecting from this rich pool are disinclined to consider candidates who appear simply to be looking for an easier alternative to life at the bench. For those displaying genuine interest and ability, however, there are opportunities to join organizations that typically provide excellent training and working environments staffed by kindred spirits who have lost none of their love of science.

What should be most encouraging to readers is that the contributors to this book find their jobs so exciting and rewarding. One hears this time and time again from those who have taken these different scientific paths. They delight in their work and rarely express any regret. We hope that this book will help other scientists to choose paths that suit them and that they enjoy similarly fulfilling careers.

REFERENCES

Cyranoski D, Gilbert N, Ledford H, Nayar A, Yahia M. 2011. Education: The PhD factory. *Nature* **472**: 276–279.

National Institutes of Health. 2012. Biomedical research workforce working group report. National Institutes of Health, Bethesda, MD. http://acd.od.nih.gov/biomedical_research_wgreport.pdf.

Schillebeeckx M, Maricque B, Lewis C. 2013. The missing piece to changing the university culture. *Nat Biotechnol* **31**: 938–941.

2

A Career at a Small Liberal Arts College

Jennifer Punt

Haverford College, Haverford, Pennsylvania 19041

A career as a tenure-track professor at a liberal arts college provides the opportunity to combine serious interests in teaching with research. The basic goals of the liberal arts institution are to educate the student broadly while encouraging mastery of a particular area of interest. Preparing for such a career requires not only a commitment to teaching but also a productive PhD and postdoctoral experience, regardless of the expectations for active research within the job. The application and interview processes require one to be informed, flexible, energetic, and clear—in writing and in speaking. Establishing an invigorating teaching and research program will allow you to balance realism and ambition as you find a way to bring the best science to the undergraduate setting. The exposure to students whose thinking is often more unfettered and creative, and to colleagues whose scholarships span many disciplines, makes a position at a liberal arts college one of the most intellectually stimulating careers available to a scientist.

Many young scientists have a keen interest in pursuing a career at institutions that focus on the education of undergraduates. These are referred to formally as baccalaureate institutions (as distinguished from research universities), and the most common institution in this category is the liberal arts college.

Largely an American invention, the liberal arts college offers a broad education to students usually between the ages of 18 and 22. Hundreds of institutions that focus on undergraduates are found within the United States; however, several countries outside of the United States (Britain, the Netherlands, Canada, Japan, etc.) have adopted variants of this model and more are likely to do so. Some U.S. liberal arts institutions are private (e.g., Allegheny College, Pomona College, Reed College), some are public (e.g., The College of New Jersey), some have current connections to religious organizations (Earlham College and the Quakers, St. Olaf's and the Lutheran Church), some have historical connections (Swarthmore and Bryn Mawr College were founded by Quakers), and many are secular (Amherst College). Most are coeducational, but some enroll only women (e.g., Smith, Barnard). Most have fewer than 3000 students, although some are considerably smaller than others (Pitzer College has just more than 1000 students; Wellesley has more than 3000).

In their ideal, liberal arts colleges educate the "whole student," exposing young adults to a breadth of educational opportunities that develop their intellects and prepare them to become thinking, working, governing citizens. This emphasis on breadth is accompanied by requirements for a depth of mastery and scholarship in a major discipline of choice. Although the general, overall mission of most liberal arts colleges is similar, their approaches, philosophies, and emphases vary. This is especially true in the sciences, where the emphasis on and resources for original research differ widely. At one end of the spectrum are colleges that are active undergraduate research institutions, where faculty and students both are expected to continually engage in original scholarly efforts. At the other end, are liberal arts colleges where active research is not a part of job expectations and may not be possible with the available resources. Most fall between these extremes and each college prides itself on an individual philosophy that is reflected in their curricular offerings and hiring preferences.

Regardless of these distinctions, and regardless of the emphasis placed on active research productivity among faculty, applicants with strong research backgrounds and active publication records have a real advantage. A clear commitment to teaching at the undergraduate level is critically important, of course, although the specific type of teaching experience a college will be looking for differs considerably from none to an expectation of formal in-classroom experience. Those who are most successful and happy in a career at any of the liberal arts institutions are those who derive energy from students and classroom engagement, as well as those who find ways to stay active in their fields, in whatever capacity they can.

JOBS

Jobs within a liberal arts college fall within a typical academic structure and are broadly divided into tenure-track and nontenure-track positions (see Fig. 1). Tenure was originally developed to protect a faculty member's

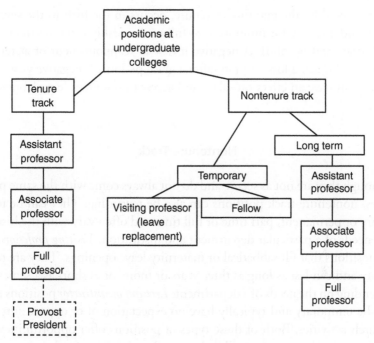

Figure 1. Schematic of academic positions.

position and autonomy from the whims of institutional donors and other decision-making members of an academic community. It is more narrowly perceived as a guarantee of employment for life, although it does not protect individuals for all transgressions. Often critiqued, it can inhibit an institution's ability to respond to professors who are underperforming. However, arguments for its role in protecting academic freedom have trumped many attempts to dislodge it from academic traditions and tenure is likely here to stay for the considerable future.

Tenure Track

The positions along the tenure track provide the most autonomy, the greatest access to institutional resources, and potential job security. They progress from assistant professorships, to associate professorships, to full professorships. The teaching and research performance of all professors is thoroughly reviewed at defined intervals. A reappointment review often occurs in the third year. A review for promotion to associate professor, which is often accompanied by the granting of tenure, occurs in the fifth to the seventh years, and a review for promotion to full professorship often occurs in the 10th year (and beyond). A negative review at reappointment or at tenure review will mean a loss of a job (after a grace period). A negative view after tenure can have an effect on salary and access to resources (e.g., laboratory space).

Nontenure Track

Although they are not as secure and do not always come with the same privileges, nontenure-track positions can also be rewarding. They can be temporary or permanent, part time or full time and often vary with the history and needs of a particular department and institution. *Visiting professorships* are positions that fill sabbatical or maternity leave openings. They are temporary and can last as long as three years or more, or as short as a semester, depending on the needs of a department. *Lecturer or instructor* positions may also be temporary and typically have no expectation of or opportunity for research activities. Both of these types of positions offer opportunities for a young scientist to try on a liberal arts college job "for size."

Some nontenure teaching positions are also long term and virtually indistinguishable from a tenure-track position. These positions are often the products of historical anomaly rather than intentional hiring practices and are less dependable as job options. Each college uses its own terminology for these positions (e.g., "continuing appointment," "regular faculty") and you will have to verify the meaning of these by doing some research and asking questions.

Administration

Finally, faculty members can also assume more administrative positions, particularly in the later stages of their careers. *Department chairs* are usually tenured or full professors. Depending on the institution, these can either be long-term or rotating positions. Department concerns are shared by all faculty, but chairs coordinate the efforts and can take a key role in shaping the direction and ambitions of a department, and in some institutions play an important role in hiring decisions. Most faculties are also headed by a *dean* or *provost*, many of whom started their careers as professors who developed interests (and skills) in administration through their service. These are either selected from the internal faculty ranks or hired from another institution. They oversee faculty hiring, development, and academic programs. *Presidents of colleges* may also have held an academic position at another college or university, and typically have had previous substantive administrative experience (e.g., as a successful provost). They govern all programming and personnel—faculty, staff, and students—and are usually hired by and report to the institutional board of managers.

SKILLS AND QUALIFICATIONS

Perhaps the most frequent question asked by graduate students interested in a career at an undergraduate institution is, "Do I need a postdoc for a job in a liberal arts college?" If you are looking for a tenure-track professorial job, a PhD is absolutely required and postdoctoral experience is highly desirable. Where an active research program is an expectation, a postdoc (of two years or more) is a necessity. Even places where research programs are not as intense, and a postdoc not absolutely required, a strong, active research and publication record will give you a competitive edge as a candidate.

There are several ways to infer a college's expectations of research activity. The institution's own website and that of the relevant science departments reveals much about their educational and research philosophy. The curriculum vitae of its current faculty, which are often available on the website, provide you with an excellent sense of research activity. Look at publication and funding records before and after the arrival of a faculty member to gain a sense of expectations.

College rankings serve as another indicator of research emphasis. These rankings are controversial within the academic world and should be viewed with the kind of scholarly skepticism that you have acquired during your training. *U.S. News and World Report*, perhaps the most influential rating agency, bases its rankings on multiple variables, including faculty and student resources, graduation rates, as well as the more intangible and arguably less reliable "reputation." The top ranked liberal arts colleges on these lists tend to emphasize active research in their programs; however, the correlation is not absolute. Other journals rank institutions differently and can offer additional insights. *The Washington Monthly* ranks institutions on the basis of their "contribution to the public good" and *Forbes* ranks institutions on their assessments of the overall value of the education received (including career prospects and debt incurred). Finally, the perspectives of current students, alumni, and colleagues will round out your understanding of institution expectations.

"What kind of teaching experience do I need to be competitive for a job in a liberal arts college?" is another frequently asked question. The answer also depends on the specific institution as well as the collection of your own experiences and your ability to communicate these. A successful application must clearly convey a genuine and thoughtful commitment to teaching and mentoring undergraduates. It should also provide evidence for teaching potential, which can take many forms, ranging from experience as a teaching assistant in a class as a graduate student, to teaching a class or two in any undergraduate setting, to actually holding a position as a visiting professor at a liberal arts college. Do not underestimate the importance of your teaching statement, which is typically requested as part of your application. In this, you can thoughtfully describe your unique collection of experiences and aspirations as an educator.

Although many successful applicants to liberal arts colleges have never taught a full course or received formal student evaluations, few successful applicants have arrived with no experience with undergraduate research. How do you gain this? Opportunities to teach in a small college setting arise informally, via contacts that you or your supervisor have with college professors, or formally when colleges advertise (typically in the spring) for leave replacements. These visiting professorships provide rewarding and valuable experiences and can enhance your application considerably. However, it is important to recognize that they are designed to be temporary—not as a stepping-stone to a tenure-track position at that institution. If they remove you too long from research momentum, they actually can put you at a competitive disadvantage with other job candidates who are actively publishing at the time of the application. Avoid extending your visit beyond one or two years. Your expectations of and attachment to the institution can easily grow beyond what the position can offer.

Some colleges offer formal *teaching fellowships* specifically designed for postdocs interested in a career with undergraduates. These fellowships are sponsored by the National Institutes of Health (NIH), Howard Hughes Medical Institute (HHMI), and other private organizations (http://www.nationalpostdoc.org/careers/career-planning-resources/186-postdoctoral-teaching-fellowships). The motivation behind their development is impeccable and the experiences can also be rewarding and valuable. However, similar caveats apply. Some teaching fellowships interrupt experimental momentum in ways that are hard to restore, putting you at a disadvantage with other candidates. The best programs are those that support a mentored teaching experience without requiring you to step away from your postdoctoral research training for too long.

"Should I develop a research program in a field that is more easily adapted to an undergraduate setting?" is an insightful question with a relatively simple answer. Although you should certainly be realistic about the resources that are required for research at an institution that does not have the same core facilities as a university, it is also critically important that you avoid shaping your scientific aspirations on the basis of anticipated limitations. Undergraduates can do more than some suspect and ambition is rewarded in the classroom, the laboratory, and if articulated well, among funding agencies. As we will describe below, substantive funding opportunities are, indeed, available to professors at undergraduate institutions. Institutions committed to faculty and student scholarship will also provide internal funding sources.

GETTING A FOOT IN THE DOOR

The most important way to get a "foot in the door" is to apply for the job. Where are jobs at undergraduate institutions advertised? Most institutions will advertise in several places. The *Science* online Science Careers site is one of the best places to look (http://scjobs.sciencemag.org/JobSeekerX/SearchJobsForm.asp). Liberal arts college positions are also listed in the *Chronicles of Higher Education* and can be announced in online and paper publications associated with specific scientific societies. Many institutions want to enhance the diversity of their faculty and will list their jobs on sites that are directed specifically to individuals from underrepresented groups (e.g., http://equity.missouri.edu/recruitment-hiring/resources.php). Finally, word of mouth is powerful: Let colleagues and supervisors know about your interest in this career angle.

What should be included in an application? The requirements are listed in the advertisement and typically include a request for a curriculum vitae, three outside letters of recommendation, as well as both teaching and research statements. It is ideal to get your application in no later than the date specified and to gently but firmly make sure that your outside reviewers also get their letters in on time. Applications that do not include all components may not be reviewed.

Who reviews the applications? The composition of search committees varies from institution to institution. Some are composed predominantly of department members, some include faculty members who are in allied departments in the sciences, and some include faculty outside the science divisions. Many committees at liberal arts colleges include undergraduates too. Each member, regardless of background, has a very important say in the fit of a candidate for a department and a college.

What are they looking for? Again, this depends on the philosophy of the institution, as well as the department; it helps to gain a sense of this before you apply. Regardless, energy, clarity, engagement, and genuine, informed interest are all features of successful candidates. Your teaching and research statements should be thoughtfully prepared and clearly articulated (share them with colleagues before sending them). The best research statements outline several possible projects that will be the basis for an independent scientific career. They also describe how undergraduates could participate in this development and contribute in original ways. They include recognition of the resources required, as well as an interest in developing the funding or support needed to garner those resources and answer the questions that interest you. The best teaching statements describe a candidate's experiences as well as their teaching philosophy. They include clear ideas for courses and approaches you are interested in developing (and why).

Applicants often ask how closely they need to fit the description of an advertisement. If, for instance, you are a biochemist, and the ad describes a position in cellular biology, will your application be considered? The more specific an ad is, the more unlikely it is that an applicant outside the field will be considered. However, if you are in an allied field and can clearly describe your connection to the field(s) described—and if your application is strong—you should certainly send the application in. Successful candidates do not always fulfill every descriptive requirement and a very strong application will be noted.

If you are short-listed by the committee, you will be asked for an interview. Some institutions may whittle a shortlist down even farther via phone interviews. These can be anxiety provoking because you and your interviewers cannot see or "read" each other; however, it is better to view them as liberating. Take advantage of the opportunity to take the call in any environment that you find particularly relaxing. The committee will ultimately offer on-site interviews to two to five candidates, who will usually be asked to prepare a research seminar and a teaching syllabus, or even a class. These candidates will meet with all members of the search committee and department, as well as students.

Prepare your presentations with an awareness of your audience. Will you be speaking to first year students? Majors? A variety? Faculty in the department? Faculty in other departments? Provost? President? If you are asked to give a seminar try to develop one that engages students and faculty who are not experts in your field, but also progresses to a level that would be appreciated by an expert. (This is a tall order, but a rewarding one. Practice!) The question/answer session after the lecture is more revealing than the lecture itself—this is where someone who knows their work and enjoys communicating science to students and faculty will shine, and be revealed to members of the committee.

If you are asked to give a class, develop a short outline, a set of slides, and/or a handout for the students. Do not pack your lecture with too many details or too many slides—give students time to digest a fact and put them into context. Do not be afraid to use a chalkboard or a white board—students often prefer this as an alternative to the rapidity of Power-Point slides. Try to remember that "less is (almost) always more" and perfection is overrated.

What questions should you be prepared for? You are likely to be asked how you would design your research program with undergraduates, how you would contribute to and develop a particular course, and how you might be interested in contributing to other college-wide efforts. You may also be asked how you would help struggling students in a classroom, or how your undergraduate experience might inform your approach, where you think your field is going over the next decade, and what might be the greatest challenges you might face in the position. Do not be afraid to say you "don't know"—praise the question if it inspires you to think of something new and offer a brief, speculative answer. If students are involved, speak to them directly, as colleagues. Show an interest in the questioner and their experiences.

What questions should you ask? Speculative scientific questions that generate discussion are wonderful. But specific questions about the position that show that you are informed, thoughtful, and serious about the job are also welcome. How do professors balance teaching and research opportunities and expectations? How are professors mentored? Are faculty offered leaves? Course releases? How are they distributed? If the college has a robust research program, do students get credit for research in the laboratories? Do faculty get teaching credit for mentoring students in the laboratory? How are students attracted to the laboratories? What internal research resources are there? What external funds have been or can be attracted? Most importantly, questions should be asked out of genuine interest, not anxiety or strategy.

Above all, if you can, enjoy the process. Follow up with thank-yous and then relax. If you do not get the offer, do not take it personally. Those who are offered an interview are not just evaluated for their own prowess but for their academic "fit" in the department—a feature that you cannot always control. Your particular scientific bent or other research emphases may overlap too much with a potential colleague, for instance. Another candidate could unexpectedly synergize or fill gaps in appealing and unanticipated ways. It is impossible to anticipate all. Feel free to call the head of the search committee for feedback, and recognize that being short-listed is a genuine accomplishment.

If you are offered the job, congratulations! You may want to make a return visit with a significant other to determine if you want to take the offer. And you will also have an important opportunity to negotiate for start-up funds and other resources prior to accepting the job—one of the only intervals in an academic career when you truly have the "upper hand." Although you should be gracious and respectful of an institution's limitations, do not be afraid to ask for what you really need. Develop lists of equipment that will really help you develop the best program for you, your colleagues, and your students. If research productivity is an important part of the job, funds to support a research technician for a year and a reduced teaching schedule in your first or second semester can help you hit the ground running.

Most institutions will give you two weeks or so to make a decision; try to respect this time limit.

However, if you are genuinely serious about the job and have real reasons to delay, ask for an extension. Do compare offers, but do not simply use an offer that you are not serious about to enhance another package. Small colleges are part of a small world.

CAREER PROGRESSION

The application process is the first of many evaluations that will span your career as a liberal arts college professor. Typically, you are given a three-year contract as an *assistant professor*; two to three years later, you are reviewed for *reappointment*, a process that determines if your contract is extended for future consideration for tenure. The reappointment process is often used as an opportunity for both you and the institution to enhance or correct your trajectory. If reappointed, you will be assessed for promotion to *associate professor* (which often is accompanied by tenure) sometime between your fifth and seventh year. At least three and often more years after this promotion, you will be assessed for promotion to *full professor*.

Typically, three types of efforts are assessed during each of these evaluations: research progress, productivity, and quality; teaching quality and innovation; and service. Teaching and research are arguably the most important elements of all evaluations, but service (or "citizenship"— contributions on committees, on outreach efforts, etc.) should not be dismissed.

Teaching

No matter how gifted a teacher one may be or have the potential to be, the learning curve in the classroom is very steep; the first two years will be the most exhausting (and exhilarating) as you develop the material you want to teach as well as your classroom delivery. Students are forgiving of occasional lapses in clarity if you are enthusiastic and responsive to their concerns, and bring a sense of self and sense of humor to the classroom. Getting students involved in the learning process is important—and much more easily said than done. "Clicker" technology is attractive to some, but technology is less important than on-the-spot engagement. Interrupting a lecture with a question that you allow students to discuss briefly, asking them to scribble a model or write down an answer to a problem can also involve and invigorate students, even in a large classroom.

Make time for your students. You will be given much advice about setting boundaries. Indeed, protecting your time and striking balances are important. However, the quality of your teaching and your students' education—and arguably your enjoyment of the job—is enhanced by a willingness to engage questions and concerns, sometimes even outside of standard office hours.

Take your students' input seriously—they can often see things more clearly than you and can be more direct in their concerns. Try to avoid feeling defensive and try not to internalize negative comments—dismiss them quickly if they are outliers, but respond to them in the next setting if they resonate with your and others' honest assessments. Enjoy the positive ones, always.

Research

It should be clear by now that research expectations as a liberal arts professor vary widely. Some want you to be funded and actively publishing, although at a lower rate than at research universities. Some do not require active bench research at all. If active research is a requirement, how can you sustain a program without the resources offered by a university? Sheer will is an important first requirement, but other resources facilitate the effort.

Funding

Multiple agencies provide funding specific for faculty from small colleges. National Science Foundation (NSF) offers a Research at Undergraduate Institution (RUI) grant, which is evaluated for quality in the same pool as all other grants, but takes into account differences in resources, publication pace, as well as the educational bonus. The NIH R21 award is another granting opportunity specific for small college laboratories. Both NSF and NIH offer opportunities to fund equipment purchases and welcome proposals from groups of professors. Some scientific societies and private organizations can supplement your students' research goals with smaller awards. Finally, internal funds at some institutions can be a big help, especially early in your career. If your first grant does not succeed, speak to your program director, share your work with colleagues, and try again. Critique often enhances quality.

Institutional Support

Institutional commitment to resources that support research is also invaluable; it is difficult to work in an environment where your ambitions are the exception, even if you have funding. Ideally, institutions serious about research need to offer start-up funds; some existing facilities and the means to keep them up; matching costs for equipment requested in grants; personnel to help with grant preparation, submission, and instrument maintenance; funds for work-study and summer students; and a genuine expectation that all faculty maintain an active research program. In reality, some institutions are in a position to offer more than others. However, even less-well-off institutions can support and inspire excellent research.

Your own efforts are an important part of maintaining research quality, culture, and resources.

Connection to Your Profession

At a small college you are often more isolated from your immediate scientific colleagues, and it is important to maintain contact with your profession. Attend meetings at least once a year, serve on review panels, and give seminars at other institutions. Develop collaborations with colleagues at other universities. And bring your students to your meetings—ask them to present their work. This provides all of you with a unique exposure—and contributes to your balancing act by combining professional and educational ambitions.

Service

Throughout your career, you will be asked to assume department-wide and college-wide responsibilities in addition to your teaching and research efforts. Young professors are typically protected from too much service, which is often performed in committees. However, some committee work is worthwhile, exposing you to colleagues, experiences, and resources that enhance your development as a teacher and scholar. Some also inspire interests and opportunities that shape or alter your career goals. Be a good citizen when you need to be, be selective when you can be, and do not be afraid to embrace opportunities that excite you.

Who will evaluate your performance in these three categories? At each interval, an elected or selected committee of respected colleagues and administrative representatives (e.g., the dean or provost) will review an assembled portfolio of your accomplishments, as well as internal and external assessments of these accomplishments and make a recommendation to the president, who has the final word. Students, departmental colleagues, other faculty, and outside scholars will all be asked for perspectives. The weight given to each input varies with the institution and with the promotion under consideration. Tenure reviews are the most demanding, but in some institutions, reappointment and full professor promotions are as intensive. Familiarize yourself with the requirements and procedures associated with promotion at your institution, but do not overly strategize or politicize the process. High internal standards are often an excellent guide to success.

Balancing Work and Family

Careers at small colleges are considered by many to be "family friendly." It is true that a small institution can provide a community that is both receptive to and nurturing of the "whole faculty member" and their families, and it is also true that the autonomy of the job can provide you the freedom to be flexible with schedules. Nonetheless, it is important to understand that being a faculty member at a small college is a 24/7 job that you cannot easily leave "at work." Your grading, your course development, your mentoring, your research, and your guilt for not reading enough literature will often invade your family life—and vice versa. However, with energy and wisdom, attention to boundaries and flexibility, it can be done and you are likely to discover real rewards in the occasional synergy inspired by raising children and mentoring students. Remember that there is never one "right" time to grow a family; the choice is an important one and a personal one.

WAY OUT

Those who join the faculty of a small liberal arts college and receive tenure often stay in the position for a long time. However, some do pursue other opportunities. Most frequently, senior faculty who have developed administrative skills are attracted to provost or dean positions. Science faculty also assume leadership positions in government and private funding agencies. Some scientists who have maintained a productive professional profile are wooed by other academic institutions—other small colleges, research universities, or pharmaceutical companies. Regardless, the options one has depend on the record you have developed. They narrow considerably if your productivity and/or profile wane, particularly after tenure.

Box 1. My Experience

In an unseasonably cold May of 1996, I was offered a job as tenure-track Assistant Professor of Biology at Haverford College, a small (1200 students) coeducational liberal arts college where the integration of research and teaching is valued highly. I could not have "chosen" a more intellectually stimulating or personally rewarding career, and know I have been very fortunate. From the first, I have been surrounded by ambitious, kind, and intellectually agile students, fascinating colleagues from within and outside the sciences, and a host of opportunities to challenge traditional boundaries.

Viewed from my CV, my route to this position seems linear. I graduated from Bryn Mawr College, with a major in biology at Haverford, where senior research was a requirement for all majors, not simply honors students. I did a research thesis with biochemical bent, and also became fascinated by immunology in an inspiring senior seminar course. I spent a year as a technician in an immunology laboratory at Stanford University, and then pursued a combined (VMD-PhD) degree program at the University of Pennsylvania, becoming a veterinarian and earning a PhD in Immunology. I did my postdoctoral fellowship at the NIH and got the job at Haverford in my fourth year.

However, the CV masks the dilemmas and serendipity that really marked my career progression. My veterinary background was a peculiarity that did not necessarily fit a career at a small college, and as a senior graduate student I seriously considered pursuing an interest in conservation genetics. Instead I was persuaded by an intellectually electric postdoctoral supervisor as well as by a budding relationship with someone whom I would eventually marry to pursue immunology and stay on the east coast.

I was not yet in the "job market" when I received a call from what I now know was a partly desperate search committee at Haverford. They had made an offer that was turned down at the last minute and someone mentioned me as a possible candidate. I leapt at the chance, but knew it was a long shot. They were looking for a biochemist who could teach metabolic pathways. I was an immunologist who had once disliked metabolic biochemistry lectures. As a Haverford biology alum I was greeted with justifiable "suspicion" by newer faculty members concerned that I was driven by nostalgia. At one point, resenting the implication, I said with some pique, "I am coming here to start my career, not end it!" My very first gray hairs appeared after this interview and I was willing to walk away from the opportunity. I was told later that my feisty objection was a turning point in their view of my candidacy.

My NIH supervisor and fellow senior scientists were as distressed by the job offer as I was thrilled. One told me I was ruining my career by going to just a "teaching institution." My postdoc supervisor ultimately came around, however, and gave me some excellent advice. Negotiate for a good salary, he said. Gender-based income inequality can start at the beginning, when men are sometimes more willing to negotiate for higher starting salaries than women; the difference then simply compounds. Indeed, I had been happy to be offered less than I was making as a postdoc, but on his advice negotiated a modest increase.

(Continued.)

The first year at Haverford was the hardest—I do not think I have worked as many hours at any other time of my life. I had a little girl and could only start preparing for lectures after she went to bed. I stayed up until 3:00 a.m. routinely and taught on fumes. But it was also wonderful. I learned more than I ever had as a student and slowly became a real teacher who not only desperately tried to deliver material to an audience, but began to craft it for the students, learning with them day by day. I came to understand that research is and always will be 75% troubleshooting and that pathological optimism is as important a skill as any other in the laboratory. By attending meetings, serving on study sections, taking advantage of collaborations, and by recognizing the talent and insights of my students, we developed a functioning and productive laboratory together. With results, publications, and student presentations at national meetings, I was able to "silence" those in my profession who assumed I would have to "drop out of research." I wrote my first NSF grant and was told it was "too ambitious." I wrote my second grant within two weeks of this news and have been funded ever since, although not without additional gray hairs. I had my second daughter prior to tenure and with the support of loving parents and stepparents, the two girls have grown into wonderful young women who speak with fondness about growing up in and around campus.

I was promoted with tenure in 2001, then to full professor in 2007. I have loved almost everything about the job (except grading) and almost every moment. There are times when the demands are exhausting and I admit that I have rarely taken the good advice about protecting one's time. Yet I credit a willingness to say "yes" for my most fulfilling experiences in the classroom, the laboratory, and with students. The best description I have for this career choice is that it offers you all the freedom in the world, but no time. And I could not recommend it more highly.

Box 2. Ten Dos and Don'ts

---

1. Do engage yourself fully in a postdoctoral research experience.

2. Do apply when you have publication momentum.

3. Do take advantage of teaching opportunities but try not to sacrifice your development as an independent scientist, even if your position will not require active laboratory research.

4. Do become informed about the institution(s) to which you apply—know their resources, ambitions, "mission," and the full nature of the position.

5. Do bring enthusiasm and ambition to your interview, your students, and your job.

6. Do not just say things that you think your interviewers want to hear; be true to yourself and interested in them.

7. Do prepare a job seminar that can reach not only those in your discipline, but also nonscientists and students—and communicate to all why the work really matters and why it inspires you.

8. Do focus on teaching and research, but do not be afraid to say "yes" to other activities when inspired.

9. Do not "strategize" too much when applying for the job or preparing for tenure—your internal standards are often your best guide.

10. Do apply for external funds, remain engaged in your profession outside the college, and do not give up.

WWW RESOURCES

http://equity.missouri.edu/recruitment-hiring/resources.php Resources for recruiting and hiring women and minority faculty candidates, University of Missouri Equity Office.

http://www.nationalpostdoc.org/careers/career-planning-resources/186-postdoctoral-teaching-fellowships National Postdoctoral Association, Postdoctoral Teaching Fellowships.

http://scjobs.sciencemag.org/JobSeekerX/SearchJobsForm.asp AAAS jobs in science and technology from Science Careers.

3

Core Facility Management

Claire M. Brown

McGill University Life Sciences Complex, Advanced BioImaging Facility (ABIF), Montreal, Quebec, Canada H3G OB1

The need for centralized shared core facilities and highly qualified core facility staff is becoming increasingly important in universities, research institutes, and commercial laboratories. With the continued advancement and sophistication of scientific equipment typically comes a larger price tag than can be handled by individual research laboratories. Moreover, the ever-increasing need for researchers to think and act in cross-disciplinary environments, coupled with the increasing sophistication of both the instrumentation and associated technologies, prevents most researchers from becoming "experts" in all areas.

At all levels, core facility positions involve a love of technology, working with people, working on many diverse scientific questions, and days full of multitasking. Entry-level positions include basic and advanced technicians that require a BSc or MSc degree and some experience in the field. Midlevel management positions require experience in the field and an MSc or PhD degree. Management experience is a plus but not always required. Scientific directorship positions require a PhD and a keen interest in the technologies that are typically applied in the director's research program. Associate deans of core resources are often former core managers or scientific directors with a vision for the core and who are strong administrators.

A career as a core facility staff member can be very rewarding. Successful managers and directors must be able to multitask, reassess priorities, and be adept at using logical reasoning to identify and solve issues as they arise. These positions will continue to be available over the long term with the increasing complexity and continued fast pace of technology development.

During the last decade, technology has advanced by leaps and bounds. Researchers are also moving into more cross-disciplinary research programs that involve complementary but highly diverse technologies, making it nearly impossible for principal investigators to keep up with all of the intricate details of the rapidly changing technologies used in their research programs. As technologies become more sophisticated, the cost of implementing them increases. It is rare, therefore, that individual research laboratory budgets can allow a given laboratory to acquire, run, and maintain advanced technological platforms. Most importantly, to implement these technologies to their fullest potential, highly trained PhD-level scientists must be hired, engaged in the research programs, and retained over the long term.

To stay competitive and recruit top scientists, many institutions are moving toward centralized shared facilities in many areas. In some countries, as in the United States, the push for centralized resources comes from the granting agencies themselves through programs such as the National Institutes of Health (NIH) shared instrumentation grants. These grants require researchers to demonstrate need, show that the technologies will support numerous research programs, and show that the institution has the infrastructure and support, including highly qualified personnel, to support state-of-the-art equipment over the long term. This equipment is then required to be placed in accessible centralized facilities. In a relatively unique initiative, the state of Victoria in Australia has developed a state-funded centralized network (Victorian Platform Technologies Network, http://www.platformtechnologies.org) for all biotechnology platforms in the state to maximize the use of shared resources and expertise and to minimize the duplication of costly technology platforms and services across the state. In many other countries, including Canada, initiatives come mainly from groups of researchers who see the need to share resources and, most importantly, highly specialized expertise.

Institutions are recognizing the need for appropriate, clear, and well-defined career paths in order to recruit and retain highly qualified personnel to train, manage, and direct these specialized technology platforms. These positions cannot simply be management or training based, although these aspects are important. Managing scientists should remain engaged in research projects and programs, both to stimulate their scientific curiosity and to keep them involved and current in the technologies that they are supporting. Ideally, core facility scientists should be engaged in grant writing, publishing, experimental design, implementation, and data analysis and interpretation.

Core facilities offer many services for the use of advanced technologies. In a typical consultation between researchers and core facility experts, the experts provide recommendations for the most appropriate core facility technology to address the research in question, as well as how to properly prepare samples and collect, analyze, and interpret data. A brief (30–60 min) meeting typically will save researchers weeks of research time, and information and assistance with the development of proper sample preparation techniques can potentially save months of work. The net result is more rapid results and higher-quality data.

Many core facilities—including microscopy, screening facilities, and cell analyzer technologies in flow cytometer cores—typically operate under a model in which users are trained to use equipment independently. Other centralized technologies—such as fluorescence-activated cell sorting (FACS), next-generation sequencing, and mass spectrometry—often operate with a full service model. For user-trained cores, training is typically conducted one on one by core facility staff, and the researcher, once sufficiently trained, can use the equipment unsupervised. Typical training sessions focus on key aspects of the technology that are specific to the users' need. Another key role of core facilities is training and education, which provide users with opportunities for a more in-depth understanding of the technologies that they are using in their research. Most facilities offer internal and external educational opportunities in the form of one-on-one training, workshops, tutorials, and courses. Several large-scale intensive microscopy-specific training programs exist across North America and Europe. One way to find out about these opportunities is through notices posted on a highly active international confocal listing service (http://lists.umn.edu/cgi-bin/wa?A0=confocalmicroscopy). The name implies that the list server is about confocal microscopy, but it really is a tremendous resource for anything related to light microscopy. The list is archived and searchable back to 1991.

Core facilities must also maintain equipment in a good state of repair and operation, requiring a tremendous amount of time and funding. Service contracts for high-end confocal microscopes, for example, start at ~$20,000 per year/per instrument and can run as high as $30,000–$40,000 per year. In addition, it is crucial for facility staff to clean, service, and monitor instrument performance on a regular basis to detect and deal with problems before they begin to affect user data or result in equipment downtime. In my experience, many issues are not obvious with routine use of the equipment and are not apparent to instrument users, but they can have a severe impact on quantitative data analysis and interpretation (Stack et al. 2011).

There is no sign that technological development will slow down or that the complexity of instrumentation will lessen in the foreseeable future. Therefore, core facility job opportunities will continue to grow during the next 5–10 years.

JOBS

Below, I consider the features and issues of core facilities in general and, in particular, of the microscopy facility, which is my own area of expertise. In fact, the microscopy core facility represents a good model for other facilities.

Core facility positions range from the routine technical to the highly technical to management and scientific oversight. Many entry-level positions can be seen as wonderful training opportunities and do not necessarily require a Master's or PhD-level degree. I have undergraduate students working in my facility and a few graduate students working part time to gain experience in microscopy. The ideal hierarchy for an efficient, well-run core facility is shown in Figure 1. With the expanding number of core technologies, most major U.S. institutions now have a highly trained scientist and administrator in the lead role. However, many institutions are far from this ideal model, with a single core facility staff member taking on all of the management, training, and technical roles. In these cases, the core facility typically is unable to achieve all of the aspects discussed here but can only focus on training and use of existing technologies.

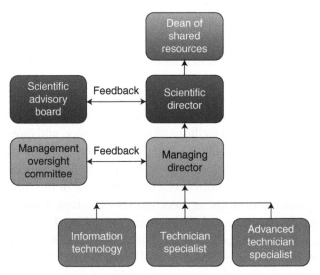

Figure 1. Hierarchy of core facility staff, oversight and administration, and career development paths.

Entry-Level Positions

Entry-level positions will vary with the nature of the core facility and its technology but usually fall under the title of technician, responsible either for the general operation of the equipment or information technology support.

Technician Specialist

The technician specialist assists with the general operation of the core, such as ordering supplies, maintenance and quality control of instruments, and keeping training records up to date. Other responsibilities include basic training on equipment use, data collection, and perhaps data interpretation. Troubleshooting is also expected; that is, addressing questions that users have throughout the day, evaluating and solving problems with equipment, and addressing experimental design issues that arise. Assistance with educational opportunities, such as workshops and courses, is also an important part of this job. This ensures that the specialist stays current on existing and new technologies and learns how to communicate them to facility users.

Information Technology

Information technology (IT) is often undersupported in academic environments, but its importance for a smooth running core, ready access to research data, and support of file processing and analysis cannot be overstated. Most core facilities could not support a full-time IT staff member, but access to 25% of someone's time is a minimum requirement. Four general areas of IT expertise are required to support the facility. First, overseeing database and networking involves monitoring networking equipment and storing and backing up images, databases for instruments such as sequencing information, chemical libraries, RNAi (RNA interference) libraries, and image databases (e.g., high-content screening microscopes). Second, a large role of any core involves data handling; that is, giving researchers access to their data and the software required to analyze the information that they generate on core facility equipment. In microscopy cores, this includes postimage acquisition data processing, so advanced workstations, image processing software, and image analysis software are required. Third, keeping equipment running smoothly involves keeping computer operating systems (MS Windows/Apple OS) running efficiently, routinely updating software interfaces and component drivers, and assuring that these are virus free. The fourth responsibility is development and maintenance of the facility web pages that provide the interface among facility users, management, and technology platforms. This includes fee information, equipment specifics, papers published with data generated by use of the core, and equipment booking and billing software. Having an effective web page is tightly linked to core facility efficiency, appeal, and communication.

Mid Level

Advanced Technician Specialist

The position of advanced technician specialist is similar to the entry-level technician/microscopy specialist but requires more expertise and knowledge of advanced applications, instrumentation, and troubleshooting issues. For example, training experiences for higher-end microscopy systems could involve training in advanced technologies such as fluorescence photobleaching, live-cell microscopy, fluorescence resonance energy transfer (FRET), and multiphoton microscopy. Assistance in developing and implementing educational opportunities would also be a central role in this position.

Manager or Managing Director

The manager or managing director of the core oversees all aspects of the day-to-day operations of the facility and provides staff within the facility adequate supervision and support in order to fulfill their roles within the facility. Importantly, the manager must keep abreast of advances in technology and, together with the scientific director, makes recommendations to the scientific advisory board (Fig. 1) regarding new equipment purchases. The manager additionally consults and works with researchers to determine the appropriate equipment to address specific research questions and assist and guide researchers to develop and implement their experimental designs. Once data is available, the manager may assist users in analyzing and interpreting the data, preparing information for presentations and publications, and presenting preliminary data for grant applications.

The manager oversees basic and advanced training and develops and modifies standard operating protocols (SOPs) or manuals for training sessions, ensures that high-quality training is offered by all facility staff, and ensures the regular maintenance of equipment. In being responsible for interpreting quality control information and initiating repairs and keeping track of repair histories, managers are the key liaison with instrument service departments and must ensure rapid and efficient service to minimize costly instrument downtime.

The manager must ensure that policies are updated to reflect the changing needs and infrastructure, appropriate access to equipment is available for all facility users, and facility users adhere to facility policies and procedures. Oversight of the facility budget, cost recovery system, and monthly and annual reporting is crucial for identifying equipment that is not being used efficiently or is out of date, and for ensuring efficient operation and budget management of the core over the long term. Identification of and application to internal and external funding sources is essential.

The manager must create and develop educational opportunities that cover both the fundamentals of the core technologies as well as the emerging technologies that are relevant for facility users. This includes the development and implementation of workshops, tutorials, and courses. Finally, the manager must initiate and build on corporate relationships with vendors in the field in order to develop partnerships with companies and to have access to appropriate technologies when purchases are being made. This also allows for alpha and beta testing of new state-of-the-art equipment and software and valuable input into how technologies develop.

Upper Level

The two primary positions at the upper division level are scientific director of the facility (a highly trained scientist) and associate dean of shared resources (having primarily administrative duties).

Scientific Director

The scientific director must oversee the core facility operations and the managing director, evaluating reports and working with the manager to ensure efficient operation and oversight of SOPs for training and equipment maintenance and of educational initiatives developed and implemented by the core. The director also is typically engaged in research in the field and should have a vested interest in the maintenance, application, and future development of the technologies. This will ensure that the director has adequate knowledge of the ongoing research and the directions in which the field should move toward in the future. In light of this, the scientific director must keep abreast of technological advances in the field in order to make informed decisions.

A third responsibility is to interact with the scientific advisory board to ensure that the core resources stay current and relevant and also move toward newer state-of-the-art technologies in a timely manner. In turn, the advisory board must ensure that the goals of the scientific director serve the entire scientific community and not just the research area of the director. This is crucial for oversight of core operations and decisions about future equipment purchases. In light microscopy, as in other fields, new technologies carry a considerable price tag and with the diversity of equipment, buying decisions must be strategic and in line with long-term planning in the core and the institution.

Associate Dean of Shared Resources

The associate dean of shared resources (core resources; shared instrumentation) provides institutional support and oversight for multiple core facilities in the institution. As an advocate for core technologies, the dean is involved in long-term planning for the viability of existing cores and the implementation of new core resource platforms. Technologies change and evolve, and constant evaluation of and synergy among institutional goals, overall research aims, and relevance of core technologies is required. Thus, in working with scientific directors, the team makes decisions on overall institutional directions for core facility growth and advancement or—alternatively—determining when cores are no longer viable and need to be closed.

Finally, the dean is responsible both for oversight of the scientific director and advisory board and of the core facility staff. It is preferable if the core facility staff are under the direction of the dean's office with broad research mandates, rather than department or research units that may have more narrow research needs.

SKILLS AND QUALIFICATIONS

All core facility positions require certain common sets of skills. Among the most important qualifications are a love of learning, the ability to learn quickly to keep up with new technologies, and a passion and determination for solving problems. Time management and the ability to adjust to changing priorities are essential. The nature of facilities is that there are many instruments and users, so being able to troubleshoot equipment problems, act in a service/customer-support-type manner, and react to changing tasks and priorities throughout the day is crucial. Without the ability to multitask and reassess priorities, the core facility is not the place for you. Personnel must use linear, logical reasoning to get at the root of issues and quickly come up with solutions. Hundreds of people use core facilities; thus, an ability to work with individuals with very different personalities, from shy and mild mannered to curt and abrupt, is required. Being personable with a customer support attitude is essential for working with different staff members and facilities users on diverse projects in a service-based environment.

Entry-Level Positions

The technician or IT specialist typically has a BSc or Master's degree, although in my facility we do have some undergraduate students working in this capacity.

Technician Specialist

A facility technician should come with experience with core facility technologies and software and be open to additional on-the-job training for highly specific equipment. Some expertise in a specific area may be desirable, for example, in microscopy fluorescent probes, live-cell or organism imaging, or photobleaching and photoactivation. Some technicians may be specifically trained for equipment maintenance and quality control. Being well organized and paying attention to detail are essential for tracking, modifying, and developing effective and efficient SOPs and facility records. Another important aspect of the job is the ability to learn quickly, perform literature reviews, and prepare PowerPoint presentations for teaching basic microscopy principles. Particularly ambitious individuals will have the potential for developing, and even teaching, workshops, tutorials, and courses.

Information Technology

In addition to the skills described in the introduction to this section, the ideal IT person should have expertise with database, networking, image processing and analysis, data handling, MS Windows and other workstation operating systems, computer equipment interfaces and communication, web design, and maintenance.

Mid-Level Positions

These positions (advanced technician specialist and managing director) are typically held by a PhD-level scientist. However, an ambitious person with a BSc or Master's-level degree combined with some experience as an entry-level microscopy specialist could be appropriate. The positions require those who can both serve as a leader and work as part of a team, are interested in learning new technologies and applications, and have excellent communication skills to present complex ideas and explain the technology at tutorials, courses, meetings, and workshops and to other upper-level administrators in the institution.

Advanced Technician Specialist

The technical specialist should have extensive experience with both diverse technology platforms and advanced technologies in the field (e.g., for microscopy: FRET, fluorescence lifetime imaging microscopy [FLIM], live-cell or intravital imaging, image correlation spectroscopy [ICM], nanoscopy, and advanced image processing). When advising users of the facility, the specialist should be able to communicate and interact with researchers on advanced projects, have a role in experimental design and implementation, and advise on or assist with grant and manuscript writing.

Managing Director

The director is expected to have superior management skills and the ability to supervise core facility personnel and coordinate a diverse set of obligations on a daily basis with rapidly changing demands and priorities.

Financial management experience is also an asset for preparing budgets and budget reports and delivering these to the management oversight committee.

Networking skills are highly desirable to facilitate interaction with facility users, principal investigators, and potential new clients within the research community. Here too, the ability to develop and maintain strong ties with corporations, including their research and development arms, is an advantage both to influence technology development and to engage in research and development of advanced technologies with commercial companies. Finally, the director must have a long-term vision for maintenance, growth, and development of the core and enhance the flow of information among the management oversight committee, scientific director, and scientific advisory board.

Upper-Level Positions

The positions of scientific director and dean of shared resources both require a PhD-level scientist with expertise in the field. In addition to the skills described in the preceding sections, these positions involve having and promoting a long-term vision of the available technologies, the development of the core facility, and the ability to maintain synergy with technological developments.

Scientific Director

The director must be a strong leader with good communication skills to integrate ideas from the scientific advisory board at the level of the core facility operations and to impress upon the associate dean of shared resources the importance of the core activities and long-term direction.

Dean of Shared Resources

The dean must have a big-picture vision—both short and long term—of how the activities of the facility fit into the overall research goals and mission of the institution, how to phase out technologies (sometimes entire cores), and the ability to continue to develop existing cores and identify and embrace new technologies. Clearly, significant management experience is an asset, as is interest in and familiarity with a wide array of technologies and their applications to problems across multidisciplinary fields.

GETTING A FOOT IN THE DOOR

During your studies, make sure to take any and all opportunities to learn the intricate details of the technologies that you use in your research work. With increasing expertise in many technologies, you will find that you will have more opportunities in core laboratories. Take technical and theory-based courses to gain an understanding of the fundamentals behind technologies of interest. Take advantage of opportunities at scientific meetings to network with vendors and find out about existing and new state-of-the-art technologies. Ask lots of questions and determine what the difficult areas are and what kinds of solutions could move the technologies forward. Sales and technical specialists from corporations are wonderful resources.

Volunteer to help out in core facilities at your institution. Perhaps if you help organize a workshop, you can attend the sessions free of charge. You will likely have networking opportunities to meet core facility staff and company representatives in the process. Consider becoming a superuser on some of the equipment and then help with training on a part-time basis.

Find core facilities in your area using the Association of Biomolecular Resource Facilities (ABRF) Core Facility Marketplace (http://www.abrf. org/index.cfm/page/resources/ABRF_Core_Marketplace.htm). When given the opportunity, take advantage of workshops offered in the field. Do not be shy about asking your supervisor; maybe you can attend a scientific meeting or perhaps you can use your budget to attend an intensive course instead. Consider the following opportunities and course listings.

- Cold Spring Harbor courses (http://meetings.cshl.edu/courses.html)

- Molecular Biology Labs in Woods Hole (http://hermes.mbl.edu/education/index.html)

- Montreal Light Microscopy Course: Fundamentals and Frontiers (www.mlmc.ca) at McGill University (held biannually)

- Canadian Cytometry and Microscopy Symposium (held biannually, typically in the spring) in Eastern Canada. This meeting has a strong focus and devotes time to a core facility manager meeting and many detailed workshops (www.cytometry.ca).

Perhaps you can find similar associations in your area. If you are truly interested in core facility work, definitely attend the annual meeting of ABRF, an international association that is rooted in protein- and genetics-based core technologies but is rapidly expanding to include light microscopy as well as many other fields. This annual meeting puts together a wonderful scientific program combined with a focus on workshops, tutorials, and round table discussions, including those regarding core technologies, core facility management, and administration. Check out their website—a resource for all things "core facility" (www.abrf.org).

CAREER PROGRESSION

Because core resource facilities are still relatively new at academic institutions, many universities do not have clear career paths for highly qualified academic staff. Dr. Jay Fox, Professor of Microbiology and Assistant Dean for Research Support at the University of Virginia, has been a pioneer in developing clear career tracks for resource facility personnel (http://www.medicine.virginia.edu/basic-science/departments/microbiology/research/research-core-facilities.html). This type of plan is crucial for the long-term retention of highly trained and qualified core facility personnel but is not well defined at many institutions. There are, however, some generalizations to be made on career progression.

From an entry-level position, MSc- or PhD-level scientists could expect to be considered for manager/managing director–type positions after at least five years of experience in their graduate/postdoctoral studies or as a microscopy specialist or similar position. Initiative to take on additional responsibility, keeping up on technology developments and advances, and the ability to work well with facility users and colleagues will all go a long way in getting a promotion. Core facility management positions are limited and positions tend to be highly specialized, so be prepared to relocate in order to move up to a management position unless you are within a large institution or large urban center with many research institutions. Promotions from a position such as a technician specialist to an advanced technician specialist are more likely to occur internally within a single core facility.

Depending on the background and experience of a core facility manager, there may be opportunities to move from this position to that of a core facility scientific director or associate dean of core resources. To move into a position of scientific director would require having a PhD and an independent research program. If you were not initially hired to start up an independent research program, this could still be achieved through collaborative efforts within the core facility. After 5–10 years of experience and the development of independent research projects, it would be possible (although not common) to be promoted to scientific director. More typical is the scenario in which a scientific director is an established independent investigator at the institution or a midlevel career scientist recruited to the institution for this position. Movement from core facility management to associate dean of core resources would be a more typical career path. Figure 1 shows the hierarchy of reporting, but a manager could move directly into a core facility administrator position without becoming a scientific director. This is a logical transition, if strong management skills are developed and the manager has a clear understanding of multiple core technologies and how they are applied to research questions. This kind of promotion would be considered only for PhD-level scientists after at least 10 years of experience as a core manager. In this case also, these positions are limited and relocation may be necessary.

WAY OUT

Training that is obtained in a core facility is highly applicable to many other job sectors. Lateral moves into corporate positions and biotechnology and pharmaceutical companies are possible, because core facility staff have tremendous expertise in technologies with broad applications.

Lateral moves into sales positions at companies selling instrumentation in the field or reagents/consumables associated with the technology are possible at many stages during a core facility career. It is not advisable to consider this type of move until you have at least a couple of years' experience with the technology. Sales positions require detailed knowledge of the products and how they are used, and it is logical for core facility staff to have this kind of expertise. When making a lateral move to a company, make sure that you do your research first. Know the company and their products. This makes a transition into a sales or technical specialist position much easier. An appreciation for the breadth of applications of the technology is also important. In turn, the potential customers are likely already familiar and the same core facility network can be used as an initial sales base. Be aware, however, that the work environment and goals in the corporate world are very different from the academic environment; therefore, be prepared for sales quotas and hard and fast deadlines.

Technical specialist positions within companies are ideal lateral moves for core facility staff with their tremendous expertise and training. These moves should be made only after three–four years in a core facility after appropriate expertise has been developed. One-on-one training in a core facility is very similar to one-on-one scientific support from a company specialist. The customer-based focus also translates well to a corporate environment. Extensive experience with technology, pitfalls, and trouble-shooting is an asset. Technical specialists also spend a lot of their time educating existing or potential customers. Experience with workshops, tutorials, and courses in the core facility will develop these same skills for use as a technical specialist.

Lateral moves can also be made into biotechnology or pharmaceutical companies that use the same technologies as the core facility. Many companies are now running core facilities with shared instrumentation in a very similar way to academic institutions. Again, do your research, know the companies, and sell yourself based on your expertise and training.

Lateral moves into academic positions to set up an independent research program can be difficult even for a core facility manager. If research is not a major component of the core facility position from the beginning, this door may be closed. Most academics hiring into research positions want researchers to follow the traditional career track of graduate work, postdoctoral work, and then a faculty position. Although not impossible, this is not typical. Therefore, before moving into a core facility job, be sure that you do not want to run your own independent research program unless it is part of the position or long-term plan from the beginning.

Finally, creating a business with core facility tools and talents is possible. Offering expertise for research projects and grant applications, training scientists to use equipment in their laboratories, maintaining equipment, and training in data analysis and presentation for publication can all be done within the framework of a consulting service for researchers at multiple institutions. All of the benefits of having your own business, making your own schedule, working at your own pace, and making decisions will follow. Be sure, however, that there is sufficient market for your expertise in your area before taking the plunge.

Box 1. My Experience

I never set out on a career track for core facility management. However, in looking back, I see it is a position that perfectly suits my interests, expertise, and personality traits. My scientific interests are diverse, and I love to learn new things, network, and work with people. I like to multitask and enjoy teaching, and I have the privilege of going to work each day to a job that I truly enjoy.

My formal training is in physical chemistry; however, I have always liked the interface among the scientific disciplines where routine knowledge in one field can revolutionize another. At the interface among chemistry, physics, and cell biology, I have developed my specific expertise in applying biophysical tools to problems in cell biology. While working in physics, chemistry, and cell biology laboratories, I have picked up tricks of the trade and developed a real sense of how these three communities of scientists operate and what scientific questions that they find important. Because I like working with people and helping them reach their goals, in graduate school I became involved in many projects with other graduate students and postdocs. During my first postdoctoral fellowship position at the Curie Institute in Paris, I worked with a group of physicists on a home-built multiphoton microscope (pretty rare in 1998), applying it to a beautifully developed system of intestinal cells expressing brush border myosin I green fluorescent protein (GFP). The cell biologists prepared all of the mutants and controls, with the GFP-fusion protein placed under an inducible promoter to avoid cellular compensation for overexpression of the protein, and I found myself looking at the dynamics of myosin in live cells.

I moved back to Canada for the birth of my son in 2000, unsure of what was coming next. During a 10-month teaching position in the chemistry department at Mount Allison University in New Brunswick, I discovered that I loved teaching. (I also had a newfound appreciation for all of my former teachers; it is a lot of work!) Nevertheless, I felt the novelty and excitement of primary research calling me back. After a brief and disappointing postdoctoral position in a dysfunctional laboratory (an experience that helped me with my "dos and don'ts" list below), I joined the first-rate laboratory of Rick Horwitz at the University of Virginia. That laboratory was very multidisciplinary, and I learned many more intricacies of live-cell microscopy. Quickly becoming the go-to person for any technical aspects of the microscopes, I learned a great deal more about cell biology, signaling, migration, and, of course, about microscopes. Then, taking the position of the core facility manager at McGill enabled me to move back to Canada, work on many research projects, and fulfill my broad research interests.

Now, I work on projects ranging from materials science to live organisms. I contribute to hundreds of other projects and collaborate with many students and postdoctoral fellows. I also enjoy working with companies and having a role in technology development. Networking, engaging the sales representatives and technical specialists, and working to improve the instrumentation, software, and reagents on the market enables me to help the community to better address novel scientific questions. The constantly evolving nature of the field of microscopy satisfies my love for continually learning new things. I quickly identified education as the key to a successful core facility. As a result, during my eight years at McGill, I have run more than 60 workshops, tutorials, and courses. The technology is available; we just need to ensure that we use it well to perform high-quality science for scientific advancements and reputable publications. I have recently been appointed assistant professor and I am currently setting up my own research laboratory, studying the dynamics and interactions of proteins during cell migration using advanced techniques including image correlation microscopy. I never set out to be a core facility manager, but I realize now that it perfectly suits my personality, my interests, and all that I love about science.

Box 2. Ten Dos and Don'ts

---

1. Do make phone calls and send mail. In this information age, people often receive hundreds of e-mail messages a day. Stand out by calling or sending a hard copy of your CV by old-fashioned snail mail. Join online professional sites such as LinkedIn (http://www.linkedin.com). In addition, join and watch discipline-specific listing services such as the confocal list.

2. Do get everything in writing. When interviewing for jobs, many promises are often made; make sure there are specific milestones and dates in order to ensure that the promises do not become forgotten and unfulfilled.

3. Do talk to people at many levels on a one-on-one basis so that they have an opportunity to be candid with you about the work environment and whether it is healthy.

4. Do find out in advance what type of career track the institution is offering for core resource facility staff. Determine exactly the type of funding model used for the core.

(Continued.)

5. Do not get too friendly with prospective employers. It comes across as being unprofessional.

6. Do not overprepare. I once got a binder full of every certificate and letter a potential candidate ever received in their career. You need to do the work to highlight a few key achievements in your interview, so as not to overwhelm.

7. Do not expect to get long-term stable employment contracts with core facilities (at least not in the current climate). You may luck out, but most are completely or partially funded on soft money, and institutional support is on the decline (Riley 2011).

8. Do not get discouraged. At a talk I attended, the speaker showed his rejection letter from a prominent journal saying his future Nobel Prize–winning work was not novel or relevant to the readership of the journal.

9. Do choose a career doing what you love. Nothing makes you more productive than looking forward to going to work each day.

10. Do not undervalue an alternative scientific career. Some people feel the ultimate goal of any scientist should be to start their own independent research program. This is not for everyone and there is equal value in many other careers. Go where you will use your gifts and talents to their full potential and where you will be happy.

REFERENCES

Riley MB. 2011. University multi-user facility survey: 2010. *J Biomol Tech* **22**: 131–135.

Stack RF, Bayles CJ, Girard AM, Martin K, Opansky C, Schulz K, Cole RW. 2011. Quality assurance testing for modern optical imaging systems. *Microsc Microanal* **17**: 598–606.

WWW RESOURCES

www.abrf.org The Association of Biomolecular Resource Facilities (ABRF), an international society dedicated to advancing core and research biotechnology laboratories through research, communication, and education.

http://www.bio21.com.au/projects/view/1 The Bio21 Cluster—Victoria's leading health and medical cluster.

www.cytometry.ca Canadian Cytometry & Microscopy Association, Montreal, Quebec.

http://hermes.mbl.edu/education/index.html The Marine Biological Laboratory (MBL) education programs, Woods Hole, Massachusetts.

http://www.linkedin.com LinkedIn, the professional network homepage.

http://lists.umn.edu/cgi-bin/wa?A0=confocalmicroscopy Confocal Microscopy, University of Minnesota.

http://www.medicine.virginia.edu/basic-science/departments/microbiology/research/research-core-facilities.html University of Virginia School of Medicine login page.

http://meetings.cshl.edu/courses.html Cold Spring Harbor Laboratory Meetings & Courses Program.

www.mlmc.ca Montreal Light Microscopy Course (MLMC).

4

Academic Administration

Lydia Villa-Komaroff

Cytonome/ST, LLC, Boston, Massachusetts 02210

Academic administration can be an extension of an academic career at the bench or it can run parallel to a career of discovery. To be an academic administrator at the executive level in a college or university generally requires advancement through the academic ranks to the professorial level. These positions include department chair, dean of a college, head of a center or institute, provost, senior research officer, and university or college president. Positions that can begin immediately after attaining a PhD or after a postdoctoral position include being named assistant dean and positions in technology transfer, grants management, and laboratory management, among many others. Many of the skills developed during the pursuit of an advanced degree in the life sciences are directly applicable to these jobs. All require problem solving, critical thinking, collaboration, and the ability to communicate clearly.

There are approximately 6900 accredited postsecondary institutions in the United States (http://www2.ed.gov/admins/finaid/accred/accredita tion_pg4. html#Diploma-Mills). These institutions are classified by the Carnegie Foundation into six broad categories (http://classifications.carnegiefounda tion.org/descriptions/basic.php) as follows:

1. Associate's colleges are institutions that award only associate's level degrees or where bachelor's degrees account for less than 10% of all undergraduate degrees.

2. Doctorate-granting universities are institutions that award at least 20 research doctoral degrees excluding professional degrees such as JD, MD, or PharmD.

3. Master's-degree-granting colleges and universities generally include institutions that award at least 50 master's degrees and fewer than 20 doctoral degrees.

4. Baccalaureate colleges are institutions where baccalaureate degrees represent at least 10% of all undergraduate degrees and where fewer than 50 master's degrees or 20 doctoral degrees are awarded.

5. Special-focus institutions award 75% or more baccalaureate or higher-level degrees in a single field or set of related fields.

6. Tribal colleges are members of the American Indian Higher Education Consortium and are excluded from all other categories.

The number and variety of academic institutions provide a broad array of positions in academic administration. Academic administration provides a career track in which a scientist can enable the work of other scientists, provide direction in the development of training programs, guide programs within a university or college setting, or run an institution. Life scientists are increasingly found in leadership positions in all kinds of academic institutions. Training in life sciences provides a strong background for evaluating some of the most exciting science in an institution and enabling its transfer to the business world or for having a key role in science training. Skills learned as a scientist are strong preparation for problem solving in any type of academic institution. Because most of the academic institutions in the United States responsible for the education and recruitment of scientists do not revolve around research, the presence of well-trained scientists in these institutions is a prerequisite for inspiring and training the next generation of research scientists.

JOBS

Jobs in academic administration include executive and nonexecutive positions. Executive positions include department chair, dean, senior research officer, provost, and president. These jobs generally require advancement through the academic ranks to a tenured position. Although some nonexecutive jobs involve laboratory work, many do not. Nonexecutive jobs are generally not on the tenure track.

Figure 1 shows the relationship of the component parts of an academic institution. Every component of the institution has jobs in academic

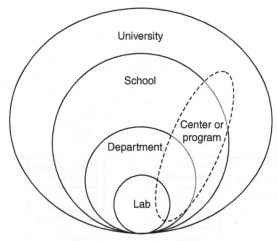

Figure 1. Components of an academic institution and their relationship to each other. The figure shows the most common organization for a research-intense school. If there is a medical school, departments may be subdivided into divisions that contain individual laboratories. Small colleges may not have separate schools. Departments are the basic components of a university, and it can be difficult to close existing departments or start new ones. Academic programs or centers are more fluid entities and can be established or closed more readily. These entities often cross departmental and school boundaries. The dual structure of fluid programs and centers imposed on a very stable structure of departments allows an institution the flexibility to respond rapidly to new fields or new opportunities while providing an anchor for faculty affiliation.

administration. Figure 2 shows a generic organization chart for an academic institution. The titles in bold are areas where PhDs in science can be found; however, opportunities may be found in almost all areas of the institution. Every academic institution in the United States has its own unique culture and practices; titles of the executive positions may differ or responsibilities may be consolidated.

Executive Positions

These positions require vision, leadership, interpersonal skills, and the ability to assess and respond to a changing environment. They also require strategic thinking and the ability to build consensus, arbitrate disagreements, and deal with inadequate resources (there is never enough money to do everything that needs to be, or could be, done). One important consideration is the desire and ability to showcase the work of others. Many different management styles can be successful in these positions as long as the leader is consistent and honest with faculty and other administrators.

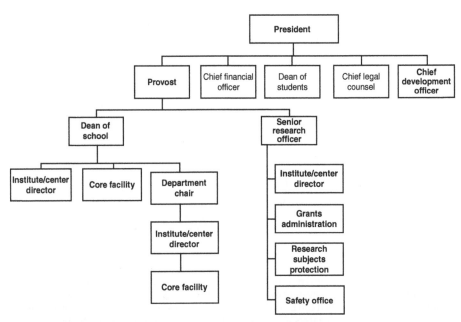

Figure 2. Organization chart for an academic institution. The chart shown is representative of the central administration of a research-intense university with many schools. The larger the institution, the more likely it is that functions such as grants administration or student affairs will have school-based offices as well as central administration offices. Not every institution has all possible schools. Schools where life scientists may have faculty or administrative roles include arts and sciences, medical, engineering, dental, veterinary, pharmacy, nursing, education, communication (formerly called schools of speech, these have programs in the science of human speech, hearing, and learning), and business. Often, a graduate school oversees all graduate education. The autonomy of schools within an institution also varies. Medical schools, business schools, and other professional schools that may or may not offer undergraduate courses generally have the most autonomy. For medical schools, this is based on the size and complexity of modern medicine. Medical schools are affiliated with hospitals, and the hospitals may be independent of the medical school and the university or may be part of the complex. Independence means that governance and budget of the hospital are separate from the medical school or university. Other offices that may exist at institutions include public affairs, alumni affairs, and information technology. Smaller institutions often consolidate functions and titles may differ. Although offices within the institution are generally described on an institution's website, the organization chart is usually not found on the website but can sometimes be obtained by searching for it directly.

First, we deal with the career track to an executive position in a research university. Figure 3 illustrates some of the pathways that are available. To be successful on this track, you must first focus on a traditional academic career and work your way up to a tenured position. In a research-intensive organization, this requires meeting the institution's criteria for excellence

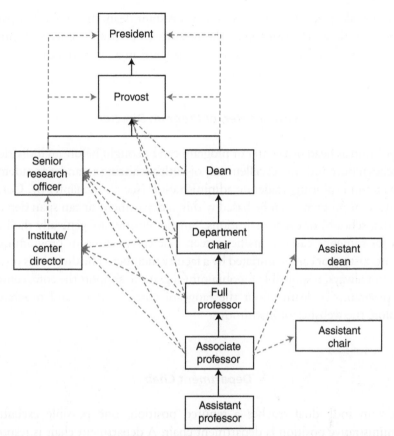

Figure 3. Paths to executive positions in academic administration. The traditional pathway is to achieve tenure in your discipline and then to move into a senior executive position. The black arrows in the figure illustrate the career pathway that is the most conventional and dashed arrows indicate the myriad of possibilities that exist. Presidents most often come from the ranks of provosts and deans but can also come from other central administrators that have executive experience, such as SROs, center directors, or chairs of complex departments such as a department of medicine.

in research as well as satisfactory performance in teaching and service. You can determine your taste and fit for administrative work by participation in departmental and university committees. Finding the right balance between your scientific work and your work for the good of the institution is in itself useful preparation and training in setting priorities, delegating, and the critically important skill of saying "no" firmly and diplomatically.

In many cases, you can sample administrative work by taking on a short-term responsibility such as organizing a seminar series, organizing a new class, or taking a role as assistant chair, assistant dean, or some other part-time role. In some institutions, the president's or dean's office has short-term assignments for faculty who show interest in administration.

Core, Center, or Program Director

A position as head of a center or program can be sought before an individual reaches tenure and is an excellent way of both advancing a standard academic career and exploring academic administration (see also Chapter 3). Cores, centers, or programs can be based within a department or can span departments, schools, or even institutions. Smaller entities are generally the best bet for someone early in his/her career. The core, center, or program may be preexisting or can be initiated by a faculty member. The director is often, but not always, responsible for obtaining a grant to support the core, center, or program. To learn about the range of cores, centers, and programs, explore the websites of institutions.

Department Chair

After an individual reaches a tenured position, one possible executive administrative position is department chair. A department chair is responsible for the academic and research activities of a department and reports to the dean of the school, the provost, or the president, depending on the size of the institution. The department chair is responsible for setting the research direction of a department. To that end, the chair recruits faculty, oversees the academic programs of the department, and develops department budgets. In institutions that are research intensive, most chairs maintain active research laboratories.

A department chair is responsible for the overall direction and quality of the department. He or she must also distribute resources, often including space. The chair works with the faculty to set the teaching agenda of the department, recruits new members to the faculty, and negotiates with the deans and others for resources for his or her department. The department chair will have a budget and is responsible for working within it. A successful chair will have an overview of the field and a vision for where the field is going. This vision guides the hires and curriculum of the department.

Dean

"Dean" is a title used for a variety of academic administrative jobs. Dean is the title given to the person who is responsible for a school, such as arts and sciences, engineering, or medicine, within a university. Deans of schools generally report to the provost. A dean is responsible for hiring department chairs, promotions within the school, fund-raising for the school, negotiating with the central administration for start-up packages, or the development of cross-departmental entities within the school, which can be either service centers or intellectual entities that bring together members of different departments. The dean will also collaborate with other deans in the formation of cross-school centers and facilities. Deans oversee much of the curriculum as well.

A dean of graduate studies often oversees the graduate programs across schools and reports to the provost. The dean of the graduate school generally has only an advisory role in hiring faculty but is responsible for approving and coordinating the graduate curriculum. The dean of a graduate school has a key role in developing new graduate programs.

"Dean" can also refer to the person in charge of student affairs. This position is most often held by someone with a degree in academic administration, but assistant and associate deans can be found in many offices of an academic institution.

Senior Research Officer

This is a relatively new office in research institutions. The title of this position can be vice president for research or vice provost for research. In most cases, the position reports to the provost but often is a member of the president's staff. The senior research officer (SRO) is generally responsible for the infrastructure offices of the institution: grants and contracts, animal research subjects, human subjects, safety, and technology transfer. In addition, the SRO may be responsible for the oversight of university-wide centers.

Provost

The provost is the chief academic officer of the university or college and reports to the president. The provost is usually responsible for the academic budget of the institution and works closely with the president and the chief financial officer to set the budget for the institution. The provost is responsible for hiring school deans as well as graduate deans and SROs. The provost, in collaboration with deans and chairs, sets the academic criteria for tenure.

President

The president of a research university is responsible for setting and implementing a vision for the institution and reports to the trustees of the institution. The president is also the public face of the institution and the chief fund-raiser for the institution—current presidents spend a great deal of time raising money.

Nonexecutive Positions

A large number of positions within an institution are not necessarily related to a laboratory but are where a PhD, with postdoctoral experience or some experience as a faculty member, is useful. These include assistant chair, assistant dean, teaching position, diversity offices, technology transfer, and grants management.

Laboratory Manager

Large laboratories often have a laboratory manager who not only does bench work but coordinates ordering, plans laboratory meetings, and generally oversees the activities of the laboratory. In some cases, these are temporary positions held by senior postdoctoral fellows, but there are an increasing number of long-term positions with various titles, including laboratory manager, research associate, or research assistant professor.

Core Director

A position that allows a fair degree of autonomy is a position as a core director. There are many kinds of scientific cores and the larger the institution, the more cores there are. Some cores are departmental but most serve several departments and may serve several schools. Some are transient and depend on funding of a center or program project grant. Some are supported by a combination of institutional funds, user fees, and grants. In some institutions, the head of the core is a faculty member on the tenure track; in others, a core director not on the tenure track runs the core and can report to a faculty member or the department chair. These positions generally require a special skill such as cytometry, cell culture, microscopy, or bioinformatics (see also Chapter 3).

Technology Transfer

Most research institutions have an office that is responsible for the commercialization of intellectual property (IP) developed by university faculty. The technology transfer office is generally responsible for licensing IP to commercial entities and is often responsible for deciding which technology to patent. In the last decade or so, many tech transfer offices have been expanded or new offices have been set up to encourage entrepreneurial activity among the faculty. These duties include identifying funding for new companies, and deciding when a technology is best for a start-up versus licensing to an established company.

Grants Management

All research institutions have offices that are responsible for ensuring that grants submitted by faculty meet institutional, local, state, and federal regulatory requirements (see also Chapter 5). A PhD is not required for a grants management position but can be of value. Some departments and some large laboratories hire a PhD to write grants.

Research Subjects Protection

Research using humans or animals is heavily regulated by the federal government. Human subjects' offices in medical schools are generally headed by an MD, and a veterinarian degree is generally required for the head of an animal facility. However, scientists in the life sciences can serve as staff or associate heads. These positions require knowledge of Food and Drug Administration (FDA) and U.S. Department of Agriculture (USDA) regulations. Start by browsing the websites of these federal agencies. In addition, speak with individuals within the office at your institution and learn how the office works.

Safety Office

The safety office is responsible for inspection of laboratories and facilities to ensure safety and for training of personnel that use the facilities. These positions do not require a PhD but sometimes require a certificate, in addition to an undergraduate degree in a science discipline.

Diversity Positions

These positions cover a wide array of options within the offices of student affairs, provost, school, or department. They may include teaching but most often include oversight of programs meant to recruit and retain students from populations that have been underrepresented in university or college settings.

Assistant Department Chair

In some cases, the position of assistant chair is a temporary position for a tenure-track assistant or associate professor who wants to try administration. In other cases, this is a permanent position off the tenure track. In either case, this person is generally the chief operating officer of the department and handles many of the administrative tasks within a department.

SKILLS AND QUALIFICATIONS

To be an academic administrator at an executive position in a college or university generally requires advancement through the academic ranks to the professorial level. These positions include head of a center or institute, department chair, dean of a college, provost, SRO, and university or college president. Many positions can begin immediately after attaining a PhD or after completing a postdoctoral position, including positions ranging from providing laboratory services, grant management, intellectual property management, student recruitment, student resources, teaching services, to others.

Two essential areas of competence are financial acumen and decisiveness. Financial acumen means the ability to work within the resources available, to be aware of sources of revenue, and to obtain additional resources. Practically speaking, it is also means the ability to read and interpret the three standard financial statements: balance sheet, income statement, and cash flow statement. These three documents summarize where the money of an institution comes from, where it is, and how it is used. Although you may have experience in setting up and administering a laboratory budget, you will need to develop an understanding of financial documents.

Decisiveness is the ability to make decisions rapidly and with only partial information. The ability to set priorities based on a vision for the unit you lead, be it your laboratory or the whole institution, is a critical skill. The inability to make a decision can have a worse effect than a mistaken decision. This does not mean that decisions are made in a vacuum; on the contrary, part of the process is seeking appropriate input—the trick is learning how to define "appropriate" and knowing whom to consult. These positions require the desire and ability to showcase the work of others.

You already have some administrative experience if you have assisted in the preparation of grants as a graduate student or a postdoc. You can gain additional experience by volunteering for committees in your institution such as those concerned with safety and intellectual property or by helping to plan department events such as retreats. You can also get involved in committees in professional societies. Please note that each institution and each department and school within the institution has a unique character. As an assistant professor, you can get a taste of academic administration by taking part in the committee work of the department and in the institution. However, remember that your first responsibility is to do the things that you need to do to advance in your career, particularly if you aspire to an executive academic position.

Every science-related job involves some administration. At a minimum, an assistant professor must organize and manage his or her laboratory. This involves time management, financial management, people skills, writing skills, and setting priorities—all of which are basic administrative skills. If you want to be a provost, dean, or president at a research institution, at this point in your career focus on establishing yourself as an independent and productive scientist so that you can get promoted. Although you will need to do your share of the teaching and service requirements of your department, you must focus on publishing and getting research funding. If you have decided that you aspire to an executive position in a nonresearch institution, you must fulfill the requirements for promotion, which are generally teaching and scholarly activities related to your PhD area. You may develop courses, obtain grants for novel programs, or become a mentor to students who enter life science majors. An indication that the administrative route is for you is finding that you enjoy and even seek out administrative tasks within the institution.

One skill that is rarely taught in graduate science programs is financial management and budgeting. This is a critically important skill in any administrative post. Even if you have a financial professional on your staff, you must understand the basics in order to effectively carry out your responsibilities. This knowledge can be gained from books or an introductory course from the American Management Association (AMA). The courses are effective, are available in cities throughout the country, or can be taken online. Start with AMA's *Fundamentals of Finance and Accounting for Non-Financial Managers*; as of spring 2013, the three-day course cost $2345.

Early preparation includes time management in the laboratory, interactions with colleagues and collaborators, as well as the ability to change direction of focus quickly. These are skills that can be developed during postdoctoral training and are essential during the early years of work in your own laboratory or as you prepare for your teaching responsibilities. Although you want to focus on fulfilling the responsibilities as an assistant professor, you also need to pay attention to how your department and institution work.

CAREER PROGRESSION: WAYS IN, UP, AND OUT

Although participating in all activities of a department is important, it is also important to focus on publications if you are a member of a research-intense institution. In smaller, non-research-intense institutions, it is still important to demonstrate that you keep up with developments in life sciences through the literature and professional meetings. In all cases, it is critically important that you learn the requirements for promotion in your institution. Seek advice from faculty members in your department and also from faculty in other departments. It is possible to move from a research-intense institution to one where teaching is the focus; it is very difficult to move in the other direction if you want to be in an executive position. Once a commitment has been made to a particular kind of institution, it can be difficult to move to institutions of a different type, so if you aspire to lead a small undergraduate institution, consider a move to this kind of institution early in your career.

Figure 3 illustrates possible career pathways in executive academic administration. Although president is perhaps the pinnacle of academic administration, your final goal should be determined by your interests and aptitudes. For someone who enjoys being deeply involved in all aspects of a particular area, a position as center director, chair, or dean of a specialized school is an ideal goal. For those with broad interests, graduate dean, dean of a school of arts and sciences, provost, or SRO provide exposure to a wide array of fields.

Figure 4 illustrates career pathways in nonexecutive positions. There are many ways to use your training in science in positions throughout the academic institution. As you consider alternatives to a career in science that do not involve running a laboratory in a research-intensive institution such as the one that you have trained in, consider your interests, aptitudes, and the skills you have acquired, not the specialization that is reflected in your thesis.

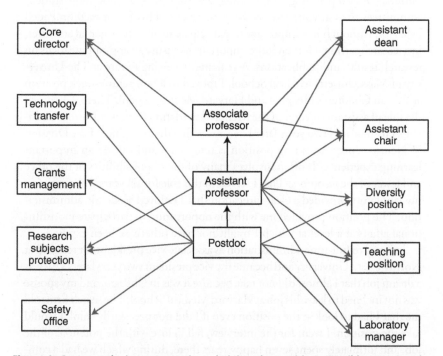

Figure 4. Career paths in nonexecutive administrative positions. Possible nonexecutive positions are myriad and can be found in every nook and cranny of an institution. These are generally selected during the early phase of a career and may require some additional licensure or specialized training.

Box 1. My Experience

My foray into academic administration began as a graduate student at Massachusetts Institute of Technology. As second-year students, three of us successfully proposed a change in format for the initial preliminary exam. We developed the plan with our fellow students and prepared both a written and verbal presentation to the graduate officer. In addition to being thoroughly engrossed in laboratory work, I was also the member of the laboratory most interested in organizing laboratory events and building a comfortable couch for our laboratory library. Another early indicator of my affinity for administrative positions was the role that I had as a postdoctoral fellow when Arg Efstratiadis, Stephanie Broome, and I accompanied Wally Gilbert to England to try to clone the human insulin gene at Porton Down, a high-containment facility. I coordinated the packing of the reagents and equipment that we would need, made the checklists, and oversaw the packing of the large trunks that I bought for the trip.

As a new faculty member, I accepted membership to many university committees, enjoyed planning and teaching new courses, and sat on more student committees than anyone else in the department. This is not recommended behavior: Although it is important to participate in all departmental activities, in a research setting it is even more important to ensure an appropriate focus on research results and publications. A year after receiving tenure at The University of Massachusetts Medical School, I moved to a non-tenure-track position at Boston Children's Hospital and Harvard Medical School. There, I assumed the role of assistant director of the Mental Retardation Center at Boston Children's Hospital and two years later I became acting division chief of the Division of Neuroscience. An acting position is temporary and can be an important learning experience. It often involves many of the responsibilities of the office and fewer of the resources. That I served in this role for six years while running my laboratory provided a clear indication that I enjoyed academic administration. The position provided me with the opportunity to participate in institutional affairs at a level at which I might not have otherwise been exposed.

I moved to full-time administration as associate vice president for research at Northwestern University and became the vice president two years later. This was a dream job that I almost did not take because it was in Chicago, and my spouse was not inclined to leave his job at Harvard Medical School. The search firm told me that I had to look at the position even if I did not necessarily think I would take the position. I went for the interview, fell in love with the potential of the job, and ultimately spent seven happy years there, during which we had a commuter marriage. When I returned to Boston, I first took a job in academic administration as chief operating officer (COO) and vice president for research

(VPR) at Whitehead in Cambridge with the opportunity to work with two dynamic women: Susan Lindquist as director and Maxine Singer as chair of the board. When Susan decided to return to research full time, I joined a start-up company—but that is another story.

Box 2. Ten Dos and Don'ts

---

1. Do learn how to read a financial spread sheet and manage a budget.

2. Do learn how your institution works: Who are the key figures? What are the administrative offices and what do they do?

3. Do get to know departmental secretaries—they are a rich source of information on the inner workings of a department.

4. Do try administrative work before committing to it; every job has difficult aspects and it's important to enjoy most of the day-to-day that a job entails.

5. Do apply for jobs that are like those you think you might want.

6. Do not disregard a position without investigating it.

7. Do seek advice from people who are in positions similar to those you wish to consider.

8. Do think of your skills, not your specialty.

9. Do read literature on management and academic institutions.

10. Do not consider your PhD a degree that limits your job options.

WWW RESOURCES

---

http://classifications.carnegiefoundation.org/descriptions/basic.php Carnegie Foundation for the Advancement of Teaching Classification Description.

http://www2.ed.gov/admins/finaid/accred/accreditation_pg4.html#Diploma-Mills U.S. Department of Education Database of Accredited Programs and Institutions.

5

Careers in Science and Grant Administration: View from the National Institutes of Health

Marion Zatz[1] and Sherry Dupere[2]

[1]National Institute of General Medical Sciences, Bethesda, Maryland 20892

[2]Eunice Kennedy Shriver National Institute of Child Health and Human Development, National Institutes of Health, Bethesda, Maryland 20892

Scientist administrators at the National Institutes of Health fall into two categories: program officers and scientific review officers. Program officers provide advice to applicants and grantees, make funding recommendations, oversee grantees' research progress, and facilitate research opportunities in emerging areas of science. Scientific review officers oversee all aspects of the initial (peer) review of grant applications.

As scientists progress through their research careers, they must think about how they can obtain funding to support their research. They can of course observe their mentors' efforts to apply for grants but often do not have a clear idea of what happens at the other end, that is, how grant applications are reviewed and how funding decisions are made. They may need someone who can provide advice, answer questions, and guide them through the maze of the grant application and funding process. A scientist administrator is that person. There are many funding agencies, both private and governmental, in the United States, and the nature of the job of a scientist administrator varies considerably with the funding agency. The National Institutes of Health (NIH) is the largest example, with an annual budget of ~$31 billion. More than 80% of that budget is devoted to supporting approximately 50,000 research and training grants to academic and research institutions across the U.S. As a result, there are thousands of scientist administrator jobs located in the NIH Center for Scientific Review (CSR) and the 27 institutes and centers (ICs) that comprise the NIH, and these individuals provide the merit review and funding recommendations of applications and the oversight of funded grants. Figure 1 shows the place of the NIH within the overall structure of government.

This chapter describes the job of an NIH health scientist administrator (HSA) and, more specifically, the roles of two types of scientist ad-

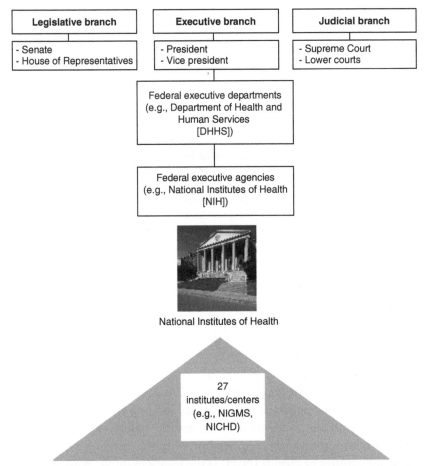

National Institutes of Health

Figure 1. National Institutes of Health (NIH) as an agency of the Department of Health and Human Services within the executive branch of the United States government. The impact of all three federal branches on science and medicine is a rich aspect of careers in government. For example, the health scientist administrator may receive congressional inquiries from the legislative branch or, less commonly, become involved with a court of the judicial branch.

ministrators, the program officer (PO) and the scientific review officer (SRO), who form the administrative team that serves the biomedical and behavioral research community. Potential principal investigators (PIs) often contact POs before submitting a grant application, seeking advice on a number of issues, including the appropriateness of a research project or training program for an institute's scientific mission or whether the application would be suited to a specific funding announcement. Trainees seeking fellowship support also may contact POs for advice on their applications. Once an application is received at the NIH, the SRO is responsible for all aspects of peer review, including selecting scientists for scientific review group (study section) service, overseeing the review committee meeting, and generating the summary statements that capture the essence of the study section members' reviews. Once the initial scientific review is completed, responsibility shifts to the PO, who advises applicants on their prospects for funding, makes funding recommendations, and, if the grant is funded, oversees the progress of the research. The PO also has responsibility for encouraging scientific opportunities, and both the PO and the SRO often provide advice on NIH policy.

Typically, there are three application submission deadlines a year and therefore three rounds of review and funding each fiscal year, so a PO or SRO may be juggling several different responsibilities simultaneously. These roles, described in greater detail below, are both scientifically and administratively challenging, but also highly rewarding and essential for the health of the country's biomedical and behavioral research enterprise.

Although the current funding climate at the NIH is uncertain at best, the NIH will continue to support the best research and the training of outstanding scientists, preparing them for independent careers in academia and the many other rewarding career options available. Although shrinking budgets may make it harder to make funding decisions and more difficult and time-consuming to advise applicants and grantees, the job of a scientist administrator becomes increasingly important in helping to sustain the enthusiasm and progress of the research and training enterprise.

JOBS

Positions for HSAs are found throughout the many institutes of the NIH. The organizational structure of one of these, the National Institute of Child Health and Human Development (NICHD), is represented in Figure 2.

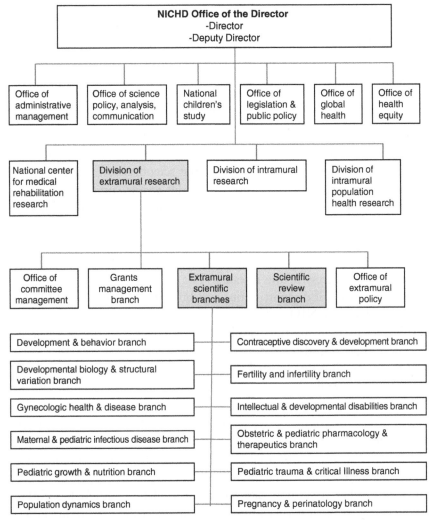

Figure 2. Organization chart of an NIH Institute (NICHD). Health scientist administrator positions reside within the division of extramural research, where the program officers administer grants and contract proposals within an extramural scientific branch, whereas the scientific review officers administer peer review of applications and contract proposals assigned to all extramural scientific branches of the NICHD for funding consideration.

Program Officer

The job of a PO will vary with the individual IC in which the position is located, although many of the basics are shared across the NIH. Most ICs have a research and training mission that is related to a specific disease or health focus, for example, the National Cancer Institute. There also is one institute, the National Institute of General Medical Sciences (NIGMS), whose mission is to support basic research and research training that is not tied to a particular disease or tissue/organ system. Because this reflects the NIGMS perspective of a PO's responsibilities, it is worth noting that NIGMS, just one of the 27 ICs, supports more than 3500 research grants and approximately 4300 trainees on fellowships and training grants.

Advice

Grant applicants may need advice at every step of the way, from whether their project is of interest to an IC's scientific mission or is responsive to a special initiative, to what the chances of funding are, or the next steps in revising and improving an application. An important part of a PO's job is to guide investigators and trainees through changing policies, practices, and budgets, providing as much information as possible along the way. Each fiscal year is different, and when research budgets become more limited and NIH budget appropriations are not finalized until several months into the fiscal year, the job of a PO is even more important for providing accurate and timely information and advice.

Funding Decisions

This area varies considerably among ICs. In NIGMS, each PO is responsible for a defined scientific area in which he/she is particularly knowledgeable and has what is called a "portfolio" of applications and grants. The PO has an active role in making funding recommendations, starting with attendance at study section discussions, where the scientific merit of an application is discussed, and reading the summary statements that are generated for applications undergoing peer review. The next step is preparing for a second level of review by the NIGMS advisory council, during which council members may provide advice on applicant concerns and the relative merits of the scored applications; every application that is funded by the NIH must receive this second level of review by the relevant IC council. After the council meeting, POs discuss and recommend those applications that should be funded. This process is driven primarily by the availability of funds (each IC receives its own budget appropriation from Congress) and the initial peer review evaluation. However, many other important factors are taken into consideration, including information gained from the study section discussion, council advice, the novelty of the scientific area, the applicant's status as a new or more established investigator, and the availability or lack of other support for the PI. The NIGMS establishes a "nominal" pay line for each council round, based on the availability of dollars to fund all applications through a given ranking. POs look at a range of applications on either side of the nominal pay line and consider all of the relevant factors in making the final funding recommendation. POs also recommend the level of funding, making budget adjustments on a case-by-case basis that, on average, must meet NIH-mandated cost-containment guidelines.

Oversight

Once an application is funded and becomes part of a PO's portfolio, annual progress reports are read and evaluated for scientific advances and changes in direction. Grantees also may seek advice on strategies for their competing renewals, changes in project goals, and other issues that arise in the course of a four- to five-year grant award. However, responsibility for oversight goes well beyond the individual grantees in a program portfolio. POs must stay abreast of the latest advances in their area of science by attending conferences, meeting with grantees, and reading relevant journals. These activities in turn enable POs to perform a crucial part of their job, which is to identify emerging opportunities.

Facilitating Scientific Opportunities

One of the most gratifying activities for a PO is to identify an emerging area of science and foster its development. A perfect example is stem cell research. The development of human embryonic stem cell lines in the late 1990s provided an exciting opportunity to address some of the most fundamental questions in developmental biology, but one that required nurturing and overcoming technical as well as policy hurdles. In the NIGMS, a series of workshops were organized and initiatives developed to encourage scientists to enter the field, master the necessary methodologies, and obtain needed resources to facilitate the study of the basic biology of stem cells. These efforts have led to a substantial commitment of the NIGMS to the support of basic stem cell research.

Scientific Review Officer

At some time in their careers, many researchers will avail themselves of various funding opportunities provided by the NIH. The SRO bears the critical responsibility for ensuring that the NIH peer review process, which determines the merit of research and training applications for funding, is conducted fairly, expertly, and in accordance with NIH policy. SROs may administer the initial peer review of applications for a broad spectrum of funding mechanisms, including research grants, training grants, contracts, cooperative agreements, fellowships, and many other complex and large mechanisms. This is a sizable operation at the NIH, involving hundreds of SROs and tens of thousands of applications and proposals each year. Peer review at NIH may be conducted either in the CSR or in an institute review locus (some but not all ICs have a review branch or office). The CSR is NIH's central review organization that receives and reviews most of the "investigator-initiated" research projects, that is, those that represent investigators' own research ideas. Applications reviewed in the CSR are assigned to one of more than 100 study sections, based on the scientific match between the project and the study section's expertise, regardless of which IC will have ultimate funding responsibility. Many of the grant applications reviewed by the CSR may be of interest to several NIH institutes for funding. Projects that are very closely aligned with the scientific "mission" of a single IC, or are submitted in response to an IC-specific initiative, generally will be reviewed by that institute's internal review branch or office. These include large complex projects, training grants, research and development (R&D) contracts, and career development awards. Nevertheless, whether a project is reviewed in the CSR or an IC review branch, adherence to NIH peer review policies is rigorously maintained.

Organizing and Overseeing Peer Review

The peer review process at the NIH initially involves a formal evaluation of the scientific merit of the researchers' applications, as judged by a panel of experts in the field(s) involved. A major responsibility of the SRO is to carefully assess the expertise needed to provide an informed and unbiased review of each application and to recruit persons with the appropriate expertise for formal deliberations, so that the initial review proceedings can be used by POs to identify those applications most worthy of funding. SROs recruit scientific experts from academic institutions, the private sector, and specialized groups, such as community/public representatives, when required. Notably, the SRO must avoid conflicts of interest between the investigators (and their institutions) seeking funds and the reviewers assessing the merit of their applications and proposals, while striving for balanced geographic, gender, and ethnic/racial representation on study sections to achieve a fair merit review process, free from outside influences.

Once the initial review is completed the SRO has the important responsibility to provide feedback to applicants and POs. This includes, at a minimum, the composite numerical score reflecting each reviewer's assessment of the overall scientific/technical merit of an application or other recommendation as well as a formal report of the review, called the **summary statement**. This document provides essentially unedited critiques from the individual experts who review the application, a "resume and summary of discussion" for applications in the top tier of those applications considered by the panel of reviewers, and other panel recommendations, such as the appropriate budget and duration of award. The SRO assures that all applicants receive this important document as a timely and accurate report of the review panel outcome, with a roster of panel members attached. The summary statement also is provided to each IC's advisory board or council for a second level of review that may include consideration of applicant concerns regarding the integrity and accuracy of the initial review. Applicants who believe that the initial peer review of their application was flawed may appeal the outcome to the council, and when this occurs, the SRO will be involved, conferring with the PO and providing additional information to the advisory council regarding the initial review process.

Although oversight of the initial peer review process is the heart of the duties of an SRO, and this is a sizable responsibility, it is by no means the job in its entirety. There are many opportunities for SROs to be involved in a multitude of exciting and career-building activities.

Contributing to New NIH Policies

SROs have opportunities to contribute to the development of new policies governing peer review in an ongoing effort to best serve the mission of the NIH. For example, beginning in 2009, many procedures that prevailed for more than 50 years were overhauled in an NIH-wide movement called "enhancing peer review." SROs still provide feedback on how various facets of this massive overhaul are faring in a "Continuous Review of Peer Review" mandate that invites feedback from applicants, SROs, POs, and peer reviewers for an indefinite period.

Teaming with Other Government Agencies

The NIH, as a government agency, has a time-honored system for extramural administration of biomedical and behavioral science; and partnering between the NIH and other governmental agencies is increasingly common and attests to the importance of embracing the growing emphasis on interdisciplinary science. One recent example was initiated by the NIH and the U.S. Agency for International Development (USAID), with assistance from the National Academy of Sciences (NAS). The "PEER (Partnerships for the Enhanced Engagement in Research) Health" program seeks to improve rates of child survival in low- and middle-income countries by developing interventions that reduce under-five mortality. The initial review for this new program was conducted in two stages: A "preproposal concept" application was reviewed by the NAS followed by a formal initial peer review of full grant applications of the top-tier selected preproposals conducted by SROs in the NICHD/NIH scientific review branch according to NIH peer review policies.

Participating in and Organizing Workshops

Joint workshops are often held by POs and SROs to provide an understanding glimpse of the NIH extramural granting process to prospective applicants. A "mock peer review meeting" is a common activity one might encounter at a scientific meeting in a workshop designed for new investigators. In addition, participating in videos of "mock study sections," webinars between NIH staff and prospective researchers for new funding initiatives, and web-based training for the scientific community are increasingly commonplace functions for SROs and POs at the NIH.

Designing and/or Testing New Technologies

As an alternative to in-person meetings of reviewers, which has traditionally been the gold standard for NIH peer review, the NIH is developing and continuously improving several "platforms" for the conduct of initial peer review. These are evolving at an impressive speed but always with the intent of providing a fair and optimal venue for the peer review process. In addition to novel review meeting strategies and accompanying technology development, new software is continuously under design and trial, often initiated and tested by creative SROs.

Participating in Training Opportunities

Requests from foreign institutions and scientific societies present opportunities for workshops with SROs that often lead to publications of workshop proceedings and/or white papers.

Congressional Inquiries

SROs may partner with other NIH staff, such as POs and legal counsel, to address congressional inquiries in response to requests from constituencies, seeking clarification for funding of certain projects, outcomes of peer review, or other issues.

SKILLS AND QUALIFICATIONS

All science administrators at the NIH are expected to have a doctorate-level degree, such as a PhD, and many have combined degrees; for example, PhD/JD, MD/PhD, PhD/DVM, DDS/PhD, or PhD/MPH. Many seek this position after a career as an independent research scientist, although some enter the profession immediately following postdoctoral training. There appears to be a growing number of investigators not long out of postdoctoral training that are now seeking administrative jobs in science as their first choice of career. Either way, most scientists have developed numerous skills that are essential not only for being a successful researcher or teacher but also for being an administrator. The most important qualification for the job is a love and appreciation of good science; that is why POs and SROs are officially called *scientist* administrators. One also needs excellent organizational skills, a talent for verbal and written communication, the ability to work well with others as a team, a tolerance for multitasking, and good common sense. Once in a position, there are many training opportunities to hone existing skills and to acquire on-the-job training.

Two key questions when considering a new career are the following: (1) What are the rewards? and (2) Is this career a good fit for you and your skills and talents? If you are interested in becoming a PO, will you enjoy the "social worker" part of the job—the gratification that comes from helping applicants and grantees—or will you dread speaking with disappointed grant applicants? Will you enjoy being at the forefront of science where one gets a broad overview of how areas connect and evolve over time, or will you miss the opportunity to drill down into the details of a specific problem? Some of the challenges of the position are linked to constrained NIH budgets. At the time that the NIH budget was doubling, the success rate for new grants was in the 35%–40% range. Currently, the NIH success rate for new grants is less than 20%, a record low. Although it is more important than ever to be able to guide and advise grantees at a time of tight budgets, it also means that difficult and unpopular funding decisions have to be made. Over the longer term, if you think it would be great fun to learn new areas of science and watch them morph, driven in large part by the scientific community, but also with a little help from you and the NIH, a PO may be a good career to consider.

For an SRO, there are additional rewards and challenges worth mentioning. One reward, which also is a challenge, is to oversee, in a neutral and unbiased manner, the peer review of projects similar to the research that you previously performed, without inserting yourself into the review of an area with which you are very familiar. Another example involves overseeing the review of applications on topics that are politically sensitive, such as applications on the uses of human embryonic stem cells, or vulnerable research populations, such as prisoners and pregnant women.

GETTING A FOOT IN THE DOOR

Program and review jobs are constantly turning over at the NIH. Specific jobs are posted on usajobs.gov and a global job registry periodically accepts resumes from individuals interested in scientist administrator positions. When someone at the NIH is interested in hiring a science administrator, they often search the global registry for promising candidates before posting a job announcement to the community via society and journal advertisements. A good way to start a search for a scientist administrator job is to contact a PO or SRO with whom you or your mentors have had previous interactions.

A strong publication record may be useful, but it is not necessary—note that many enter this arena directly from a postdoctoral position. Perhaps more advantageous is the demonstration of the skills and qualifications described previously; for example, excellent organizational skills, a talent for verbal and written communication, and the ability to work effectively in a team.

To demonstrate these broader talents, consider becoming involved in student organizations, organizing academic events, or taking advantage of writing opportunities (particularly related to science and technology). Then, ensure that your resume reflects the administrative/organizational and communication skills that you have developed.

CAREER PROGRESSION

Whether you opt for a position as a PO or SRO, the career paths for an HSA are certainly not dead-ended. The ability to keep abreast of cutting-edge science and make a significant impact is there for both types of administrators, as is the ample opportunity for lateral movement back and forth in a vast number of organizational settings within the federal workplace (Fig. 2).

Once one enters an administrative career at the NIH as a junior- or mid-level scientist, there are many pathways to follow and many opportunities for upward mobility (see Fig. 3). Within the career track of a scientist administrator, it is not uncommon to switch from being an SRO to a PO or vice versa, to move from one IC to another, or move to a policy position within the central NIH Office of the Director (see Chapter 6), often with responsibility for broader areas of science and supervision of personnel. In addition, armed with the skills and knowledge of a PO or SRO, many more-senior scientist administrators move into administrative positions of leadership and responsibility in other funding agencies and organizations, academic institutions, or professional societies. Scientist administrators should expect to have highly rewarding careers that build on their training, knowledge, and identity as a scientist.

WAY OUT

Taking a position as a scientist administrator does not have to be a one-way street; however, the longer you are in an administrative position, the harder it is to resume a research career. Therefore, scientists who make

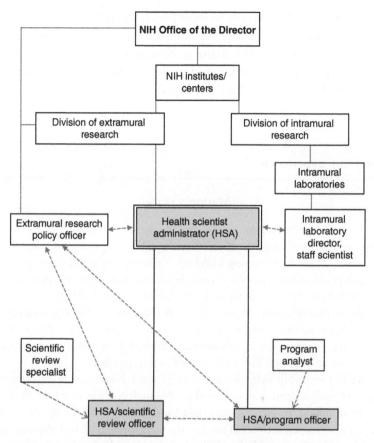

Figure 3. Typical career paths for health scientist administrators (HSAs) at NIH. Within the 27 institutes and centers, HSAs may serve various functions with lateral movement between them as program officers, scientific review officers, and in fewer cases, extramural policy officers. whereas HSAs are usually under the auspices of an NIH Institute (or center in some cases), extramural policy officers generally report to the Office of the NIH Director, although some institutes or centers have in-house offices for extramural policy. The NIH Institutes typically support divisions of extramural research and intramural research, although centers do not. Intramural staff scientists may seek HSA positions, and vice versa for career changes within NIH. Growth potential is particularly notable for program analysts or scientific review specialists (usually junior-level PhDs with postdoctoral training) that seek promotion to HSAs. Solid gray vertical lines depict lines of authority; dashed gray lines with arrows represent typical movements between positions.

this transition should be ready to leave bench research and move on to the rewards of a new career in science. In moving out of a position of science administration, consider the many opportunities that exist elsewhere in the government, in universities, and in the private sector that require the skills and abilities that you have developed.

Box 1. Our Experience

Marion's Story

I began my research career as an academic research immunologist and Clinical Director of a tissue transplantation laboratory. After a hiatus in my career during which I raised two young children, I returned to a full-time academic research position but soon discovered that I was ready for new opportunities and challenges. After speaking with the PO for my own NIH research grant, I realized that research administration could provide the opportunity to approach science from a broader perspective and to develop my "social worker" side. Service to the scientific community, coupled with a continuing connection to science, seemed like an ideal direction to pursue.

As a PO at the NIGMS for more than 27 years, I have seen many swings of the NIH budget pendulum—from the 1990 budget crisis, to the 1998–2003 budget doubling, to the currently tight fiscal situation. I have also witnessed the evolution of science overall because the areas for which I had responsibility continuously changed. My first PO job at the NIGMS involved developing a new program in molecular immunobiology that built on my previous immunology background, as well as assuming responsibility for a program in cell growth and differentiation, an area about which I knew little. Over time, the program area in cell growth and differentiation grew to include the rapidly emerging area of cell cycle control. Later, the area of programmed cell death blossomed and became a new focus for my program responsibilities. The most recent evolution of my program came to encompass the exciting new area of basic stem cell research. Clearly, while remaining at the NIGMS for many years, the nature of the science that I administered was constantly changing, as were my other activities.

Although my initial role as PO focused on administration of research grants, I acquired new responsibilities for administering training support mechanisms, such as individual postdoctoral fellowships and institutional predoctoral training grants. Training strategies must keep pace with workforce needs as well as the increasingly more complex and multidisciplinary practice of science. I have had the opportunity to develop new PhD training grant programs in two emerging areas: bioinformatics and computational biology, and molecular medicine. Equally important has been the challenge of promoting diversity in the biomedical and behavioral workforce. I have been involved in many activities over the years with this goal in mind, including organizing a workshop for training grant program directors, "Achieving Scientific Excellence Through Diversity," developing a new NIGMS website for diversity recruitment and retention strategies, and serving on the NIGMS Committee for Biomedical Workforce Diversity. My current responsibilities are to manage NIGMS diversity and reentry supplements programs that provide supplemental funds to research grants to recruit and train underrepresented individuals, from high school students through postdoctoral fellows, with the goal of increasing the diversity of the biomedical and behavioral workforce.

Although I never expected to become a science administrator when I entered graduate school, and never even knew that such a job existed, I clearly discovered a career that blends my love of science with the rewards of serving the research community. In 2012, I retired from my position as PO and from the federal government, but I have been fortunate enough to be able to continue some of my professional activities as a part-time contractor overseeing the NIGMS diversity and re-entry supplement programs. This has been a career that keeps on giving!

Sherry's Story

I financed my undergraduate education leading to a BS in zoology/microbiology through full- or part-time employment in clinical laboratories (as a technician in a university endocrine-metabolism research laboratory and subsequently as head of a serology laboratory in a large mid-western hospital). After gaining accreditation of the serology laboratory as a state reference laboratory, I returned to graduate school and earned an MS in cell biology, followed by a PhD in immunology. I acquired my initial postdoctoral training in a national laboratory with research on chromatin neoantigens in carcinogenesis. A second postdoctoral stint at a large cancer center was spent specifically conducting research on proto-oncogenes and oncogenes in "viral carcinogenesis," and I was finally involved in phase I–II clinical trials of rH-tumor necrosis factor at this cancer center on a contract with a Japanese pharmaceutical company.

Eventually I joined the NIH as a "microbiologist" at the National Institute of Allergy and Infectious Diseases (NIAID), division of extramural activities,

(Continued.)

where I functioned as an SRO (then called an "executive secretary") heavily involved in the administration of peer review for grant and cooperative agreement applications and contract proposals related to HIV AIDS. From there, I became review officer at the Fogarty International Center/NIH for initial review of research and research training grant applications in international biodiversity, international HIV epidemiology training, and international bioethics training, among others.

After a subsequent move to the NIH Center for Scientific Review, I initially administered a federally chartered review panel ("study section") that availed of my previous research in proto-oncogenes in development and cancer, plus molecular and genetic aspects of development, cancer, and aging. At the CSR, I rose through the ranks to the position of chief, biology of development and aging integrated review group. In this role, I helped to create and administer a group of study sections that still exist and have served many of the NIH ICs, including the NIGMS, and my coauthor Dr. Marion Zatz, whose portfolio consisted in part of applications that underwent peer review in some of my study sections. One of the most gratifying of my SRO duties at the CSR was in serving as the point person for review of human embryonic stem cells and a member of the NIH stem cell implementation committee, at a time when the topic of regenerative medicine/stem cells began to emerge as an integrated NIH-wide effort (due largely to the efforts of HSAs such as Marion Zatz as a PO, heavily involved in projects involving stem cells).

In 2010, I was honored to join the Eunice Kennedy Shriver National Institute of Child Health and Human Development (NICHD) as Director, Division of Scientific Review. The NICHD celebrated its 50th anniversary in 2012, and for me, the main attraction for joining this IC was (and remains) its mission: "to ensure that every person is born healthy and wanted, that women suffer no harmful effects from reproductive processes, and that all children have the chance to achieve their full potential for healthy and productive lives, free from disease or disability, and to ensure the health, productivity, independence, and well-being of all people through optimal rehabilitation." With a mission of such breadth, the opportunities for making a meaningful contribution are immense for anyone seeking a career in biomedical and behavioral research administration and training.

In summary, my 23 years at NIH have consisted of the administration of initial peer review in four institutes/centers. Looking back over two decades, I have not regretted the move to the NIH as an HSA at any stage; this remains a challenging and dynamic position that I heartily recommend to anyone seeking a meaningful and rewarding science career.

Box 2. Ten Dos and Don'ts

1. Do be ready to leave the bench.

2. Do develop a sense of whether you would prefer serving as an SRO or a PO.

3. Do not disregard the possibilities of moving among SRO, PO, and policy officer positions as you contemplate the HSA career route for long-term growth prospects within the NIH.

4. Do speak to people in administrative positions and colleagues who have interacted with NIH scientist administrators.

5. Do keep up with current events in scientific areas relevant to your field(s) of interest and training; the HSA is a scientist in his/her own right.

6. Do not forget to explore the value of formally "mentoring" through sharing the wisdom of your life experiences and thereby filling the "brain drain" as more senior HSAs leave the workforce.

7. Do develop a resume that highlights the administrative and science skills that you have developed.

8. Do not view a position as an administrator as a dead end. There are many opportunities for administrators in academia, government, and private industry.

9. Do not consider an administrative position to be a dead end; it can lead to other administrative positions in academia, government, or private industry.

10. Do not view yourself as a failure if you wish to leave bench research; focus on how you can use your training to further science in a new way.

Within the government, it is possible to move within or between federal agencies to gain experience and take on new leadership roles in other areas of administration or in policy. Similarly—outside of the government—pharmaceutical and biotech companies, nonprofits, and private foundations all offer many positions well suited for government administration professionals. Finally, universities and other research institutes typically sponsor research programs or other projects that may require grant specialists or program managers or those capable of communicating science to a broader audience. Any of these careers may be a good fit for some individuals with experience in science administration.

WWW RESOURCE

usajobs.gov A global job registry.

6

At the Crossroads of Science and Society: Careers in Science Policy

Amy P. Patterson, Mary E. Groesch, Allan C. Shipp, and Christopher J. Viggiani

Office of Science Policy, National Institutes of Health, Bethesda, Maryland 20892

Science policy offers a challenging and rewarding career path for scientists interested in the social, ethical, and legal implications of their field. This topic encompasses a broad spectrum of activities all in support of advancing the scientific enterprise. Science policy spans various sectors, and policy careers are found in many different organizations, including the federal government, scientific societies, and professional organizations. Although their specific duties may vary greatly, science policy professionals generally apply their scientific training to ensure that the scientific enterprise advances in a responsible and ethical manner and to solve challenges with broad scientific and societal implications.

Science policy is an area of public policy concerned with the course and conduct of the scientific enterprise. A thriving scientific enterprise is a vital national priority that is intertwined with broader national interests such as economic competitiveness, public health, environmental health, energy production and consumption, education, food production and safety, international relations, and national security. Science directly and indirectly impacts almost every area of life and, as such, developing science policy requires an ongoing dialog among scientists, policy makers, and the public. It is this realm, at the center of the dialog between science and society, where policy professionals work to shape the policies that advance the scientific enterprise in a manner that is ethical and acceptable to society as a whole. This chapter describes science policy careers as they pertain to the life sciences, with a focus on those in biomedical research. We primarily discuss careers in the U.S. government but will touch on policy careers in other sectors.

In the biomedical context, science policy is aimed at advancing basic and applied research to address public health priorities. Advancing biomedical research and developing new disease treatments are essential, but doing so in a responsible, ethical manner is equally important. Striking this balance can be challenging, given how rapidly many life sciences disciplines are advancing. But as scientific frontiers advance and discoveries and technologies push the boundaries of what is possible, new questions with scientific, ethical, legal, social, and political dimensions emerge and must be addressed.

For instance, our office—the Office of Science Policy, within the Office of the Director at the National Institutes of Health—deals with a broad range of constantly evolving policy issues. Some of our current areas of focus include policies related to clinical research, genomic data sharing and oversight, biosafety, biosecurity, emerging biotechnologies, and the return on public investment in research. In seeking to advance the life sciences in a manner that is responsive to both public health needs and any ethical or other concerns associated with the science, we grapple with a host of challenging questions. For example, how can the privacy of human subjects involved in clinical or genomic research be protected? When published, could some of the information from research on dangerous pathogens provide a blueprint for bioterrorists? How should ethical concerns surrounding embryonic stem cell research be addressed? What are the risks associated with emerging fields, such as synthetic biology or nanotechnology? What potential burden will a new policy place on the research community? Is that burden acceptable? Answers to these types of questions are embodied in the policy responses that guide how research is conducted, technologies are pursued, and treatments are developed.

The policy process begins with the identification of a problem or issue. Then, policy makers begin to develop policy options or recommendations. In doing so, they consult with the public, subject matter experts, and other stakeholders to determine how best to address the issue. Stakeholders for a given issue might include scientists, medical and public health professionals, research institutions and hospitals, pharmaceutical and biotech industries, patients, the scientific publishing community, the public at large, and many more. Ultimately, policy makers decide on and implement a course of action and periodically review the policy to ensure that it adequately addresses the problem and keeps pace with the changing scientific landscape. Science policy professionals fulfill key roles at each step in this process with their leadership, policy analysis, scientific expertise, and advocacy efforts.

There are many areas of science policy, and science policy careers can be found in many sectors. In this chapter, we primarily discuss careers in biomedical science policy, the skills required to succeed in science policy, strategies for moving from the laboratory or clinic into science policy, and different policy career paths. Regardless of the path, the ever-changing and unpredictable nature of scientific progress makes science policy a dynamic and rewarding career choice.

JOBS

There is no "typical" science policy job. But careers in science policy generally involve "the bigger picture" and offer individuals an opportunity to work at the intersection of science and society. The exact role of a science policy professional varies depending on the mission of their organization and its role in the policy process. Below, we describe science policy in the executive branch of the federal government and note some of the other sectors involved in science policy.

Almost every federal department or agency invests in or has an interest in life sciences research and they therefore use policy professionals to shape their research programs or contribute scientific input to their policy activities. The federal government funds all types of life sciences research, typically through extramural programs (i.e., research conducted by independent scientists supported by federal funds) and intramural programs (i.e., research conducted by government scientists). Basic and applied biomedical research is supported by the U.S. Department of Health and Human Services and its component agencies.

- The National Institutes of Health (NIH) funds and conducts basic and applied life sciences research aimed at enhancing health, lengthening life, and reducing illness and disability.

- The Centers for Disease Control and Prevention (CDC) conducts scientific research and provides health information to protect the public against health threats.

- The Food and Drug Administration (FDA) helps to ensure the safety and effectiveness of various life sciences research products, such as vaccines, drugs, and medical devices.

Many other federal agencies fund or have a direct interest in life sciences research as well, including the National Science Foundation, Environmental Protection Agency, and the Departments of Energy, Homeland Security, Defense, and Veterans Affairs. The Office of Science and Technology Policy, within the Executive Office of the President, coordinates science-related policy development activities for the executive branch and also provides the President and senior staff with sound scientific and technical advice on policy matters.

Policy professionals at these and other federal agencies coordinate the policy process, analyze or develop policies, and work to implement policies. They may conceptualize or advance a research agenda or initiative or develop policies that help to ensure that the scientific enterprise advances, and new innovations are developed in a safe, responsible manner. Policy professionals also commonly manage working groups or committees of experts who are enlisted to make policy recommendations on a given issue. These activities generally occur at many levels, ranging from the broad (i.e., government-wide policy development and coordination) to the more specific (i.e., policy analysis and development specific to a division, branch, or research area). Science policy professionals commonly review policy documents and consider them according to their impact on the scientific enterprise and their agency's mission. When developing policies, policy professionals routinely organize meetings, workshops, or conferences to solicit important feedback from stakeholders.

Science policy jobs exist outside of the government as well. These jobs vary greatly based on the scope of the organization's work, structure, and role in the policy process. Some of these organizations are federally funded; others are private research institutions (which can be for- or not-for-profit). Typically, these organizations are commissioned by the government to provide objective expert advice and analysis, coordinate studies, or manage projects at the request of a federal department or agency. For instance, the National Academies (which consists of the National Academy of Sciences, National Academy of Engineering, Institute of Medicine, and National Research Council) regularly issue reports that help to shape policy, inform public opinion, and advance the pursuit of science, engineering, and medicine. Scientific and professional societies also conduct studies on how policies impact their constituents, and many universities have academic centers devoted to the study of specific areas of science policy. Numerous other research and development centers—sometimes called think tanks—provide specialized expertise and support.

Other opportunities in science policy are found in scientific societies or professional associations that represent the interests of their scientific communities, institutions, or other stakeholders. These organizations form a conduit between their communities and the federal policy makers. They regularly communicate with their constituents and policy makers, stay abreast of relevant policy issues, and shape policy discussions with their analysis and input. Examples of such organizations include the American Association for the Advancement of Science, the Federation of American Societies for Experimental Biology, the American Society for Microbiology, the Association of Public and Land-Grant Universities, the Association of American Universities, the Association of American Medical Colleges, the Pharmaceutical Research and Manufacturers of America, the Biotechnology Industry Organization, and countless others representing constituents with a stake in the scientific enterprise. Government relations specialists at individual biotech and pharmaceutical companies, as well as universities and medical centers, also routinely interface with policy makers, monitor relevant policy developments, and advocate their entity's position on given policy issues.

Finally, there are policy jobs that are less about developing policies that guide the conduct of scientific research and more about ensuring that science *informs* policy development. The FDA, for instance, uses scientific information when developing science-based regulatory approaches for new drugs and medical devices. These approaches range from pre-market review of efficacy and safety to post-market product surveillance to review of product quality. The CDC also relies on scientific input in its efforts to detect and monitor existing and emerging health threats. This information informs various policy responses, such as determining how much and what types of vaccines should be produced. In addition, there are federal agencies whose primary missions do not involve supporting research activities but nevertheless have an interest in the scientific enterprise or how scientific findings affect and inform their areas of focus (e.g., the State Department). Budgetary issues impact all policy decisions, including those related to science and technology; as such, the Office of Management and Budget employs individuals with scientific expertise. The legislative branch also deals with a host of policy issues, many of which directly involve scientific research, whereas other issues are informed by scientific consensus. Policy professionals working in regulatory science, in "nonscience" agencies, or serving as staff to senators, representatives, or congressional committees may communicate science to policy makers and contribute an understanding of scientific issues related to the development of broader public policy.

SKILLS AND QUALIFICATIONS

Although few academic degrees are offered in science policy, the skills one acquires by earning an advanced degree in the natural or social sciences, medicine, public or international health, public policy administration, law, ethics, economics, or other related fields are immensely beneficial. In general, an advanced degree, such as a master's degree, MD, PhD, or JD, is required to get a start in science policy, and such degrees may help individuals to advance as a science policy professional. Generally, but not universally, senior-level life sciences policy professionals have doctoral degrees in a medical or scientific discipline. A master's degree in public health can be valuable for certain positions and other master's degrees can help to get a foot in the door or provide a candidate with a particularly desirable area of expertise. Postdoctoral research experience or additional training is not necessary but may be beneficial if it allows a candidate to strengthen their analytic skills or develop expertise in an area that is particularly desirable to a given policy office or organization.

Strong analytic skills are crucial to succeed in science policy. A policy analyst needs to be able to quickly hone in on the bottom line of a particular issue. What is the underlying challenge or hurdle? What are the implications for the agency or the research community? Analysts need to be able to quickly distill many pages of scientific or policy rhetoric down to the essential key points and come up with a plan or options for addressing the issues. An analyst also needs to be able to recognize common threads among seemingly disparate items.

In science policy, it is absolutely essential to be able to communicate clearly, both orally and in writing. Writing skills are particularly important. One of the biggest challenges in transitioning from bench science to science policy involves the different writing styles required for each field. Scientific writing and science policy writing both require an ability to communicate ideas clearly and precisely, but proficiency in writing scientific papers does not necessarily translate into being an effective writer in the science policy arena. An essential part of communicating in the policy arena is the ability to communicate effectively to nonscientists or experts in other fields about complex science and policy issues. In policy, it is often necessary to focus on the implications of scientific results rather than on the scientific details per se. Shifting focus away from nitty gritty scientific details to a bigger picture can be one of the most challenging aspects of the transition from the bench to science policy.

In addition, science policy sometimes focuses on controversial, sensitive, or polarizing issues (e.g., embryonic stem cell research, animal research, or genetic testing) that can be especially challenging to address if the personal views of a policy professional differ from the organization's position. Policy professionals should generally be comfortable working in support of their organization's mission.

Science policy work can be exciting and challenging, especially when it involves short time frames, uncertainty, change, politics, and bureaucracy. Policy professionals should be flexible and able to roll with the punches because they are often required to draft and analyze policy documents or respond to requests in a matter of days—and often, hours. Many times, policy analysts do not immediately see the outcome or end result of their work; often, they are asked to contribute to an ongoing process or meet a tight deadline only to wait on other input or contributions before the process moves forward. As new policy challenges arise, policy professionals are often expected to develop additional expertise that may be outside of the scientific area in which they are trained. This all makes for exciting—and unpredictable—work that often requires policy professionals to adapt and rapidly shift gears.

For careers in science policy, the old adage that "no man is an island" holds particularly true. Although an individual may be the lead on developing a report or organizing a workshop, policy analysts always bounce ideas off others and get input from colleagues who test and hone these ideas. This input may come from within the office, the agency or department, elsewhere within the government, and/or from private sectors. To be successful in science policy, one must be aware of and open to different perspectives.

Further, to be successful in science policy, policy professionals should be service-oriented and comfortable with the fact that they do not make policy by themselves. Rather, they contribute to a large, collaborative policy development process that often involves managing or working within groups and developing consensus. Developing policy is never the activity of a single individual, and the sphere of influence of science policy professionals is typically behind the scenes; federal policies and reports for public dissemination rarely have authors. This can be a bit of a culture shock for students, postdocs, or clinicians who are used to "owning" their research projects and authoring manuscripts. But policy professionals often derive satisfaction in knowing that they advanced their organization's mission or were a substantive participant in the dialog surrounding an important issue.

Finally, policy professionals must value the consultative process. Policy issues evolve over time but rarely disappear or are fully "solved." Policy professionals should be able to "enjoy the conversation" and not always expect discrete, tangible outputs for each project.

Careers in policy are challenging and incredibly interesting and satisfying. Policy professionals are integral participants in truly important discussions and policy efforts; their work helps to advance the scientific enterprise in ways that broadly benefit society.

GETTING A FOOT IN THE DOOR

Moving from academia, the laboratory, or the clinic into a career in science policy can be challenging, but it is not impossible. Graduate students, postdoctoral fellows, or early-stage clinicians should begin by developing an area of scientific expertise and demonstrating academic success with research publications, presentations, awards, and other accomplishments. Although a strong publication record may be helpful, researchers with a more modest publication history can still be very competitive for science policy jobs because the other skills and qualifications described above are truly important in science policy. Stand-out candidates are those who supplement their scientific achievements with a broader understanding of the social, ethical, legal, or other implications of scientific research.

To demonstrate this broader interest and understanding, one should explore opportunities outside of the laboratory or clinic. This might include becoming active in student organizations; organizing academic events, workshops, or symposia; or pursuing writing opportunities (particularly related to science, technology, or policy) with newspapers, newsletters, or magazines that are published by universities or professional societies. Volunteer experience related to science or broader policy areas—such as experience with nonprofit organizations, technology transfer offices, academic public policy research centers, or any experience interacting with the public to explain scientific issues—may also be helpful. Teaching experience can be leveraged to demonstrate communication skills and an ability to clearly convey complex scientific information. Numerous other activities can help a candidate prepare for a career in science policy; the idea is to explore opportunities and demonstrate leadership, initiative, an ability to work with others to accomplish goals, and importantly, an interest in the broader implications of science.

Toward this end, it is also important to stay abreast of science policy issues and demonstrate some understanding of the policy process. Many scientific journals have sections devoted to scientific news, editorials, and policy perspectives. Professional societies also typically publish newsletters and have sections on their websites devoted to policy issues that impact their research community. It is not expected that a student or postdoc be an expert on science policy, but knowledge of some of the "hot button" issues and a basic understanding of how the government works serve a candidate well.

When seeking a science policy job with the U.S. government, begin the search at USAJOBS (see the end of the chapter for URLs) for a comprehensive listing of the job vacancies at federal departments and agencies. Many positions require some prior policy experience, but entry-level positions are available. Science policy or policy-related jobs may also be available through contractor positions that can be sought out through other online job-listing services.

Formal science policy fellowships are also an excellent way for candidates to get a foot in the door of government agencies. These fellowships provide training and experience in science policy offices, exposure to different types of science policy work, and opportunities for networking and making contacts. Such fellowships often lead to permanent positions or provide a stepping stone to other opportunities. The Science and Technology Policy Fellowship, sponsored by the American Association for the Advancement of Science, is one of the most well-known science policy fellowship programs. Other programs include the Presidential Management Fellows Program and the Christine Mirzayan Science and Technology Policy Graduate Fellowship Program. Many scientific societies and associations have science policy fellowship programs as well, including fellowships in congressional offices.

It may also be possible to secure a brief internship (full or part time) in a science policy office within the government or a professional society, either through an internship program or on a volunteer basis. Any kind of regular participation in a policy office is an opportunity to demonstrate passion and suitability for the work. Whether an internship can be secured or not, informational interviews with science policy professionals are quite useful. Not only do these interviews provide a sense of what a career in science policy entails, but they are an opportunity to identify other individuals with whom to confer.

Scientific associations, professional societies, nonprofit organizations, private research centers, think tanks, and academic centers are also sources of policy-related jobs. Positions in such organizations provide opportunities to influence the policy process, become steeped in the issues, conduct studies or analyze policy, and make important contacts in the policy arena.

CAREER PROGRESSION

Because science policy includes a broad spectrum of activities, policy domains, and sectors, careers can be quite fluid and rarely will any two science policy careers follow the same trajectory. Furthermore, the precise hierarchy of an office or organization involved in science policy varies significantly. In general, however, a career in policy progresses from analytic or technical responsibilities to positions of management. Typical policy offices might have junior analysts, senior analysts, senior advisors, program directors, and an office director who may be in a senior leadership position for their agency or organization.

Analysts typically monitor policy developments and provide policy options to their leadership. They typically work in teams to prepare reports, issue briefs, option papers, slide presentations, talking points, memos, meeting summaries, fact sheets, and FAQs. They may also help to organize meetings or workshops aimed at exploring issues and gathering stakeholder input. More senior analysts are likely to lead individual projects and may have the responsibility of managing or coordinating the efforts of others. As policy analysts gain experience, they often become subject matter experts on particular research or policy areas and may be asked to represent their agency on a particular issue.

Senior advisors or program directors have even more supervisory responsibility and oversee the operation of larger programs or portfolios. These senior policy professionals anticipate emerging policy issues, set priorities for their program, develop a plan for achieving desired goals, and coordinate the efforts of policy analysts and others to achieve those goals. These individuals lead major policy development or other efforts and manage projects. Senior advisors and program directors are typically counted on to provide their organization's leadership with policy analysis and advice about issues that are particularly challenging and perhaps controversial.

A director of an office involved in science policy is in charge of leading and managing all of the policy efforts of their office, branch, division, and/or organization. This involves working with an organization's leadership, federal partners, and other stakeholders to identify policy needs and set priorities. Ultimately, a director mobilizes an office and allocates resources to accomplish tasks in support of their office's mission. An office director sets the short- and long-term goals for their office and responds quickly to emerging policy issues.

As with any career, advancement in science policy is based on how well candidates perform their tasks. Generally, individuals who advance in science policy careers are those who demonstrate a keen grasp of complex issues, take direction, welcome new challenges, and work well with others. Individuals who effectively analyze and draft policy documents, manage larger projects, help coordinate the efforts of a team, or effectively represent their organization at meetings are often assigned more responsibility, which can lead to career advances. Networking is also important to advancing in science policy and is an excellent way to find new opportunities within federal agencies or other organizations or sectors. Developing strong relationships with colleagues often opens the door to new, sometimes unexpected, opportunities.

There are many ways for science policy professionals to advance their careers. In the government, for example, one can move within or among federal agencies to gain experience in new policy areas, interact with new industries and sectors, and take on leadership responsibilities. Career advancement in science policy can also occur through moves among the public, private, or nonprofit sectors. For example, at the NIH, one may work on a policy issue that has international dimensions that may translate well to a policy position promoting global health at another federal agency or a private foundation focused on international development. As a general rule, individuals should advance their policy careers by seeking out new challenges and responsibilities while continuing to pursue their passions.

CAREER TRANSITIONS

Although opportunities in science policy exist elsewhere, policy careers are concentrated in the Washington, D.C. area, because analyzing, developing, and implementing science policy occurs largely within, and in association with, the federal government. For this reason, science policy is not one of the most "portable" careers. However, the skills and experiences gained in the policy arena are applicable to other areas, and because science policy professionals interact with stakeholders in many sectors, they can often develop a diverse network of colleagues "outside the beltway."

Private sector positions in government relations or regulatory affairs may be a natural transition for some. For instance, an individual with experience working in regulatory policy at the FDA, or fostering public–private partnerships at the NIH, may be well suited for a career with a biotech or pharmaceutical company. Nonprofits, private foundations, and universities also employ government relations professionals.

Universities or other research institutes may be another logical transition for individuals with experience in science policy. Universities often sponsor research programs or other initiatives with specified goals that may require grant specialists, program managers, technology transfer professionals, compliance officers, and individuals with experience in public relations and communicating science to a broader audience. These careers may be a good fit for some individuals with experience in science policy.

Box 1. Our Experience

The authors of this chapter all entered science policy through different paths.

Amy's Story

I am currently the Associate Director for Science Policy at the NIH, but my career in science and science policy took several unexpected turns. After completing medical school, a residency in internal medicine, and a postdoctoral research fellowship in endocrinology and metabolism, I had accepted an academic appointment. However, "life" intervened, and in order to take care of an ill family member in the Washington D.C. area, I postponed my academic position and worked as a medical officer at the FDA. Instead of being the temporary position that I anticipated, my tenure at the FDA lasted five years. My work in the Center for Biologics Evaluation and Research introduced me to the world of drug development, policy, and regulation. I learned first-hand about product development, clinical trial design, and public health. I was also selected to represent the U.S. Department of Health and Human Services at a World Health Organization meeting on an emerging and controversial area of research, and together with scientists and ethicists representing more than 30 other nations, I helped to develop international guidelines that are still in place today.

My experiences at the FDA opened my eyes to the critical role of policy development and the importance and diversity of global vantage points and profoundly influenced my career path toward science policy. I realized that a career in science policy offered ample opportunity for problem solving and public service while delving into the crossroads of science, ethics, law, and society. I knew that this was the career path for me.

After five years at the FDA, I accepted a position as the Director of the Office of Biotechnology Activities (OBA) within the NIH Office of Science Policy (OSP). OBA analyzes, develops, and implements policies to address ethical, legal, and social concerns associated with basic and clinical research involving recombinant DNA, genetic technologies, and other emerging biotechnologies. After several years, I took on an even broader range of issues as the Associate Director for Science Policy and the Director of OSP. At OSP, we provide leadership on science policy issues of significance to the NIH, the medical research community, and the public, with particular focus on cross-cutting issues. At OSP, in addition to emerging biotechnology policy issues, we are also involved in policy issues associated with clinical research, genetic testing, data sharing and privacy, health care research, biosafety, biosecurity, return on scientific investments, and more. As an integral part of our policy development process, we conduct extensive consultations and routinely engage with the public and scientific communities.

Mary's Story

During my postdoc in a cell biology laboratory, I became increasingly aware that I did not want to stay at the bench and have my whole world revolve around the role of one protein in one step of a subcellular process, nor did I

(Continued.)

want to teach or work in industry. Instead, I wanted the focus of my career to be "the bigger picture." It was also important that what I worked on could truly have the potential to make a difference in science at a level beyond the bench.

At that time—we are talking more than 20 years ago—science policy was not a very visible nor well-recognized career option. After considerable exploration, I finally learned about science policy and the AAAS fellowship and was told by many that this was the *only* way to break into the policy arena. I applied for the fellowship with great excitement, absolutely sure that this was my destiny and unable to imagine a future without that fellowship. But, as you might guess...I was not selected for the program!

I did not give up, but continued to pursue every possible lead and contact, and eventually was put in touch with the Director of the science policy unit within the Office of the Director at the NIH. She was looking for someone with a strong scientific background (there were very few scientists in science policy at that time) and was willing to teach that person about policy. Something I said to her in my first interview caught her attention—that it is important to be able to explain even the most complex science in an understandable way to members of the public. I was hired, and one of my favorite tasks for the next several years was writing about the NIH's most important scientific advances for members of Congress and the public—to explain the return on the public's investment in biomedical research.

Although I was crushed at not getting the science policy fellowship, I actually ended up getting a job in science policy a year or two sooner than I would have through the fellowship. My lesson: Do not give up pursuing your passion if you encounter a roadblock—there is always another way forward!

Allan's Story

As an undergraduate, I majored in biology at a time when molecular biology was an emerging and exciting field with tremendous promise. I planned on applying to PhD programs in molecular biology but first wanted some practical laboratory experience to test whether a life as a scientist was right for me. After working for a biotechnology company for a year and a half, I realized that my interest in molecular biology, and science in general, was related to its impact on society more than to the conduct of science itself.

At the time, I was unaware of any formal degree programs in science policy, and so I investigated health policy and health-care management programs. I entered a program in health administration and upon graduation with a master's degree, I worked for a managed care company as a health economics analyst. Quickly, the scope of the job seemed quite small relative to my broader interests, and I subsequently found a position as a policy analyst in the biomedical research division of the Association of American Medical Colleges—an association representing medical schools, teaching hospitals, and academic and scientific societies. There, I worked on a broad array of issues, including the regulation of biotechnology, clinical research ethics, training the research workforce, the use of animals in research, and scientific integrity. The work was stimulating and capitalized on my skills at analysis and writing. After 13 years, though, it was not enough to simply write and think about the issues; I really wished to be working in an environment closer to the science and at the front lines of policymaking. I was fortunate to find a job in the science policy office at the NIH, where I focus on working with the research community about biosafety, biosecurity, and other research matters, and I am also able to stay steeped in policy analysis and development as well—a perfect fit!

Chris's Story

I entered science policy as an AAAS Science and Technology Policy Fellow at the NIH after completing a PhD in molecular biology. Throughout graduate school, I was an observer of national politics and became interested in how policy can drive scientific research and innovation. I was drawn to the idea of strengthening our national research portfolio through policy. With the encouragement of an understanding mentor (who himself had dabbled in policy), I became involved in student government, took on other student leadership roles in our department, and took a course in biobusiness. These experiences were essential to making me a competitive candidate for the policy fellowship.

After the policy fellowship, I realized that I had some more research left in my system, so I returned to the bench for a postdoc position with the intent of pursuing the academic track. My postdoctoral work on telomeres was interesting and exciting, my colleagues were incredible, but I soon began to miss the broader "big picture" issues that I had worked on as a policy fellow. After two years—and again with the guidance and understanding from a wonderful advisor—I returned to policy, joining the NIH Office of Science Policy to work on biosecurity and emerging technologies issues. My advice is to work hard at the bench, but be sure to explore opportunities outside the laboratory.

Box 2. Ten Dos and Don'ts

1. Do pursue your passion.

2. Do welcome challenges and enjoy problem solving.

3. Do be open to new and unanticipated opportunities, even if it takes you off the career trajectory you had originally planned to be on.

4. Do knock on doors; they usually do not open unless you do so.

5. Do build a network of contacts.

6. Do take a writing course if you are unaccustomed to nonscientific writing.

7. Do aim your efforts at excellence and shift your focus beyond yourself.

8. Do practice patience, negotiation, resiliency, conflict resolution, and time management.

9. Do familiarize yourself with science policy issues and the activities of the agency/organization in which you are interested.

10. Do not forget to stay energized and committed to personal and professional growth.

WWW RESOURCES

http://sites.nationalacademics.org/pga/policyfellows/ Christine Mirzayan Science and Technology Policy Graduate Fellowship Program.

www.usajobs.gov USA Jobs Working for America, U.S. Office of Personnel Management website.

http://www.aaas.org/program/science-technology-policy-fellowships AAAS Science and Technology Policy Fellowships.

http://www.osp.od.nih.gov/ National Institutes of Health Office of Science Policy.

http://www.phds.org/jobs/nonacademic-careers/internships-and-careers-in-science-policy Internships and Careers in Science Policy

http://www.pmf.gov/ Presidential Management Fellows Program.

7

Working for a Scientific Society

Martin Frank

American Physiological Society, Bethesda, Maryland 20814

Opportunities for employment of PhD scientists exist within the world of
scientific societies. Societies exist to serve the needs of their scientific or
engineering constituencies. As membership organizations, they provide
their constituents with access to meetings, publications (both books and
journals), educational programs, and advocacy assistance. Within many
of these societies, leadership positions and associated coordinator/analyst
positions can be filled by someone with a PhD. Examples of positions in
societies include science policy/government relations, education, publications, communications, and executive departments. Interested PhDs
should demonstrate their interest by volunteering to participate in society
outreach or committee activities. The critical element is to remember that
as a PhD you have the critical thinking and problem-solving ability to succeed in whatever career you pursue. The key is to demonstrate that these
abilities are applicable to the available positions in the association.

National scientific and engineering societies exist to fulfill a scientific or
engineering purpose or to serve the needs of a scientific or engineering audience. Typically, they have a nonprofit status and at least 100 members and
do one or more of the following: (1) publish a peer-reviewed journal; (2)
hold regularly scheduled professional or technical meetings; (3) produce
standards; and (4) offer continuing education.

The Council of Engineering and Scientific Society Executives (CESSE)
represents a small subset of the association world that is more broadly represented by the American Society of Association Executives (ASAE), a society representing more than 10,000 societies. This chapter is based on the
author's experience at the American Physiological Society (APS), but in
order to confirm that other societies provide similar opportunities for
PhD scientists, a survey was conducted among members of CESSE. There

are ~200 CESSE member societies and responses were received from 36 of these societies. The responding societies employ 1288 individuals, 75 of whom possess PhDs.

Job opportunities for PhDs in scientific societies span a wide range of positions within a multitude of departments. For example, positions exist in the following departments/areas: education, publications, communications, government relations/science policy, and executive administration. As an example of a society structure, Figure 1 shows the organizational chart for the APS.

The history of the APS (see Box 3, p. 106–107) is typical of the course taken by many associations as they progressed from organizations led and managed by volunteer leadership to organizations managed by professional staff. In many cases, the individual hired to lead the society has a doctorate in the relevant academic discipline, whereas in other cases, the leader has a business or management degree. Since its founding, the APS has grown to approximately 11,000 members and at the same time the society's staff has grown to 70 individuals. Of those, seven APS employees have PhD degrees—two in the humanities and the others in scientific fields. The five PhD scientists are employed as follows: executive director; director of education programs; education project coordinator; publications ethics manager; and science policy analyst. The two humanities PhDs are journal supervisors. This chapter describes the opportunities available to PhD scientists within the association world and provides guidance for professional scientists interested in obtaining these positions.

JOBS

The CESSE survey revealed the primary areas in which PhDs are employed, including science policy/government relations, communications, education, publications, and executive positions. Below is an overview of some of the duties individuals in these positions exercise as they strive to advance the mission of the association.

Science Policy and Government Relations

In reviewing the job titles associated with this area, one might find science policy analyst, science policy or government relations director, or legislative officer. In general, the responsibilities for all are the same and the distinguishing characteristics are the level of authority and responsibility. It is

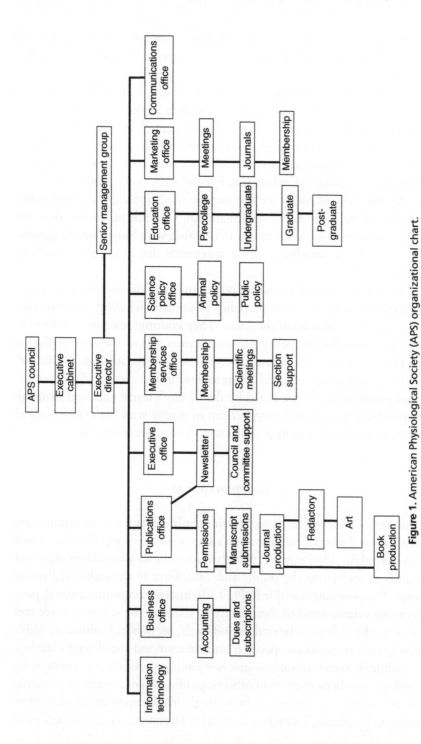

Figure 1. American Physiological Society (APS) organizational chart.

obvious that a director level position will have supervisory responsibility and provide leadership and direction for the society's overall science policy efforts.

Science policy/government relations specialists work with the society's leadership to develop the policy positions taken by the organization. Issues of interest to the organization might relate to research funding; the conduct, regulation, or management of government-funded research; or regulatory oversight. In most associations, the policy response is developed in conjunction with committees of volunteers. For the APS, two committees oversee the development of policy for the society: the Science Policy Committee and the Animal Care and Experimentation Committee. In addition, the APS, as with most societies, works in coalition with like-minded organizations in order to amplify position statements developed individually or jointly.

Science policy staff formulate policy and develop and compose documents that convey the society's policy positions, including position statements or white papers on the issue. They communicate outward to the officials responsible for policy implementation and to the membership so that they amplify the message and become an effective advocate for the policy. The policy analyst prepares letters to be sent to elected officials, congressional testimony to be presented by the society's leadership, and materials designed to encourage the membership to engage with their elected representatives so that they embrace the society's recommendations.

Communications

Increasingly, associations are recognizing the importance of communicating information about their organization's activities to their membership as well as to the public. The latter is especially important for associations that work in areas of interest to the public and contribute to the public debate on issues. The positions available to PhD scientists in communications departments are often related to their ability to translate the scientific topic area into something that can be understood by the lay public. Positions available include communications specialist and director and social media manager. Although communications involves issuing press releases announcing awards to members, election of officers, publication of a study, or presentation of research at a meeting, it increasingly involves posting of such information to Facebook, Twitter, or LinkedIn. The communications staff must be familiar with social media and the means to speed information out to their communities. In addition, associations are increasingly hiring individuals to promote their mission and activities through blogging, either on a full- or part-time basis.

At the APS, the director of communications is responsible for developing and implementing a strategic plan for communicating the benefits of, and appreciation for, the science of physiology, as well as the APS itself and its programs. This includes but is not limited to press releases for journal articles, presentations at the society's meetings, development of a consumer website, and social media outreach. The communications director and communications specialists may be PhD scientists but it is critical that the individuals within the department have excellent writing and verbal skills. In many ways, the communications issued by the department become the "face" of the organization. Individuals within the communications department must be able to work closely with members of their committee but also interact with other departments within the society to decide on the information to promote and programs to feature in press releases and social media. The communications staff is also responsible for responding to media inquiries and identifying the individuals most capable of talking with the media.

Education

Education activities in most associations cover a broad expanse of activities. These might include the management of scientific meetings but most relate to management of programs focusing on K–12 through professional education. Overseeing the former, a scientist with a PhD may serve as a meeting planner and a grant writer. For those employed in an education department, the mission might relate to development of K–12 programs, undergraduate or graduate programs, or postdoctoral certification programs. Education activities might focus on increasing diversity within the discipline, increasing the representation of women, enhancing opportunities for trainees, or providing information about career opportunities. The professional education staff is responsible for implementing the society's education programs; overseeing externally funded education projects, including development of project products; evaluation of projects; and dissemination of final project reports in the literature. They are also responsible for overseeing internally funded education activities and award programs.

The positions within such a department include education project coordinator, education or professional development specialist, or education director. In all positions, knowledge of the program and ability to write clearly are necessary. These qualifications provide opportunities for the individual to become responsible for writing proposals to federal agencies and foundations to support the society's activities and preparing annual reports on the programs for the membership and leadership.

Executive Office

PhDs often find opportunities within the executive offices of scientific societies. These jobs might be the association's executive director or deputy executive director, foundation director, or development officer. The role of the foundation director or development officer involves raising funds to advance and implement society programs. The scientific experience and expertise of the incumbent allows them to talk science with the individuals with whom they meet to raise funds. The positions require unique skills that allow the incumbent to visit with individuals and groups to solicit support by making oral presentations and submitting written proposals. In some cases, the development officer's position can be filled by an individual early in their professional career who possesses the oral and written skills as well as the personality needed to solicit program support for the association.

In general, the executive director (chief executive officer, or CEO) position is filled by a more senior individual who has had prior experiences that have demonstrated his or her management and communications skills. However, in many larger organizations, there are opportunities for a more junior PhD to become a deputy executive director with the potential for promotion to a CEO position. The executive director generally reports directly to the volunteer leadership (board or council) and is responsible for carrying out the society's functions and managing the operation. The deputy executive director reports to the CEO and is responsible for overseeing and managing a subset of the executive director's responsibilities.

The CEO serves as principal administrative officer of the society, responsible for the management of the central office and the conduct of day-to-day operations. He or she is responsible for selecting, evaluating, and promoting all personnel and coordinating these activities with the association's department heads. The CEO provides overall supervision of the department directors and all other senior managers. Working closely with the finance director to develop the annual budget, the CEO receives and distributes copies of financial reports from investment counselors managing the association's reserve funds and has discretionary and signing powers for the society's investment funds. As a PhD scientist, the CEO often speaks on behalf of the association, especially when the society's president is unavailable.

Publications

Most scientists with PhDs are knowledgeable about publications and, depending on how well versed they are in writing and editing, it is possible to develop this experience into a career in publications. A number of job opportunities are open to PhDs in this arena. These range from copy editor to positions as journal supervisors, managing editors, publication ethics officers, art editors, news staff writer, scientific editor, or publications director.

Most societies issue a newsletter on a regular basis to inform the membership of activities occurring within the organization. In some cases, as with *ASBMB Today*, the newsletter of the American Society for Biochemistry and Molecular Biology, the content includes summaries of recent papers published in their research journals and profiles of ASBMB member scientists. The preparation of these articles falls to scientific staff writers who translate the science into more readily accessible prose.

PhDs can also be hired as scientific journal editors when the journal is managed within the society. The scientific editor recruits associate editors and editorial board members, assigns manuscripts for review, and determines which articles will be published in the journal. For most societies, the scientific editor resides in an academic institution, but there are some instances where the scientific editor is a full-time employee of the association. A more likely scenario is for the PhD to work as a managing editor for the journal, interacting closely with the scientific editor to oversee the review, copyediting, and publication of manuscripts.

The APS recently hired a PhD scientist to serve as the publication ethics officer. With 14 scientific journals, we have seen an increasing number of ethical violations. It is the responsibility of the ethics officer to work with the art editors to determine whether figures have been manipulated, with copy editors and editors to determine whether text has been plagiarized, and to work with the publications committee to determine whether actions must be taken to punish the offender.

Although likely perceived as being overqualified, PhDs can be hired as copy editors, providing they have good writing and grammar skills. It is their responsibility to edit the accepted manuscripts to make them consistent with journal style.

In some cases, publication directors for scientific societies have a PhD. However, in all cases, they have extensive experience in publishing, including the business experience to develop budgets and negotiate contracts. The director prepares financial statements and budgets with input from the finance director and executive director, presenting the statements and budgets to the publications and finance committees for their approval. The director is also responsible for managing the publications staff, who, in the case of the APS, includes peer review staff, copy editors, art editors, and online editors.

SKILLS AND QUALIFICATIONS

You have completed your PhD degree, worked as a postdoctoral fellow, and possibly accepted your first position as an assistant professor. All of a sudden, you realize that you have had enough of the academic rat race and you want to try something else. What skills will you need to garner a job in the world of scientific societies? Believe it or not, the skills needed are essentially the same wherever you go with your PhD degree: people skills, problem solving, and management skills. What most PhDs fail to recognize is that although they might not have taken courses in management or communications, they are continually honing those skills while exercising their professional skills. PhD scientists manage students, technicians, and postdoctoral fellows working in their laboratories. They are responsible for developing budgets that are submitted as part of the proposal writing efforts associated with research funding, and if they are fortunate enough to get a research grant, they are responsible for managing resources to fulfill the goals of the project. Their success as scientists requires them to have outstanding oral and written skills in order to communicate the results of their science and to convince others of the relevance of the results. All of these experiences and skills will serve you well should you choose to look toward a position in a scientific society.

GETTING A FOOT IN THE DOOR

The challenge faced by each of us is how to get a "foot in the door" of a scientific society. The key is to join a society, to participate in its programs and activities, and learn as much as possible about how the organization runs. In some cases, students and early-career PhDs are able to volunteer to serve on committees that will provide some insights into the society and its programs. These experiences can serve you well when you begin considering how best to use your PhD degree.

For those interested in science policy/government relations, start by attending sessions at meetings that provide guidance on how to become a science advocate. When asked to write in support of a piece of legislation, do so and inform the society's director of science policy of the response that you received from the legislator or executive branch correspondent. Reinforce your letter by calling the local office of your elected representative and visit the office to talk with staff responsible for the management of science issues. Volunteer to serve on the science policy committee to demonstrate your interest to the association's leadership. In some associations, there are opportunities for summer or one-year internships or fellowships designed to bring PhDs into the headquarters to learn more about advocacy. In addition, the American Association for the Advancement of Science (AAAS) offers Science and Technology Fellowships (http://fellowships. aaas.org), and the National Academies offer the Christine Mirzayan Science & Technology Policy Graduate Fellowships (http://sites.nationalacademies. org/PGA/policyfellows/index.htm). Both programs are designed to help PhD scientists develop basic skills essential to working or participating in science policy at the federal, state, or local levels. Both of these programs will provide you with the skills needed to work within a scientific society.

If you are interested in communications, get involved with your association and its communications committee. PhDs can develop their communications and writing skills by contacting the press office at their academic institution. Often, the press office will welcome assistance in writing press releases promoting the scientific discoveries of the institution. In a sense, these should be considered internship opportunities because they will likely not involve remuneration or be a full-time position. It represents an opportunity for you to hone your writing skills. Similarly, explore the possibility of writing about the scientific discoveries at your institution for the college or local newspaper. For many young scientists already familiar with social media, demonstrated expertise will serve them well as associations seek out individuals who can strengthen the organization's social media presence. Develop a blog that discusses science and shares it in ways that can be understood by the public. The AAAS Mass Media Science and Engineering Fellows Program (http://www.aaas.org/programs/education/MassMedia) provides another route for interested PhDs to develop the skills that can lead to a position in an association. The program provides participants with the tools and know-how to accomplish the goal of translating science for the public.

Your desire to pursue a PhD marks you as an individual interested in education and discovery. Use that interest to get involved in the education programs of your society. Many associations have outreach programs that take PhDs into K–12 classrooms to talk about science and the joys of discovery. Become engaged with the program or volunteer to work with the society's leadership to launch such an effort. The APS program is called PhUn (Physiology Understanding) Week (http://www.the-aps.org/mm/ Education/K-12/EducationProjects/PhUn-Week) and the Society for Neuroscience program is called Brain Awareness Week (http://www.sfn.org/ index.aspx?pagename=baw_home). Volunteer for service on committees within the organization that focus on careers, diversity, and K–professional education. Serve as a judge for undergraduate poster presentations at the annual meeting or volunteer to provide assistance at a local science fair. The key is to demonstrate interest in a career focusing on the educational mission of the association.

Publications are an area in which most PhD scientists have some expertise, based naturally on their experiences writing theses, papers, and abstracts. However, those experiences are only a subset of the publishing world. The entry level is usually as a copy editor for those with excellent grammar skills. New PhDs can be hired into associations with a book program as an acquisition editor, soliciting submission of book proposals from accomplished scientists. You can also seek an internship in a publishing organization, such as a university press, to gain expertise in journal or book publishing (see also Chapter 3), an important revenue source for a society.

Developing the management and business skills associated with running a society is probably the best way to get started in the executive office of an association. Make sure that you chronicle the skills that you are developing throughout your career so that when a management position becomes available, you can provide information on how you would, for example, handle a personnel issue, management problem, or budget deficit.

CAREER PROGRESSION

As you move into the world of scientific societies, it is important to recognize that there is a need to commit three–five years to any position taken in an association. A three–five-year commitment allows you to master the intricacies of your position, observe what others do in higher positions, and identify the skills needed for you to take more responsible positions. Then, as opportunities present themselves within your current association or others, you will be prepared to move ahead.

As described earlier, entry-level jobs are usually science policy analyst, communications specialist, education program coordinator, copy editor or acquisitions editor, or development specialist. These jobs provide a skill set that allows for advancement and contributes to future successes.

You can then use that experience to rise to managerial and director positions to guide the society's science policy, communications, and education or publications program. As you gain expertise and the confidence of the volunteer leadership, you may be tapped to become the deputy executive director or ultimately the executive director of the association. Clearly, attaining a leadership position in an organization generally requires that someone with a PhD has been in a management position for 10–15 years. This chapter deals primarily with association experience; however, the leadership skills required for selection as an executive director of a society can also be developed in positions in academia or government.

WAY OUT

Having spent 28 years as the executive director of the APS, I initially wondered why there is a need for a section titled "Way Out." However, I then realized that most executive directors do not have the benefit of such long tenure in their position. Indeed, most people in the world of scientific societies are much more mobile than I.

Once one has spent the requisite three–five years in a position, it is worth considering one's future options. If the position still provides challenges and opportunities to grow programs and activities, there is every reason for you to remain in your current position, especially if it is at a managerial or directorship level. However, if the activities associated with the position have become repetitive and there is no opportunity for growth and expansion, it is time to begin looking for other opportunities. In some cases, the opportunity might reside within your current association, especially if it is large enough to have a diversity of positions. Alternatively, it may be time to shop your expertise to another association, for example one with more opportunity for growth and creativity. Such positions are advertised on job boards provided by the ASAE and the CESSE. Choose wisely by learning as much as possible about the society and its programs. Ask questions of those currently working there to determine what the work environment is like, something you did when you decided to take a postdoctoral position. Most importantly, check out the finances to ensure that the association will be around long enough for you to make a difference.

Although working in an association to advance the discipline and to serve a community is fun, you can move into the business or academic world on the basis of your management expertise. Science policy staff can move to a university to serve as government relations staff interacting with elected representatives to seek support for the institution. Similarly, with the development of university outreach programs in education and communications, opportunities exist for individuals who have developed this expertise at scientific societies. In all three areas (science policy, education, and communications), similar jobs are available in the pharmaceutical industry as well as with other business entities.

For those working in the editorial or acquisition areas of publications, positions exist within the commercial publishing houses that are responsible for the vast majority of our scientific journals and monographs. Similarly, many academic institutions have academic presses that recruit individuals with PhD degrees for positions similar to those in the publications operations of a scientific society.

Individuals in executive positions can move to larger associations or into executive/administrative positions in academia or industry. Alternatively, one can remain with an association until retirement, as I expect to do, and then become a consultant to other associations or the development officer who solicits donations for the organization.

Box 1. My Experience

Thanks to a scholarship program for caddies in financial need from the Western Golf Association, I attended the University of Illinois–Urbana–Champaign, where I majored in physiology as a result of a class taught by Dr. F.R.

Steggerda. After receiving my BS degree, I remained there for my PhD degree in physiology. To strengthen my research credentials, I held two postdoctoral positions—first at the Michigan Cancer Foundation, Detroit and then at Michigan State University in East Lansing–before accepting a position as an assistant professor in the department of physiology at George Washington University Medical School.

Being in Washington, D.C., I became interested in science policy and government support of research. Looking for a more policy-oriented career, I accepted a position at the National Institutes of Health (NIH) as executive secretary, Physiology Study Section, Division of Research Grants. As executive secretary, I was responsible for managing three review meetings per year, at which ~100 proposals were considered by members of the study section. However, I was not satisfied as the executive secretary of a study section and I was able to convince my bosses to allow me to work one day each week in the offices of senior NIH leadership. As a result, I was able to successfully compete for entrance into the Department of Health and Human Services Senior Executive Service Candidate Development Program in 1983. My first three-month assignment was in the Office of Program Planning and Evaluation, Office of the Assistant Secretary of Health, where I worked on orphan drug legislation.

While on assignment, I saw my current job advertised in *Science*. I interviewed during the summer of 1984 and started as the society's executive director in July 1985. I am now responsible for managing all aspects of the society's affairs, working cooperatively and collegially with the society's leadership and members, and directing a staff of approximately 70 individuals. During my tenure, the society has grown from an organization of 6000 members in 1985 to one of more than 11,000 members. Our annual budget has now grown to ~$18 million. I work with staff and volunteer leadership to ensure that the 14 journals published by APS have the best articles and come out on time and that the APS meetings show the best research in physiology and allow scientists to exchange ideas freely. Another goal is to ensure that the members and the general public learn about careers in physiology, the best ways to teach physiology, and new research going on in the field. We also deal with the government to make sure that there is enough money for members to do the research that is needed to move physiology forward. I have been fortunate to have been able to hire an outstanding staff and to have an excellent working relationship with the society's leadership. Working together, we have been able to advance the discipline and strengthen the APS.

Box 2. Ten Dos and Don'ts

1. Do not be afraid to take an internship in an association to gain expertise.

2. Do chronicle the skills that you have developed during the course of your doctoral training and postdoctoral experience.

3. Do not forget to review your introductory letter to ensure that it highlights your interest in the position that is actually being advertised.

4. Do consider applying for one of the fellowship programs offered by the AAAS or other societies.

5. Do not ignore opportunities to volunteer for programs sponsored by your association in your areas of interest.

6. Do discuss your interest in a nonacademic research or teaching career with your mentors so they can help you to develop the necessary expertise.

7. Do not ignore opportunities to develop your expertise by working in your academic institution.

8. Do remember that your PhD has provided you with critical thinking skills and problem-solving abilities that are applicable to a career in a scientific society.

9. Do not think that your PhD provides you with all the skills that you need to succeed; take a business or communications course to hone your skills.

10. Do contact the leadership of your association to discuss your career interests and to gain knowledge about positions and opportunities in scientific societies.

Box 3. A Brief History of the APS[1]

More than 125 years ago, the APS held its organizational meeting at Columbia University College of Physicians and Surgeons. The specific event that triggered its formation was the founding of the Congress of American Physicians and Surgeons, a federation of medical specialty societies that was conceived in 1886 with an emphasis on medical research rather than on medical practice.

[1] *History of The American Physiological Society. The First Century, 1887–1987*, ed. JR Brobeck, OE Reynolds, TA Appel (The American Physiological Society, Bethesda, MD 1987).

Participant societies were responsible for developing their own programs for the congress, and this provided the impetus for the development of the APS.

During the society's early years, its activities were managed by members serving in a voluntary manner. Indeed, the *American Journal of Physiology*, founded in 1898, the official journal of the APS, was initially managed and edited almost entirely by William Townsend Porter. It was not until the APS was 50 years of age that the burden of running it became too great on the volunteer elected leadership. Management by the volunteer leadership continued, however, throughout World War II and until 1947, when the Society hired Dr. Milton Lee, a physiologist, to serve as secretary-treasurer.

Lee hired staff to handle many of the administrative duties, eliminating the need for the volunteer offices of secretary and treasurer, and obtained its first permanent home in the offices of the National Academy of Sciences. Since the appointment of Lee as the first executive secretary-treasurer in 1947, the APS has benefited from administrative leadership provided by three additional physiologists: Ray G. Daggs (1956–1972), Orr E. Reynolds (1973–1985), and Martin Frank (1985–present).

WWW RESOURCES

http://www.aaas.org/programs/education/MassMedia Mass media science and engineering fellows program, American Association for the Advancement of Science (AAAS).

http://www.asaecenter.org American Society of Association Executives (ASAE).

http://www.asbmb.org/asbmbtoday *ASBMB Today*, a monthly publication distributed to members of the American Society for Biochemistry and Molecular Biology.

http://www.CESSE.org Council of Engineering and Scientific Society Executives (CESSE).

http://www.sfn.org/index.aspx?pagename=baw_home Brain Awareness Campaign, Society for Neuroscience.

http://www.the-aps.org American Physiological Society.

http://www.the-aps.org/mm/Education/K-12/EducationProjects/PhUn-Week Early education program, Physiology Understanding Week, American Physiological Society.

www.wgaesf.org/ Evans Scholars Foundation, Western Golf Association.

8

Leaving the Bench and Finding Your Foundation

John E. Spiro

*Simons Foundation Autism Research Initiative, Simons Foundation,
New York, New York 10010*

Scientists who leave the laboratory bench to work for biomedical foundations mobilize and focus resources on the most promising research behind a foundation's mission. They acquire a broad view of a field, interact closely with research scientists at meetings and laboratory visits, and often manage proposal review boards and monitor grant progress. Increasingly, scientists at foundations also have a more active role in catalyzing research: They are involved in organizing targeted workshops, setting research priorities, and directly creating and managing resources for a scientific community. They often work closely with patient advocacy groups, contract research organizations, government funders and regulators, and biotech and pharmaceutical companies.

Job opportunities in foundations are highly varied, reflecting the diversity of foundations and missions. For example, some foundations have general missions to support broad basic scientific research, whereas others focus specifically on a particular disease and may require different skills. Most scientific positions at foundations require a PhD or MD and often some postdoctoral or other experience, although not all do. Foundations often lack the clear career path that an academic position offers (various levels of professorship, tenure, etc.), although there is often significant potential for growth in responsibilities in terms of managing science, people, and budgets. Jobs in foundations can be challenging yet extremely rewarding, especially for those with broad interests and goal-oriented personalities. Many at foundations feel that they have the potential to have an even greater impact than if they had stayed at the bench.

What follows is a rather personal account of the state of jobs for bench scientists at foundations. I draw on my own experiences of the last six years, during which time I have worked at a foundation, as well as experience I've gained from talking with numerous friends and colleagues at other foundations; admittedly, my view is rather U.S.-centric. What is clear from even a casual survey is that there is no such thing as an "average" foundation job. Foundations differ enormously in their size, scope, and missions, and likewise, jobs at foundations differ correspondingly.

Several important distinctions stand out and have some bearing on the type of positions that may be available. One is whether the foundation was established with a broad general mission—such as the Rockefeller Foundation, founded in 1913 with a mission "to promote the well-being of humanity"—or rather, whether it was founded with a very specific cause in mind, such as the Michael J. Fox Foundation, launched in 2000 to find a cure for Parkinson's disease. Another major distinction is whether the foundation raises funds from the public to be distributed to research (known as a public charity in the U.S.). For many such foundations, money that is raised in a given year is then spent directly on research. Alternatively, other foundations are private and have a single or small number of wealthy donors or a corporate donor—and often, these foundations have a substantial endowment from which operating costs are derived.

Probably the distinction most important to a scientist considering work at a foundation concerns how research is evaluated and supported. A foundation may operate in a more traditional grant-giving mode, primarily making use of outside scientific advisors who are active independent scientists running their own laboratories; alternatively, a foundation may rely heavily on a professional scientific staff and therefore be more proactive in its approach to supporting research. In the former situation, outside advisors evaluate investigator-initiated proposals that come in following a call for applications. The latter more proactive scenario, which is seen increasingly, has created some very interesting and dynamic positions for scientists who leave the bench.

The more proactive model of foundations—especially for foundations with a disease focus—is likely to become more prevalent, leading to an expansion in possibilities for scientists who are interested in employment away from the bench. The main driving force seems to be the recognition that the standard academic (and National Institutes of Health [NIH] or National Science Foundation [NSF] funded) model that works so well for promoting creative research in individual laboratories may not, in fact, be the best model to find cures for various diseases and to put these ideas into practice with patient populations. What is needed in addition (importantly, not instead) is a more focused and targeted approach that often crosses the boundaries of traditional academic research and emphasizes highly collaborative work.

Full-time professional science staff can have a major role in helping to bring about this change. They can work with academic scientists, biotech and pharmaceutical companies, patient advocacy organizations, and others to stay focused on the problem at hand. They need not worry about many of the daily concerns of academic scientists (running a laboratory, getting grants, publishing papers, teaching) and can often very effectively build the infrastructure and teams of experts who can work together to solve complex problems that are difficult or impossible to address in a typical academic setting. Nonprofits that are scientifically nonpartisan can have significant influence in the community given their clear and unencumbered incentives. As such, foundations often have an important role in a research community of helping to set research standards and opening communication channels in various ways. For example, as a condition of a grant award, foundations can require that experiments with negative results be published. Negative results often go unpublished, to the detriment of progress.

The details of this more managed approach depend heavily on the state of knowledge of a given field. As an example, there are still major unknowns about the causes of autism, although it is clear that genetics have a major role. Therefore, the Simons Foundation Autism Research Initiative (SFARI) has made it one of its priorities to assemble a large cohort of families with autism; the families' biospecimens are made available to the basic research community and have been used to help outline the genetic landscape of the disorder. In contrast, in the case of Huntington's disease, the genetics are well established—the gene responsible for Huntington's disease has been known for ~20 years, but this has not led to effective treatments. The Cure Huntington's Disease Initiative (CHDI) Foundation (http://chdifoundation .org), a private foundation whose focus is on discovering drugs that slow the progression of Huntington's disease, therefore, operates in a space mostly beyond early discovery and is much more focused on making the transition to the clinic, a job that is often reserved for for-profit biotech and pharmaceutical companies. CHDI calls itself a "collaborative enabler." Regardless of the particular focus, foundations—and private foundations in particular, which often lack much of a bureaucracy—can be very nimble compared with other types of funding agencies. As an example, funds can sometimes be mobilized extremely quickly if an interesting opportunity arises to the foundation.

For anyone interested in learning more about foundations, I would recommend the Health Research Alliance, a loose organization of many (although by no means all) biomedical foundations. Their website (http://www.healthra.org/) can serve as a launching pad for finding out more about various foundations. Another organization, GuideStar (http://www.guidestar.org/), provides a rich data set on nonprofits. One service is to potential donors, who can use GuideStar to evaluate whether a particular nonprofit operates efficiently. But prospective employees can benefit greatly as well, because the site provides detailed information gathered from tax returns and other sources that get right to the bottom line about foundations: how much money they have and where they spend it. GuideStar presents this information without obscuring the details, as is often the case on some foundation websites.

JOBS AND CAREER PROGRESSION

Jobs for scientists at foundations vary significantly depending on the size and style of the foundation, as described above.

For foundations that primarily put out requests for applications in a focused area and review grants that come in—and rely heavily on an external board of professional scientists who review and advise—a common job title that reflects the responsibilities is "program officer." A program officer may be responsible for grants in a particular area and his/her job will largely entail writing requests for applications, helping to manage scientific review boards, monitoring progress on grants—including site visits—and dealing with principal investigator (PI) requests to change scope or budget. With increasing experience and independence, the position might entail a promotion to senior program officer.

For the more proactive foundations described above, much more weight is placed on the internal foundation scientists to evaluate, coordinate, and drive the research. Responsibilities might include launching and managing infrastructure projects, organizing targeted workshops, and evaluating grants and other projects in-house, with additional external advice taken ad hoc. In addition to giving grants, where the external PI is expected to construct and perform a research project, responsibilities of a scientist in such a foundation might include more general overview and supervision. For example, the foundation scientist would be involved in the initial phase of setting the project goal(s) and design, followed by a phase in which the work is done by an academic laboratory or contract research organization, or in some consortium arrangement that is often best described as a contract as opposed to a grant. Scientists at foundations that raise money are often involved in fundraising efforts in some way.

Titles at foundations tend to follow an NIH model (program officer, senior program officer) or a model that is familiar to academics such as assistant, associate, and senior and deputy director for research, leading up to scientific director. Alternatively, some foundations use a model that is more familiar to those in the corporate world, such as vice president (VP) for research, senior VP, chief research officer, chief scientific officer, executive director, etc.

Careers at foundations often lack the established structure/hierarchy found at universities (including tenure!). Nevertheless, despite the different types of titles, promotion at a foundation usually brings increased independence in decision making and often involves additional expectation of initiative and leadership. More senior personnel are expected to be able to represent the organization externally and to participate actively in strategic planning, goal setting, hiring, and management of staff and budgets. At some foundations (but certainly not all), the highest scientific position is often reserved for individuals who have had a distinguished career in academia (perhaps as a department chair or similar) who then decided to make a transition to a foundation at a later career stage. So, for some of the most senior positions, having run a laboratory (maybe even a big one) is something of a prerequisite.

Data on the number of jobs for scientists in foundations is hard to come by, but anecdotally the number of positions is on the rise. This is likely the result of a complex combination of limited federal funding for research and an increasing awareness of the important role for advocacy organizations to help provide, focus, and direct research spending. The rise is also likely tied to the rise of wealthy donors and favorable tax laws for foundations in the United States. Finally, foundations tend to be nice places to work, with competitive salaries and good benefits.

SKILLS AND QUALIFICATIONS

Not surprisingly, the skills required differ significantly based on a foundation's mission. On balance, however, a scientist at a foundation is expected to interact with the scientific community at a high level and will make decisions that can have a significant impact on a field, and thus is expected to have a PhD or an MD. Given the current job market and the relative plethora of scientists with postdoc experience who are looking for jobs, it is advantageous for someone to have completed a postdoc. This is not necessarily about the additional scientific training that one might get as a postdoc (although that is always good), but as much so about more life and job experience—and experience in a setting different from one's PhD laboratory.

In general, prospective foundation employees should be able to think comprehensively—and optimistically—about scientific problems while maintaining attention to detail. It is not uncommon to have to deliver difficult news to prospective grantees, so resilience in making tough calls is essential. Scientific research is inherently uncertain and involves many failures. An optimistic attitude is therefore essential, especially as foundations often position themselves as greater risk takers compared with traditional funding bodies—and thus often deal with failed experiments.

The jobs almost always involve communicating with a large number of scientists with very different backgrounds and personalities—and also working with different types of internal teams—so strong interpersonal and written/oral communication skills are very important. At foundations that raise money, the job may involve speaking with existing or potential donors, and skill in talking about science comfortably at multiple levels would be relevant. Regardless of the type of foundation, it is almost certain that the job will involve thinking more broadly about scientific questions than when one is at the bench, so a passion for learning new material is essential. Related is a willingness to travel to meetings and make laboratory visits.

Beyond these rather general statements, skills required may be specific to a given foundation. For example, for a foundation that centers on issues that primarily revolve around neuroscience, it would be highly advantageous to have training in that field. Similarly, for a foundation that operates in a space that is very advanced clinically and involves drug trials, for example, experience in a biotech or pharmaceutical company may be a prerequisite.

One active debate among those of us who have responsibility for hiring new science staff has to do with the skills that are prerequisite and those that can be learned on the job. Interpersonal and communication skills and a genuine curiosity and passion for science are essential, as is being comfortable dealing with uncertainty and a rapidly evolving knowledge base. More specific skills, such as knowledge of the best methods for managing review boards and dealing with grant management, can generally be learned on the job.

GETTING A FOOT IN THE DOOR

There is no set formula for getting your foot in the door for any foundation, but there are a few general strategies that can help.

Do not hesitate to send an email to scientists at a foundation that you admire. Perhaps you know about a foundation because it supports work in a field in which you have worked or are otherwise interested in, or perhaps you have some more direct connection to the mission of a foundation given a family member with a particular illness. Another approach is to check out the acknowledgment sections of scientific papers that you admire, or look for who supports interesting work as you browse posters at a scientific meeting.

It is important to be able to demonstrate that you can function in a situation beyond the bench. This may involve having evidence that you can be passionate about and can communicate scientific ideas that go beyond your immediate technical expertise. One way to get this type of experience is to write for a university publication or a website or other forum that seems appropriate. If you have a particular foundation in mind, offer to write for their website if they have one. Propose ideas for a workshop and/or offer to help organize it. Foundations often advertise jobs on their websites and in the job sections of various general science journals.

WAY OUT

Leaving the laboratory and a "traditional" academic career is a big career move. After being out of the laboratory for a year or two, it can be difficult to get back into laboratory research that you may have been doing, seeing as science most likely will have progressed significantly. That said, if one were to take a job as a scientist at a foundation, an ecosystem of related jobs are possible if the specifics of the job at a foundation are not working out. For example, there is substantial movement between jobs at other foundations or related jobs such as a program officer at a big government funder such as the NIH, editor at a scientific journal, university administrator, staff member at a biotech company, or as an independent consultant.

Box 1. My Experience

As a result of a very engaging mentor, I was hooked on biology, and on neuroscience in particular, as an undergraduate at Haverford College. I got my PhD at University of California, San Diego (UCSD) in the laboratory of the late Walter Heiligenberg. I then did postdoctoral work in the department of neurobiology at Duke University Medical Center in the laboratory of Richard Mooney. For both my PhD and postdoctoral work, I used multiple types of techniques (primarily electrophysiology, anatomy) to try to understand the neural basis of behavior. I enjoyed and was deeply intellectually engaged in the work that I was doing. This is probably most clearly reflected in the fact that I spent much of my time outside of the laboratory on mountain biking, hiking, or sailing trips talking about biology and neuroscience with friends, whom my teenage daughters now lovingly refer to as my "nerd friends."

At both UCSD and Duke, I was privileged to have been surrounded by an enormous variety of science. At UCSD in particular, to where scientists flocked from everywhere in the world (especially in wintertime when it was warm and sunny in La Jolla), I was very distracted by the huge assortment of excellent seminars that were available each week. With UCSD, Scripps Oceanography, the Neuroscience Institute (now closed), the Salk Institute, and Scripps Clinic, La Jolla was a science mecca.

In the back of my mind, I always harbored some doubt that I was going to thrive in an academic atmosphere. I felt that I would be forced to become a superspecialist in one particular area, which is the standard practice for someone who pursues an academic career and must make a name for oneself to get tenure. Science generalists are not usually rewarded unless they move to a position where the primary responsibilities involve teaching.

Despite these reservations, I started to apply for faculty jobs several years into my postdoc at Duke. At the same time, *Nature Neuroscience*, a new neuroscience spinoff from the weekly *Nature*, was just turning one year old, and the launch editor/editor in chief, Charles Jennings, was visiting Duke to get feedback about the journal. I attended a lunch with several other postdocs, and I was struck by how Jennings described the intellectual atmosphere at the journal. In essence, one could get paid to be a generalist in neuroscience. As a postdoc, I was also working very long hours. I was doing electrophysiology experiments that often went late into the night. With two young children and a wife who worked, it was difficult to balance. At one point, describing what I did at work to a family friend, my three-year-old daughter said that an experiment was "when Daddy doesn't come home for dinner." Working at *Nature Neuroscience* was very hard work but had more controllable hours.

I applied for a position as an assistant editor, and when I was offered the job, spent several weeks thinking deeply about leaving the laboratory. I convinced myself that I could do it for a year or two without burning any bridges to a more traditional academic path.

Fortunately, I thoroughly enjoyed the work and had excellent colleagues. I started handling manuscripts in circuits/systems neuroscience that I knew well and gradually expanded into other areas by traveling around the world to all sorts of meetings and making laboratory visits. I especially enjoyed getting to see the different types of cultures that defined different communities within neuroscience—and relished the access to top-notch scientists/advisors that comes with this type of position. It was truly eye opening to realize that two eminent referees could *completely* disagree about the importance of a particular piece of work.

I eventually worked my way through associate and senior editor at *Nature Neuroscience*, and then moved over to *Nature*, where I eventually became a senior editor on the biology team, where my responsibilities included all of neuroscience and where I oversaw a small team of other editors in neuroscience. *Nature* presented some additional opportunities as I interacted with editors in other disciplines of biology and the physical sciences, including the "front half" "News and Views" editors and various news writers and editors. It was also a time where there were major challenges (mostly driven by the web and open access) to the traditional models of publishing.

One of the main reasons for leaving the laboratory was to be able to remain a science generalist. After being at Nature Publishing Group for more than seven years and handling manuscripts and interacting with many different types of communities, I started to look around for an opportunity where I could dig a bit deeper. I was attracted by the idea of sticking with a topic for a longer period of time compared with the length of time it took for a manuscript to make it through review and publication. By taking the lead on various special focus issues at *Nature*, I developed some taste for this and I enjoyed it.

The Simons Foundation was starting an initiative to understand autism (SFARI). I was attracted to this opportunity because it was/is clear that to make progress in understanding autism spectrum disorder (ASD) one needs to make connections between the genetics, neural circuits and systems, and behavior. There were also multiple challenges inherent in coming up with constructive ways to engage and keep the research community focused on SFARI's mission and research priorities, especially in the realm of translating basic research findings into possible avenues for treatment. SFARI has given me an opportunity to stay broad in my thinking but to also dig deeply into particular issues and be involved in all stages of research, not just at the stage of a finished manuscript.

Box 2. Ten Dos and Don'ts

1. Do not assume that a PhD is about technical training. On the contrary, it is about learning how to make sense of a huge and rapidly evolving body of specific knowledge while keeping a broad view and about learning how to communicate clearly. These are highly transferable skills.

2. Do not worry about those who think you are "dropping out of science" or disappointing former mentors by not pursuing a traditional academic career.

3. Do realize that you can have a significant impact on a field even though you are not at the bench. Sometimes, even more so.

4. Do realize that although you may have an important role in research, you will likely need to be comfortable being part of a team and not necessarily the center of attention. In employment ads that I have seen, I think the phrase "low ego needs" sums it up well.

5. Do try to expand your horizons while you are at the bench by writing and reading broadly beyond your area of expertise in the laboratory.

6. Do be sure that you are comfortable with the inevitable trade-off of breadth versus depth that comes with leaving the bench. You will no longer likely be the "world's expert" in a particular subfield, but you will probably be exposed to a much larger community of scientists than if you had stayed at the bench.

7. Do write/call scientists working at foundations that may be involved in supporting the work that goes on in your laboratory.

8. Do research on foundations that you are interested in; know their mission, know where the money comes from.

9. Do research the people who work at foundations that interest you. (Use various web resources, such as GuideStar.)

10. Do practice talking to scientists who work in different disciplines. Try to understand their language and their community and practice explaining your science and community to them.

ACKNOWLEDGMENTS

I thank Dr. Brian Fiske for comments on an earlier version of this chapter.

WWW RESOURCES

http://www.healthra.org Health Research Alliance.
http://www.guidestar.org GuideStar.

9

Patent Law: At the Cutting Edge of Science, but Not at the Bench

Salim Mamajiwalla

In(sci)te IP Patent Agency, Markham, Ontario, Canada L3S 4K5

Patent law is an area that many people move into after obtaining a PhD in biomedical science. Close to the cutting edge of research, patent agents draft the detailed descriptions of new biotechnology required for patent applications and engage with patent offices during the review process known as patent prosecution. Jobs are also available as patent examiners who examine these patent applications, and it is common for individuals to move between the two jobs. A law firm is generally the best place to train as a patent agent, but biotech companies and tech-transfer offices can provide an alterative route. Although obtaining a law degree is not essential after your PhD, it is recommended, and all patent agents must pass rigorous qualifying exams. Further down the road, training in patent law offers opportunities for in-house work in biotech companies, business development, and mergers and acquisitions.

WHAT IS INTELLECTUAL PROPERTY?

Intellectual property (IP) is an umbrella term relating to creations of the mind. Unlike real property, IP is intangible. It is "intellectual" because it is derived from the work of the intellect. It is "property" because it has value and can be sold, bought, licensed, transferred, or given away like any other property. Governments have recognized the value of IP for enhancing their economies and have created laws for conferring IP rights (IPRs) to those individuals/corporations that develop certain IP in exchange for a full public disclosure of their invention. The rights conferred primarily allow the owner of the IP to exclude others from using their IP for a limited time. This creates a situation in which a competitor who wants to use the IP has to either innovate and design around the existing IP, buy it, or rent (license) it. IP owners may sue those infringing on their IPRs.

There are several forms of IPRs. The most common include patents, trademarks, trade secrets, industrial designs, and copyrights. To a knowledge-based company, such as a biotech company, the most important and valuable IPRs are patents.

A patent is a time-limited monopoly (normally 20 years from the date of filing a patent application) granted by a government to the inventor or the owner of the patent in exchange for full disclosure of the invention to the public. The exclusive right granted to the patentee allows him/her to exclude others from making, using, selling, or distributing the patented invention without permission, that is, without a license. It does not give the owner of the patent the right to make, use, sell, or distribute his/her own invention unless he/she has in turn determined that there are no earlier patents excluding him/her from performing any one or more of these activities.

Obtaining a patent can be a long, arduous, and expensive process. This is especially true for life-science-related inventions because the technology involved is often complex. Obtaining a patent begins with the preparation of the patent application. The application must be carefully drafted after having considered a multitude of factors, including the prior art,[1] the patent laws (which may differ from country to country), and the latest court decisions. Ideally, a patent application should have an abstract, a background, a summary of the invention, a detailed description of the invention, and examples of how to make the invention, and it must end with at least one claim.[2] Drawings or figures are also often provided and described, if they can aid in understanding the invention or further support the examples. The all-important claims must be carefully crafted to define the invention in words, which must also be carefully chosen. Although patent laws vary from country to country, it is universally accepted that to be patentable, the claimed invention must be novel and nonobvious to someone skilled in the art to which the subject matter of the patent application relates,

---

[1]Prior art is a term used in patent law to describe all patent and nonpatent literature (e.g., journal articles, abstracts for conferences, etc.) related to the subject matter of the invention published before the earliest filing date of the patent application.

[2]Claims are the most important part of the patent. The claims point out and distinctly delineate in words the subject matter that the inventor regards to be his or her invention.

and have some utility, that is, real-world use. Various other requirements must also be met. For example, a patent application must be drafted to satisfy the written requirements for patentability and define and enable the scope of the claimed invention.

Once the application is drafted to the satisfaction of the client, it is usually first filed with the Patent and Trademark Office (PTO) in the inventor's respective country, although many foreign inventions are often first filed in the United States PTO. The application is then examined by a patent examiner, who will most likely have academic qualifications similar to the patent lawyer. The examiner will review the application in light of the prior art and the patent rules and laws for that country. The examiner will then either allow the patent or, more often than not, issue a rejection of the patent along with a detailed explanation as to their reasoning. This reasoning is often a combination of legal and scientific arguments. The applicant is given the opportunity to respond to the examiner's rejection by amending any defects and arguing against the examiner's rejection. This back-and-forth exchange of arguments with the PTO is referred to as patent prosecution and in some instances can take many years before the application is in condition for the PTO to issue what is called a Notice of Allowance, a formal notice by the PTO that it has agreed that the invention as claimed is patentable and that the application will proceed in due course to a granted patent.[3]

JOBS

Jobs as a patent professional can be very competitive and there are only a limited number of places at which one can work as a patent agent. Law firms with IP departments will often hire PhDs to train and ultimately qualify as patent agents; these individuals work side by side with lawyers, paralegals, and other IP support staff. Alternatively, if you are currently a scientist in a biotech, pharmaceutical, or other life-science-related company with a sizable IP department, you might be able to start training there. Patent offices also hire PhDs to train as patent examiners. Finally, if you are at an academic institution, the tech-transfer office can be a good place to start.

---

[3]It is not unheard of to have applications pending in the PTO for 5 or more years.

Law Firms

A law firm is probably the best place to train to become a patent agent because you will gain valuable training and experience in IP law through exposure to a broad variety of issues in patent law. Law firms generally hire PhDs as "patent specialists," "scientific/technical advisors," or "patent agent trainees." These titles are synonymous. Firms with large IP practices or large boutique IP firms may be divided into different practice areas by subject area groups, for example, life sciences/chemistry, mechanical, or high tech, and you will most likely be placed in a group that matches your educational background. Patent specialists are usually placed under the supervision of a senior associate or a partner.

Law firms tend to have a diversified clientele and hence you will be exposed to a variety of different inventions. Thus, if you are a life scientist, you may get to work on a new chemical entity for the treatment of a particular disease, novel drug delivery systems, antibodies, genetically modified organisms, processes for purifying or isolating compounds, or, at times, even medical devices. It is not uncommon for law firms to have new hires start by drafting mechanical inventions regardless of educational background; only once the trainee becomes familiar with the fundamentals of drafting and the law will they assign you cases related to your technical specialty. With more experience, you may be pulled into other areas of IP law that require a sophisticated understanding of the underlying technologies, including assisting in due diligence, mergers and acquisitions, or litigation. When working for pharmaceutical clients, you will also likely develop a working knowledge of how regulatory law intersects with IP law and how you might be able to leverage both to obtain maximum protection for the company's innovative drugs or medical devices.

A word of caution: The law firm environment is not for everyone. The concept of the "billable hour," in which every minute of the working day must be accounted for, is foreign to scientists and can be difficult to get used to. Law firms generally set an annual "billable target" for every professional to strive to meet, and the target is dependent on many things, including, for example, your position within the firm, its size, and its geographical location. Your performance review, and hence bonus and promotion, can depend, in part, on whether you met your billable target for the previous year. Although individual experiences vary, it is not uncommon in large law firms with busy patent departments to place high demands on patent specialists. You might work 6 to 7 days a week in the beginning (which you should be used to as a postdoc anyway). Your hours will be long (again, nothing new), and expect a portion of your hours to be written down as you learn to apply your newly acquired patent skills. Nevertheless, the training you will receive at a law firm will put you on firm footing for future positions elsewhere. For example, biotech/pharmaceutical companies, although they usually prefer to hire patent agents who already have corporate experience, will also recruit from law firms.[4]

Biotech/Pharmaceutical Company

If you are a staff scientist at a biotech or pharmaceutical company with a sizable patent department, you may be able to transition into IP law by training under the supervision of a company patent agent/lawyer. Alternatively, as mentioned above, you may transition into a biotech/pharmaceutical company after having gained several years experience in a law firm. Depending on the focus of the company, you may not be exposed to the broad variety of issues you might see at a law firm. Nevertheless, working in a corporate setting can be quite rewarding. You will have the opportunity to interact with various other departments within the company, such as research and development (R&D), marketing, regulatory affairs, clinical operations, and finance, and see how the patents you are working on fit into the overall business strategy for a particular product. It is rare that you get to gain this same intimate knowledge of the overall strategy that you develop when working in-house if you work externally in a law firm that represents the client. You will likely have to formulate the optimal IP strategy based on the marketing and/or regulatory strategy for a particular product, which may not always involve procuring a patent, and provide your rationale in support of this strategy to the product team and management. You will be faced with problems that require unique solutions. Finally, you will continue to build on your patent experience and gain a unique perspective about the biotech/pharmaceutical business.

Patent Offices

The primary function of a country's PTO is to enable the protection of IP, including the granting of patents to those deserving of that protection in

---

[4]Corporate positions are often referred to as in-house positions.

accordance with the relevant laws of that country. To fulfill this function, at least where patents are concerned, the PTO hires individuals with the relevant academic background to examine patent applications. Examiners are trained to assess the patentability of the inventions in accordance with their country's law. Given the highly technical nature of chemical inventions, which include biotech/pharmaceutical inventions, the PTO hires individuals with doctoral training in the relevant scientific disciplines. The one important distinction between examiners and agents is that examiners are not trained to draft patent applications. It is not uncommon for examiners to move into law firms once they gain sufficient experience at the PTO. Having once worked as an examiner gives them the added advantage of knowing the inner workings of the PTO, including what the PTO will be looking for when examining an application.

Tech-Transfer Offices

Tech-transfer offices are dedicated to identifying technologies developed within academic institutions that have promising potential for commercialization. Once identified, patent protection is usually sought for the practical use of the technology. Large tech-transfer offices may have their own internal patent agents/lawyers, but more often than not, they outsource the drafting and prosecution of the patent application to outside patent firms. Nevertheless, tech-transfer offices provide a good place to learn about the patent process and can be a good springboard for applying for a job as a patent agent trainee at a law firm.

SKILLS AND QUALIFICATIONS REQUIRED FOR AND GAINED DURING TRAINING AS A PATENT AGENT/LAWYER

What academic qualifications do you need to transition into patent law? Must you have a PhD? Do you need to spend another 3 to 4 years getting a law degree? Do you have to be certified/registered to practice patent law?

Patent practice is unique in that it is the only branch of law where a law degree is *not* required to practice. Nonlawyer patent professionals do have significant limitations in terms of what they are qualified and licensed to do, however. For example, as a registered United States or Canadian patent agent, you are not permitted to advise a client regarding issues dealing with patent validity, infringement, or litigation. In the United States and Canada, you certainly cannot represent a client in court, even on patent-related issues. Many jurisdictions do not permit nonlawyer patent agents to enter into legal partnerships with lawyers, regardless of the number of years that they have been at the firm, the number of clients that they have, or the amount of billable hours that they have docketed.[5]

A PhD is *not* necessary either. In fact, you may transition into patent law with as little as a bachelor's degree in science (e.g., physics, engineering, math, chemistry, biochemistry, cell biology, genetics, biology, etc.). But a PhD is desirable, especially in the life sciences/chemistry, and the more technical expertise you have, the better. Most law firms looking to hire in the life sciences field will not consider applicants for a position unless they have a PhD. In other fields, such as mechanical or electrical engineering, a bachelor's degree may be sufficient. However, depending on the type and size of the law firm, a master's degree might be a minimum. At boutique IP firms,[6] the majority of nonlawyer patent professionals will have a PhD and many of the lawyers will have, at minimum, a master's degree.

Regardless of whether or not you have a law degree, as a patent professional you must become registered/certified to practice patent law before the PTO of your country by passing a rigorous examination. Certain countries require that you have a minimum amount of on-the-job experience before you can sit for the exam. Once certified, you can file and prosecute

---

[5]Law professional bodies of certain countries, such as the United States, permit individuals to obtain a law degree on a part-time basis by going to law school at night. Some countries, on the other hand, require that you attend law school on a full-time basis. Given the limitations on nonlawyer patent professionals, and if time and resources and your personal circumstances permit, ultimately obtaining a law degree is becoming increasingly the norm for PhD scientists who enter the field of patent law, and is one I highly encourage. Many law firms, especially in the United States, may even foot the bill for you to attend law school.

[6]Boutique IP firms are those that only practice IP law, including IP-related litigation. General-purpose law firms, or full-service law firms as they are sometimes called, are those that practice other areas of law in addition to IP law, such as corporate, real estate, criminal, or employment law. There are even smaller boutique IP firms that specialize in only life science IP or high-tech IP. Such firms are normally run by solo practitioners or groups of two or three professionals. It is unlikely that such small firms will take on nonlawyer PhDs as trainees.

patent applications on your own in the PTO of your country. Nonlawyer patent professionals, once they have passed the patent agent's exam, are often referred to as "patent agents" in the United States and Canada, or "patent attorneys" in the United Kingdom, Germany, and certain other jurisdictions.

Law firms, where you will most likely start your new career, look for individuals who are not only self-starters but can work and manage projects independently. The majority of your time will be spent drafting and prosecuting patent applications and communicating with your clients, examiners, and other officials at the PTO. Hence, you must be able to write and verbally communicate well. You must have excellent time management skills and work under pressure because there will be times when you will have to draft patent applications or respond to correspondence from the PTO on short notice. You must be able to quickly make sense of complex data given to you by your clients, and you must be able to think logically and have strong reasoning skills. Based on the data provided to you by your client, you must be able to ask and answer key questions that will allow you to advocate for the patentability of your client's invention, or request more data from your clients to be able to further strengthen the argument for the patentability of their invention. You will be required to come up with creative solutions to difficult problems. Now, think about it—don't you already have the skills highlighted above? These are skills that you started acquiring as a graduate student when you worked under the guidance of your PhD supervisor, and you likely perfected them as a postdoc when you worked independently in another principal investigator's laboratory.

You will also learn new skills and build on those you already have. Initially, you will find drafting a patent application, especially the claims, an exercise in pure frustration (much like writing your first grant). Drafting a patent application is part art, part science. There are plenty of texts out there that will teach you how to draft a patent application and the accompanying claims, but none of these will replace on-the-job experience. Be patient, and be prepared to have your drafts come back with a lot of red ink. Just as it took you time to develop and perfect the techniques that you learned at the bench, it can take many years before you are comfortable drafting and prosecuting patent applications without a second set of eyes looking over your work. You will also learn how to be nonconfrontational and try to understand the other person's point of view and how to give in on issues of less importance. You will likely learn aspects of IP licensing agreements and issues relating to IP when companies merge or are acquired. With those cases, you will learn how to work with a team of lawyers from different areas of law and see how IP fits into the big picture.

GETTING A FOOT IN THE DOOR

How do you market yourself for the transition to patent law? You need to reinvent yourself. The first place to start is your resume. Scientists tend to have a voluminous curriculum vitae identifying every publication, every conference at which they presented, and every poster submission. These achievements are important because they demonstrate your writing, speaking, and presentation skills, but for your new job applications these areas should be toned down. Instead, you need to highlight the skills described above—the more generic analysis, reasoning, and creative thinking skills that are transferrable and will make you marketable as a patent agent trainee or technical advisor. Highlight any other experience you may have had with patents or the patent application process. For example, you might have been fortunate enough to have your name listed as an inventor on one or more patents or patent applications while you were at the bench. Make sure to make a point of this. It will demonstrate, at the very least, that you are familiar with the patent process.

Next, flood law firms, universities, and biotech/pharmaceutical companies in your area, or the city to which you are relocating, with your new resume. If possible, become a member and attend the local IP association meetings.[7] If you are at an academic institution, contact the law school career services office for opportunities to transition into IP law or set up a meeting with a career guidance counselor.

Finally, and perhaps most importantly, network, network, network. Although there are many social and professional networking sites where

---

[7]Many cities have IP associations that organize events, usually held monthly, primarily for the benefit of the local business community. These "breakfast" or "lunch and learn" meetings are held to educate local businesses on basic issues related to IP law and the best practices for managing their patent portfolio. These events are also meant to keep businesses up to date on important issues raised by court decisions that may impact their patent strategy. Certain law firms also organize seminars that are open to the public on hot-button IP topics. Such events are good networking opportunities to meet with a wide variety of IP professionals and business leaders. Find these events by searching for them on the Internet or inquire at the law department of your academic institution.

you can post your new resume and announce that you are looking to transition into IP law online, nothing will replace the old-fashioned in-person meeting. Call up a patent agent or lawyer at a firm and offer to buy them coffee for a brief introduction and an "informational interview." Stress that you simply want to learn more about the profession. Once you are in conversation at the coffee shop, you can ask them to let you know if they hear about openings for a PhD with excellent skills such as yours. Call someone you may know who has made this transition into IP law. Ask them for advice and assistance.

Transitioning into IP law is not easy. It takes a lot of courage to step out of your comfort zone and start at the bottom of a new career that you know barely anything about. But you have the skills and most of the qualifications. The rest you will learn on the job. The road to success is filled with challenges. You have the courage and wherewithal to overcome these obstacles. After all, you could not have come this far if you had quit after the first failed experiment as a graduate student. Transitioning into IP law is no different. There will be many disappointments, but the key, as with any disappointment, is to learn and build on your experience. IP law is a challenging career, but it can also be a very rewarding one, both financially and intellectually. Persevere, and you will find that the light you see at the end of the tunnel will guide you to a very bright future where your skills and technical expertise are very much in demand.

WAY OUT

As you gain more experience in IP law, especially if you hold an in-house position, you will likely learn aspects of IP licensing and will also acquire experience related to IP issues associated with mergers and acquisitions. This knowledge, together with your science background and your IP experience, will provide you with a powerful skill set that can lead to other career opportunities in licensing and/or business development within your current organization outside of the legal department. You may, for example, be able to transition into the business development organization of the company that you work for and assist them in assessing the strength of the science and IP of a biotech company that is being considered as a target for acquisition or for licensing of their proprietary technology.

Box 1. My Experience

The opportunity to be a summer student in the Molecular and Cellular Physiology course at Woods Hole Marine Biological Laboratory while a graduate student at the University of Miami School of Medicine was a defining moment in my scientific career. Sixty of us were chosen out of 600 graduate students from all over the world who had applied for the course. It was a glorious summer, one I will never forget. I rubbed shoulders with some of the finest minds in cell and molecular biology. I was convinced, after that experience, that there was only one path to follow—the traditional academic track to having my own laboratory. I knew, even back then, that this was not going to be easy. There were already rumblings about how competitive it was going to be to get an academic position. But I believed that pedigree was an important factor and if I could postdoc at a world-renowned institution under the mentorship of a leading scientist in his/her field, I would have a leg up on the competition. I was next accepted for a postdoc at Cold Spring Harbor Laboratory, the Mecca for molecular and cellular biology. My project was to unravel the mysteries of a cell-surface receptor that had recently been cloned. We had a rough idea of what the receptor might do, but we had to prove it. I had to identify the ligands and/or substrates and elucidate the signal transduction pathway by which this receptor might exert its effects. Other postdocs had made significant progress in the same laboratory with other proteins in the family. All I had to do was follow the same strategy they used.

Fast-forward five years and I had yet to publish. The turning point came at a conference in Keystone. My laboratory colleagues and I were sitting in front of the fireplace while two laboratory mates discussed the day's presentations and how their work would tie in. Their excitement was palpable. I just could not get excited. I realized at that moment that I had lost my passion for bench work, but not science. My personal circumstances were also weighing on me. I had recently been married to a physician in Toronto, Canada. We had had a commuter marriage for the previous 3 years. One of us had to move, and given my circumstances, it only made sense that I move to Toronto. The decision to transition was a difficult one. I felt I had worked hard, perhaps for nothing. What could I possibly do with everything I had learned so far? After much research and networking, I came to know of a former Cold Spring Harbor postdoc who had made the transition into patent law and I decided to give her a call and ask for her advice. Obviously, it worked out well—very well.

I rewrote my resume and sent it out to every single law firm in Toronto. I was eventually offered a position as a patent agent trainee in the IP department of

(Continued.)

one of the biggest general-purpose law firms in the country. Six months into it, I knew that the law firm environment was not for me. Although I enjoyed patent law, I had decided that at some point I needed to work for a biotech/pharmaceutical company, that is, I needed to move in-house. That opportunity arrived eight years later, when I interviewed for a position to head up IP for Canada's largest publicly held pharmaceutical company, Biovail Corporation. In the meantime, I kept working at the law firm, not only learning as much as I could about IP law and honing my patent drafting and prosecution skills, but also networking, primarily with members of the biotech and pharmaceutical business community in and around Toronto. My mandate at Biovail was to build an IP department and be responsible for the company's global patent strategy. My primary responsibilities were to draft, prosecute, and maintain the IP related to the company's drug delivery technologies; assist R&D to ensure that projects had the necessary data to support patentability of these projects; inform senior management of potential risks to the patent portfolio; and work together with individuals from other departments such as regulatory and marketing and provide them with scenarios for what would happen to the exclusivity for a particular product in the event that the patent(s) was challenged. I also assisted corporate lawyers in the legal department on IP clauses in agreements relating to the out-licensing of our products or in-licensing of products/technologies. I started at Biovail as Manager, Patents and during the next nine years, I moved up the corporate ladder to Senior Manager, Director, and finally to Senior Director, Intellectual Property.

In September 2010, Biovail Corporation was purchased by Valeant Pharmaceuticals. The IP department was gradually dissolved and I was finally packaged-out in June 2011. I eventually came to the decision that it was time to go solo and set up my own patent agency. In(sci)te IP was formed in June 2012, at which time I had zero clients. My first course of business was to network and convince start-up life science companies to sign me on as their patent agent. The networking took me halfway around the world to Malaysia (I am a Malaysian citizen and a Canadian permanent resident), where I knew that the government was actively funding R&D in the life sciences, primarily in the herbal industry. I also believed that my experience in North America would be a significant advantage. After much networking I managed to sign on my first client and have since signed on several others. The networking, together with what I learned about the pharmaceutical business while at Biovail, however, has now led me to start up my own biotech company in Malaysia, with the help of the Malaysian government, but that is a story for another day.[8]

---

[8] "If you want to play a game, go to where it's played and find a way to get in. Things happen when you get in the game," Chris Matthews, Commencement Speech, Fordham University, May 20, 2006.

Box 2. Ten Dos and Don'ts

1. Do read the patent blogs. These websites provide useful summaries of the latest developments in patent law and summarize important court decisions. Reading the patents that were key to the decisions helps in understanding how to, or not to, draft a patent application. The following blogs focus on biotech/pharma/life science IP law: http://www.patentdocs.org, http://www.patentbaristas.com, http://www.pharmapatentsblog.com, and http://www.patents4life.com. Another popular blog can be found at http://patentlyo.com.

2. Do not highlight your area of research. Your expertise in cell-cycle research, genomics, or cancer research is not of particular relevance, but do highlight your analytical and reasoning skills. These are the transferable and valuable skills.

3. Do network, network, and network. You will have to kiss a lot of frogs before you find the position that you want.

4. Do not stop networking even after you have transitioned into IP law. You never know what opportunities might come up.

5. Do learn how to read a patent. These can be found easily at https://www.google.com/?tbm=pts. Search by keyword and you will find a ton of documents. To begin, search for patent documents in your area of research.

6. Do seek out other PhDs who have made the transition into IP law and ask for their advice.

7. Do get to know IP support staff when you have found a patent agent trainee position. They have a wealth of information on IP rules and regulations.

8. Do not be a "know-it-all." Transition with an open mind. Be humble and willing to learn. You will have to learn a new language and a new way of thinking. You will have to start at the bottom, again.

9. Do be confident of your skills.

10. Do not let criticisms of your drafting get you down early on. After all, you are learning. Persevere and you will become good at your job.

ACKNOWLEDGMENTS

I thank Lana Janes, Melanie P. Merriman, and Shaheen Doctor for their comments. Lana is a chemist who took a career path similar to mine and is now Vice President, Intellectual Property and Chief Patent Counsel at a biotechnology company in Vancouver, Canada. We were, and still are, each other's support system. Melanie was one of my PhD supervisors, and Shaheen, Medical Director of the Neonatal Intensive Care Unit at North York General Hospital in Toronto, is my wife and the reason that I moved to Toronto.

10

Biotech Start-Ups and Entrepreneurship

Susan Froshauer

Connecticut United for Research Excellence, New Haven, Connecticut 06510 and Hartford, Connecticut 06103

The world of biotechnology "start-ups" and entrepreneurship offers exciting new avenues for driving state-of-the-art research using an arsenal of multidisciplinary skills, whether your role is as part of a team or as a leader. Although traditionally these positions may not be as secure as those offered by some of the larger companies, the small start-up culture provides opportunities for contributing at many levels to a wide range of responsibilities: from scientific discovery to delivery of proof of concept and intellectual property; from analysis of market opportunities and competitive intelligence to creation of time lines and business plans for a first product. Often, if you get in on the ground level, you get to validate your own concept, pitch to potential investors, argue value, build a team, engage advisors, and then, with funding in hand, launch an entirely new research and development (R&D) enterprise. Many of the skills and much of the experience gained while pursuing a graduate degree can be put to good use in these arenas as well. This path, however, is not for the faint of heart; it requires not only a strong scientific background and organizational skills, but also the ability to work well on a team, excellent communication skills, and persistence when faced with delays or disappointment. With increasing responsibilities in the small company come the requirements for aptitudes for leadership, strategic and financial planning, networking, negotiating, and managing both projects and personnel.

Leaving the relatively well-defined, safe path of research at an academic or established biotechnology/pharmaceutical institution for a new venture can be risky but also highly challenging and rewarding. In contrast to the more narrow focus of academia, in which often the organizing principle is to contribute basic research and fundamental understanding, the clear goal in the start-up setting is to develop an application, service, or product that has value medically and commercially. It is not sufficient to simply have a clever research idea for a new product. As a member of a team, you also consider how your research/product will be differentiated, the cost and time needed to deliver it, prospects for patenting, and regulatory hurdles.

The realm and the role of the bioscience sector are rapidly changing, creating new opportunities for small start-ups and biotechs. In particular, as large pharmaceutical companies downsize their R&D workforce in response to pricing and regulatory pressures, they seek to invest in and/or acquire smaller companies and focus their efforts on product marketing, sales, and distribution. For example, to bolster its pipeline, Cubist acquired Trius and Optimer, smaller companies with antibiotic products, and Merck has taken over Idenix (admittedly no longer a "small" biotech company, but the model holds). For many of these large pharmaceutical companies, acquiring smaller or start-up biotechnology companies provides support for their own development efforts as their older products lose patent protection. Another corporate strategy is to move the research efforts from the company R&D departments into academic settings; this shift in investment is thought to be both more efficient and less expensive for the companies. In this model, generating and exploring new ideas and innovative concepts is assumed by laboratories in the universities, whereas the companies focus their attention on funding and supporting clinical trials and other developments. Principal investigators—either individually or in collaboration with colleagues—have formed small satellite companies on the basis of an idea or finding coming out of their laboratories (or sometimes coming from conversations with like-minded colleagues). Universities such as Yale and the University of Connecticut are also producing their own companies to meet the demands for healthcare information technology or advances in personalized medicine. Cutbacks in federal funding also kindle a start-up culture, as faculty spin out their very early technology to access different types of federal funding, such as small business grants.

Generally, start-up companies are where the perhaps risky but truly innovative experimental efforts are carried out. If your experience, vision, and personality are well suited to tolerating the possible lack of stability, these environments can provide a challenging and exciting career. The outlook for the small biotech company is also favorable, with biotech stocks outperforming the general market. And, according to market analysts, the increase in initial public offerings (IPOs) by start-ups in the biotech sector seems likely to continue. Clearly, the need for innovation in research is continuously expanding and is being met by a variety of original and imaginative approaches.

JOBS

We first discuss the positions likely to be found at a small start-up because this may be your starting point, allowing you to have the opportunity to gain experience in the running of a small company. This experience will serve you well, especially if you wish to consider launching your own venture.

Working in a Small Biotech Company

In an existing small start-up company, the positions will vary, depending on the maturity and the nature of the company and its focus. But there are generally a few consistent categories. Figure 1 shows relationships among the various positions as well as possible career paths.

Bench scientists typically work on a variety of projects such as target or assay development, chemical analysis or synthesis, data mining and prediction, instrumentation improvement, or systems optimization. It is more frequently the case that companies hire individuals with very specific subject matter expertise (e.g., microbiomes and obesity) rather than generalized skills (e.g., protein chemistry). In conducting their research, bench scientists may also become involved in analyzing data, publishing results, and filing patents. These activities are often team efforts. With increasing success, the bench scientist will come to make a decision whether to continue at the bench as a senior research scientist or to move into a managerial or leadership position.

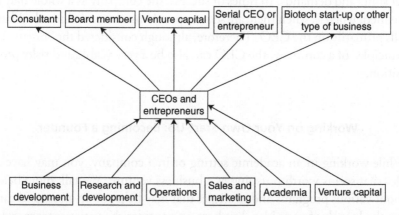

Figure 1. Common career paths for CEOs and entrepreneurs. (Modified, with permission, from Freedman 2008. © Cold Spring Harbor Laboratory Press, Cold Spring Harbor, NY.)

Group leaders often assume their positions as a result of taking a leadership role among a small group of researchers working together as a team. The leader assumes responsibility for coordinating the efforts of the team, evaluating results, and assigning specific tasks to be undertaken. They must be experts on data and able to articulate the research findings clearly to senior managers.

Managers and directors expand the scope of responsibility to overseeing the activities of a few groups of research teams. They generally set the goals and expectations of a project or program and track the directions, budgets, and time lines for achievement. They must present data well to senior management and in the context of the business strategy and customer needs and be open to leading individuals through dramatic shifts in project funding or corporate strategy. Beyond hiring and supervising personnel, managers are also responsible for creating an environment that encourages the research groups and supports morale. Often, these individuals have important roles in interfacing with external advisors or scientists, or—depending on the size of the company—speaking to investors. Clearly, in this arena, having strong interpersonal and communication skills, as well as scientific and analytical expertise, becomes increasingly important.

Finally, the top tier of the company is occupied by "C-level" positions, including chief executive officer (CEO), chief financial officer (CFO), and chief scientific officer or chief operating officer (CSO or COO). Responsible for establishing the strategy for the overall direction of the company and reporting to the board of directors, these executives continually develop and revise business plans, engage in fundraising, and respond to general market shifts and demands. In times of success, the company as a whole may be credited, whereas when there are serious problems or even failure, the blame falls primarily on the CEO. Therefore, although considered the "organizing principle" of a company, the CEO can also be a very visible and risky proposition.

Working on Your Own Start-Up: Becoming a Founder

While working in an academic setting or in a company, you may have an idea that seems worth pursuing as a business venture. We talk more below about various programs and strategies that may help you to assess and carry out the launch of your idea, but here we consider the various stages, roles, and responsibilities of the founder.

The first step is to determine whether the idea is both competitive and fundable. To address this question, it is best to turn to a mentor (a respected professor or supervisor and experienced entrepreneur) for expert and dispassionate advice. With support and encouragement, the next step is to develop a compelling business strategy ("a pitch") to present to possible team members and investors. Consider the following: Do you want to undertake this on your own or enlist the help of a savvy colleague or two? Understand that as a start-up CEO, you will likely have many roles, serving at first as finance and operations officer as well as the primary "human resource." The uniqueness and soundness of the business story ("the special sauce") and your own enthusiasm and sense of vision are critical to raising support for your company. This plan is often presented as a very logical and engaging set of PowerPoint slides that describe in detail to your potential investors how you intend to implement your idea and make it profitable (showing how investors will make money). The presentation can serve also as the basis for applying for government support via a small business grant.

Performing proof-of-concept activities serves to validate your business concept. These activities vary with the nature of the business and may include building prototype software, testing marketing hypotheses, continuing biological assays on drugs, developing patents, and accessing key people. The overall goal of your proof of concept is to win the confidence of both investors and potential customers by demonstrating the value and validity of the proposal and its likely outcomes. Often, small sums of money are available from angel investors or the state to support proof-of-concept work.

Acquiring successful capital investment provides the true beginning, enabling you to entice others to join you and begin to form a team that can make your vision a reality. You set the "culture" or style of management of your enterprise to motivate and encourage those whom you have enlisted and to ensure an inspiring and collegial workplace. Your investors may often serve as business advisors or board members to track budget and progress against corporate goals. Creating a scientific advisory board provides the technical balance and expertise to assess and encourage your research activities.

Finally, while working at or establishing a start-up venture can be wonderfully adventurous and rewarding, the day-to-day work may also be challenging and stressful, often demoralizing. The opportunities exist to have a role in many different aspects of the company, sometimes simultaneously. Clearly, these career paths should not be undertaken without careful consideration of what may best suit you personally as well as professionally.

SKILLS/QUALIFICATIONS

Your graduate and postdoctoral training provide a strong background that enables you to evaluate novel and exciting scientific developments and to envision their possibility for transfer into a business setting. As is true for management positions described in other chapters, the rising executive also requires vision, leadership, and decisiveness—the ability to respond quickly but deliberately to an unexpected changing situation. Similarly, having excellent communication skills, both oral and written, provides a strong advantage. You will need to present your ideas and strategies to a variety of disparate groups. Senior scientists present at team meetings and scientific conferences; managers report to colleagues and to potential investors, and when difficult decisions must be made, managers defend these decisions. Strong analytical and problem-solving skills are necessary features for success. To some degree, many or all these skills come from your experience in pursuing a PhD.

But different abilities and qualifications are also desirable. Typically, a PhD student pursues her/his own research project, collaborating or enlisting help only for specialized parts of the project. Doing research within a company, however, typically involves working—at some level—with or on a team. Thus, the ability to share responsibilities, trust coworkers, and share knowledge and research results is essential. Other expertise needed, usually rarely part of graduate training, is in personnel or financial management. Facility in these areas is important for success in heading an academic research laboratory, as well as in a corporate setting. Any training or courses taken in these areas can only enhance your application for a position.

In terms of self-employment, a sense of ambition, confidence, and passion about your ideas and your company are all essential to promoting your cause. Because you may be called on to deal with any number of questions or problems across the broad spectrum of the business (from science to personnel to workplace operation failures), it is important to be strong-willed, resourceful, and resilient—even optimistic in the face of discouragement. Strategic planning and negotiation skills are indispensable. If you feel that you are lacking in any of these qualifications, consider enlisting a partner (perhaps a business partner) whose expertise complements your own.

A final word on "intellectual honesty": Adherence to the highest ethical standards in business practices as well as in personal interactions is absolutely essential to maintain a reputation that serves you and your company well.

GETTING A FOOT IN THE DOOR

Presenting a resume that reflects a broad range of competencies is a distinct advantage. During your tenure as a PhD student or postdoctoral fellow, engage in activities that will expand your expertise: Attend and present your results at scientific meetings, plan conferences within your institution, and develop strong writing and communication skills. You will likely have written articles for publication or submitted a research grant (or submitted a section for your advisor's application). To enhance your ability to communicate with the nonscientific sector, consider writing for the university newspaper, explaining recent advances in your department, or starting a student journal. It is also a good idea to take some classes outside of your immediate area of specialization—for example, courses in entrepreneurship, financial management, or business development. Start-ups often have nonpaid internships that flex around graduate or postdoc schedules and offer opportunities to test the culture and contribute to their investor value creation.

The term "networking" has become cliché; however, the value of networking is not to be underestimated. Reach out beyond your immediate (and comfortable) circle of colleagues to become acquainted with those who may serve as mentors or role models. Identify those at your institution who have had some success with inventions, entrepreneurship, and start-up efforts and set up meetings with those individuals. Speak at professional meetings, join local biotechnology associations as well as professional societies, and make use of their career services.

An increasing number of universities and communities now offer entrepreneurial training and support that are well worth exploring. Steve Blank's collaboration with many universities and the National Science Foundation (the I-Corps program) and his Lean Launchpad system provide excellent tools for entrepreneurs (www.steveblank.com). At the University of Massachusetts, the New Venture Creation Program offers various electives to aspiring entrepreneurs. The Yale Entrepreneurial Institute is devoted to mentoring students with ideas for new ventures, providing expert advice and bringing students together with advisors and consultants. The University of Connecticut houses incubator space and educational programming (the Technology Incubator Program). The Grove in New Haven and other Connecticut coworking spaces offer opportunities for local entrepreneurs to connect with mentors and one another and share resources to help develop and expand. The Bioscience ClubhouseCT (www.cureconnect.org) is a state-wide program sponsored by Connecticut Innovations and Connecticut United for Research Excellence (CURE) to convene students, entrepreneurs, new technology ideas, and start-ups.

CAREER PROGRESSION: THE WAY IN, UP, AND OUT

If the prospect of beginning your career at a start-up seems a precarious start, it is reasonable first to consider working at a large, better established biotech or pharmaceutical company. There you will learn how research is conducted in a more traditional company setting and, if you seek out opportunities, how business is developed and managed. This early tenure will provide valuable and instructive experience to help you determine how you wish to proceed in your career path and will transfer to and enhance your position should you choose to move to a smaller setting. Working on a research team, whether in a large or small company, will prepare you to continue in research as a senior scientist or project manager and to shift into more managerial positions in the business and operations part of a new venture. Should an opportunity arise, you will have an insider's view, even generally, of how a company is run—valuable training for launching and maintaining your own start-up. Potential investors may view this exposure as value added to a start-up. Progressing from a manager to CEO or entrepreneur opens the door to a variety of other positions in the corporate world (see Fig. 1), serving as consultant or advisor to corporations, universities, and even to state government scientific councils or analysts for venture investors.

It is important to note that entrepreneurs can come out of many different career levels. Many coming from large pharma or biotech companies have created research team projects that enabled them to spin out an idea or technology arising from their own findings when the focus of the company shifted. And, as we have seen, some entrepreneurs come out of academia, forming a company within the university or leaving to form an independent company.

It is also important to be aware that leaving academia for a career in biotechnology is no longer one way only. Success in working in (or starting) a company provides a transition to other related activities in higher education and in government.

Box 1. My Experience

My lifelong interest in nature and science came into focus with an opportunity to work, after college, as a research assistant at Cold Spring Harbor Laboratory in New York. Having grown up on Long Island, I was happy to return to a place I knew and to expand my experience in botany into the world of molecular biology.

In the 1970s, Cold Spring Harbor was flooded with scientists pursuing new technology and building new research fields. My passion for scientific excellence, the habit of arduous work hours, and the fun of the exchange of out-in-front, creative ideas began there. This experience led to the pursuit of a doctorate in microbiology and molecular genetics at Harvard and a postdoctoral research fellowship at Yale. After getting my postdoc, I took a position at Pfizer, working first as an antibiotic drug hunter and then as a member of Pfizer's Strategic Alliance Group, formed to execute and manage Pfizer's collaborations with external scientists at biotech or universities. As part of a multidisciplinary team, we were charged with creating a deal (investment) portfolio to access new technology and advance Pfizer's global research strategies.

By 2000, in conversation with a group of like-minded friends and colleagues, we developed an idea for a company that became Rib-X Pharmaceuticals Inc. (now Melinta Therapeutics) in New Haven. Our goal was to design and develop novel antibiotics for the treatment of serious drug-resistant infections by exploiting a collective expertise in drug discovery, structural biology, and computational chemistry, in particular, using the structure of the ribosome (for which one of our founders was awarded the Nobel Prize in Chemistry). To support the company, we raised ~$160 million from angels and venture capital investors. After 10 years at Rib-X, I left the company to work with the Yale Entrepreneurial Institute and as Director of the Technology Exchange Portal at University of Connecticut, assisting Connecticut entrepreneurs and others with training programs for students.

My passion for working with entrepreneurs paved the way to my new position as President and CEO of CURE (www.cureconnect.org), a nonprofit organization that serves as an advocate and network for the state's bioscience industry, involving health-related corporations, organizations, associations, and businesses involved in bioscience.

Throughout my career, I have remained involved in my community, serving on many different boards, including the advisory boards of the Yale Entrepreneurial Institute, The Grid (a resource for entrepreneurs around New

(Continued.)

Haven), UCONN Ventures, and the Angel Investor Forum. I am also a member of the board of the Creative Arts Workshop of New Haven.

My focus is to create research and education partnerships and facilitate collaborations among universities, companies, and investors that promote entrepreneurship and innovation and improve our quality of life. My work with universities and start-ups to identify talent, assess business strategies, and establish a mix of new healthcare-related companies in the state supports this long-term goal.

Box 2. Ten Dos and Don'ts

---

1. Do spend time formally and informally with a diverse team of mentors up and down the biotechnology food chain. Ask for input on issues arising, pressure testing your own assumptions and leveraging their connections.

2. Do take advantage of local business or entrepreneurial networking and educational forums. Selective, quality, industry-focused conferences can also be valuable.

3. Do learn how to introduce yourself appropriately; offer a business card and share what you do in an engaging manner to identify interesting mentors and connections. Offer a connection or an idea of your own.

4. Do take career risks. Consider joining a company that offers broad opportunities, rather than a larger salary. Move yourself outside of your area of comfortable experience to widen your knowledge and expertise. Appreciate that your first company is a start and not necessarily your destination.

5. Do not forget to serve as an advisor, mentor, or consultant for students, companies, and organizations.

6. Do think more broadly and consider joining a local angel organization, scientific society, or entrepreneurial group that invests in efforts that create community and drive the biotech community.

7. Do stay optimistic and persistent. Optimism is the secret to staying motivated. A new venture will face many challenges but a successful entrepreneur shows persistence in the face of this adversity, keeps focused on the

(Continued.)

vision, and pushes ahead despite obstacles. To scientists, details are critical and absorbing, but entrepreneurs need to focus on the big picture and avoid becoming distracted.

8. Do remain flexible and adaptable; more than simple perseverance is required. When faced with a serious setback, a successful entrepreneur can adapt the venture to the changed circumstances with a fresh positioning, a different market, a changed business model, a new source of funding, and an alternative technology application—all the while with a clear eye on getting that rock to the top of the hill. Seeking challenging and conflicting inputs from advisors, investors, and colleagues is critical.

9. Do consider a transparent communication style. Investors, colleagues, mentees, and teammates often appreciate knowing your thought process.

10. Do take a step back when you need it. The trick when demoralized is not to force yourself to work but to figure out what it takes to get you back to a state where you want to work. Create a discipline around balancing friends/family and a passion for entrepreneurship.

ADDITIONAL RESOURCES

Freedman T. 2008. *Career opportunities in biotechnology and drug development*, pp. 25–32 and 311–328. Cold Spring Harbor Laboratory Press, Cold Spring Harbor, NY.

Hill LA, Brandeau G, Truelove E, Lineback K. 2014. *Collective genius: The art and practice of leading innovation*. Harvard Business Review Press, Boston.

LaMattina JL. 2009. *Drug truths: Dispelling the myths about pharmaceutical R&D*. John Wiley & Sons, Inc. Hoboken, NJ.

MIT Technology Review: September/October 2013, 35 Innovators Under 35. http://www.technologyreview.com/lists/innovators-under-35/2013.

Spors KK. 2009. So, you want to be an entrepreneur. *The Wall Street Journal* (Journal Reports: Small Business); February 23.

WWW RESOURCES

www.cureconnect.org Connecticut United for Research Excellence.

SteveBlank.com/2013/08/21/reinventing-life-science-startups-evidence-based-entrepreneurship-2/

11

A Career for Life Scientists in Management Consulting

Rodney W. Zemmel

McKinsey & Company, Incorporated, New York, New York 10022

Compared with life sciences, management consulting is a relatively new field. Nonetheless, leading firms have assumed a central role in the global business economy and command increasing influence as advisors to corporations and organizations in the public and social sectors. Offering robust analysis, independent and expert perspectives, and—in the best cases— valuable creative input, these companies focus on helping clients to improve their performance or more effectively execute their mission.

Because the top firms tackle the most complex problems for the most successful organizations in the world, they attract top graduates. But the field is no longer the sole province of those with MBAs. In recent years, the profession has increasingly diversified and now actively recruits candidates with advanced degrees in a range of disciplines—including the life sciences.

Those who join the field will find many parallels between the consulting approach and scientific inquiry. As a result, life scientists have many of the intrinsic skills needed to thrive in the industry, which can offer an extraordinary breadth of assignments, global experience, and an accelerated way to learn. At leading firms, the intensive training and development offered can pave the way for partnership, in which consultants counsel senior executives as peers. Many of those who leave become entrepreneurs or join top organizations—sometimes their former clients—at a leadership level.

Management consulting took root in the 1920s, when James O. McKinsey, a University of Chicago management professor, launched a small business to provide financial and accounting advice to local companies. Understanding that financial data could be mined to improve business performance, he launched McKinsey & Company in 1926.

It was less than a decade after World War I, three years before the Great Depression, and a time of profound change in the U.S. economy. Ambitious young men and women were leaving rural America in droves, as McKinsey himself did, to seek unfettered opportunity in cities. Small family businesses were giving way to corporations. The success of Henry Ford's assembly line fanned interest in specialization, changing the profile of industry and the professions. And everyone, it seemed, was growing giddy (if not rich) by speculating in the stock market.

Against this dynamic backdrop, James McKinsey saw that no one was expressly serving the needs of chief executives charged with leading the growing business enterprises. When he founded his management consulting firm, it was with the idea that it would provide analytically rigorous and independent advice to top management.

Although McKinsey had the initial idea that launched the management consulting field, it was really his protégé, the lawyer Marvin Bower, who shaped the industry. Called "the father of modern management consulting" by the Harvard Business School, Bower had served on bankruptcy committees, learning how to gut businesses and retain what remained of value for bondholders. When he joined McKinsey in 1933, he hoped to serve businesses more broadly, and indeed, he did. Bower is credited with shaping the vision and culture of McKinsey, and he ultimately had enormous influence on the consulting profession as a whole.

Some of Bower's best ideas were adapted from other fields. For example, the professional conduct that distinguished law and medicine led him to author a set of guiding principles that remain—in an adapted form—a touchstone even today. Of note, these include putting clients' interests first and maintaining high ethical standards. According to Bower's "one firm" concept, offices are encouraged to cooperate rather than to compete with one another. This principle remains a core feature of the firm and the basis for its international diversity and its opportunities for mobility and entrepreneurship.

Other innovations influenced the management consulting industry as well. One of the most significant involved recruiting—specifically, the determination to emphasize talent and intrinsic intellectual strengths over experience. This led the firm to "experiment" in the mid 1950s with hiring MBAs straight from business school. It is difficult to imagine the consequences if those early MBAs had failed. Instead, they flourished. And soon after, many other consulting firms were also mining business schools for talent.

In time, the drive to build a preeminent firm with exceptional talent led McKinsey to broaden its recruiting to candidates with advanced professional degrees, such as PhDs, JDs, and MDs, as well as holders of non-MBA master's degrees. Again, McKinsey was a pioneer in this recruiting strategy, which other consulting firms soon adopted. As technology and globalization have made specialized knowledge more important to clients, McKinsey has continued to diversify. Today, more than half of its ~8000 consultants have non-MBA backgrounds. They include entrepreneurs, scientists, doctors, authors, athletes, and military officers, as well as "experienced hires" from many industries, and represent a mix of nationalities, expertise, and tenures.

With this polyglot consulting community, the firm solves many complex problems for the world's leading corporations—in industries including energy, pharmaceuticals, telecommunications, healthcare, media, consumer goods, and banking. McKinsey also works with leading organizations in the public and social sectors and invests actively in pro bono efforts, serving 70 governments and four of the top five foundations in the world. At any given time, the firm's consultants might focus on issues ranging from helping hospitals decrease wait times for patients, cell phone manufacturers to partner with music companies, schools to increase graduation rates, and consumer companies to integrate postmerger.

Since the founding of management consulting more than 85 years ago, the field has grown exponentially. Some firms focus broadly on important issues facing CEOs and other senior executives. These include The Boston Consulting Group (BCG), Bain & Company, and Booze & Company. Still other consultancies serve businesses at different levels of the corporate structure. Such firms include Deloitte Consulting and Oliver Wyman, among others. The field has also expanded to include a myriad of smaller, "boutique" firms that specialize in a variety of industries and disciplines. They serve clients more narrowly on almost any topic one can think of—from helping airlines design their route systems to helping companies upgrade information technology used by salespeople.

Consulting firms have become a fixture in the world's business landscape. And their presence seems secure: As change continues to accelerate, as globalization expands, and as the private, public, and social sectors increasingly collaborate on the world's most pressing issues, the need for rigorous problem solving and expert, unbiased advice seems unlikely to diminish.

JOBS

Unlike corporate environments, management consulting, with its client and project focus, can open up a world of opportunity to explore different industries, functions, and geographies over time and to build expertise in one or several areas. The descriptions here reflect my own personal experience at McKinsey but include some features of other management consulting firms that generally have a narrower focus and client base.

Typically, the associate position is the most common point of entry—one that offers an exceptional growth experience. At McKinsey, for example, associates work on a variety of engagements within their first year and over time have tremendous flexibility to explore, specialize, change course, or do something new, depending on their preference. In the past five years, the firm has served several thousand clients with a wide range of projects in different industries and countries at any given time. Associates receive substantial training that is designed to help them to build leadership skills as well as the ability to lead their own client project areas. The training occurs both in formal settings and on the job, as part of the firm's apprenticeship model.

For example, before starting work, most advanced-degree holders attend a three-week mini-MBA program. This follows a one-week training program that introduces the firm's approach to solving problems and communicating with clients. Many associates receive up to eight weeks of formal training within their first two years at the firm, which invests more in knowledge and capability building each year than do the leading business schools. The review processes focus as much on building individual strengths as on identifying development needs.

Learning that happens less formally is equally important. Because the firm works in teams and embraces an apprenticeship model, much development occurs in team rooms and client settings. Associates can expect to receive coaching from peers (who may have different strengths) and from engagement managers, who lead teams on a day-to-day basis. Associates also receive mentoring from associate principals (who apprentice as partners-in-training) and from partners themselves, who are responsible for the overall quality of the work and who counsel CEOs as peers. Because the firm has a culture of collaboration and a distinct way of working side by side with clients, much learning also occurs "organically" through interactions with clients. Successful associates can expect to be elected partner in

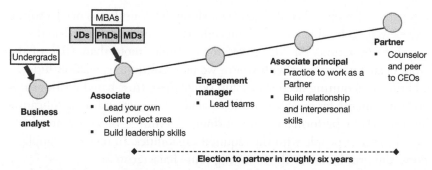

Figure 1. Career progression and related responsibilities. The example is specific to McKinsey, but may be generally applicable to other firms.

roughly six years (see Fig. 1 for a description of various positions and an illustration of career progression).

Many client engagements begin with a kickoff meeting, in which teams discuss their aspirations for a client project, its scope, timing, "boundary constraints," sources of insight or expertise, as well as the development goals of each team member. The purpose is to ensure that the team exceeds client expectations—knocking it out of the park, if you will—while simultaneously providing a rich development experience for each team member. In addition to fostering collaboration, this system promotes intellectual freedom and egalitarianism.

In the meetings, teams often agree on a set of norms to guide their approach to work as well as to manage "work style" and lifestyle preferences. This includes planning in advance how the team will balance major project milestones and individual team members' outside obligations and interests.

SKILLS/QUALIFICATIONS

The top consulting firms seek candidates who have a strong record of achievement and leadership and who exhibit a capacity for continuous development. At the most basic level, consultants must have a strong intelligence quotient (IQ) and emotional quotient (EQ). They must have strong problem-solving capabilities to appropriately frame their client's issue, and then research and analyze data, synthesize findings, develop recommendations, and communicate these effectively.

But even with exceptionally smart solutions, nothing is gained unless the client supports the answer and is motivated to implement it—and can persuade scores of colleagues to go along. So consultants need a strong EQ as well, to be able to lead clients effectively and build trust-based relationships over time. At McKinsey, for example, more than 70% of the work occurs with clients with whom we have continuous relationships. In addition to requiring deep leadership skills, these trust-based relationships give consultants far greater latitude to achieve impact and to significantly improve client performance. Accordingly, recruiting processes are finely tuned to select people with the required capabilities. In reviewing applications, the firm looks for the following four characteristics:

1. **Problem solving.** An ideal candidate reasons logically and demonstrates curiosity, creativity, good business judgment, a tolerance for ambiguity, and an intuitive feel for numbers.

2. **Achievement.** Candidates should set high aspirations, expect and achieve outstanding results, handle obstacles well, show signs of entrepreneurship, and have a willingness to take personal risks.

3. **Personal impact.** Candidates should be able to influence others in a positive way, show an interest in other people, demonstrate self-confidence without arrogance, and listen, understand, and respond well to others.

4. **Leadership.** Candidates should be able to assume leadership roles, seize opportunities and take action, help build highly effective teams with a shared vision, and be sensitive to the thoughts and feelings of other team members.

Because management consulting and scientific inquiry have many parallels, life scientists have a number of assets that can make them strong candidates and help them to excel in the industry, including the following:

• **Training.** Consistent with the approach used by management consulting teams, life scientists use logic and analysis to develop hypotheses, and then find facts to prove or disprove them.

• **Intellectual curiosity.** Similar to many management consultants, life scientists are attracted to continuous learning. In their research, they look to answer problems that others have not been able to answer and to try solutions that others have not thought of.

• **Credibility.** In some consulting work, advanced degrees give life scientists enhanced credibility with clients and occasionally relevant content knowledge.

* **Publishing.** Both fields encourage professionals to publish internally and sometimes externally.

GETTING A FOOT IN THE DOOR

Life scientists contemplating a shift to management consulting should look for opportunities to test the waters. For example, McKinsey offers postgraduate candidates, including life scientists, opportunities for an insider's look at the field. Programs range from an 8–12-week paid internship, in which candidates join a McKinsey team and work on a client project, to opportunities to work on a client case for more than three days. MDs also have an opportunity to participate in a one-day seminar that introduces the healthcare practice and provides an opportunity to meet consultants and understand their work.

Internships or summer rotations are available at other management consulting firms as well. In addition, some universities have created internal consulting functions that serve industry. The University of Pennsylvania, for example, has a club that advises biotech companies. Some universities also offer business case competitions that are typically open to non-MBA candidates as well as students seeking advanced business degrees.

Candidates have many ways, outside of an academic or research setting, to demonstrate the skills that consulting firms value. For example, extracurricular activities can distinguish candidates. Activities that demonstrate leadership—in a laboratory, in the community, or on a sports team—can help to build a profile that attracts interviewers and recruiters. Entrepreneurial ventures, such as launching a nonprofit, can demonstrate a bent for innovation or emerging business skills. Similarly, excelling in team-oriented activities can signal a talent for developing relationships.

WAY OUT

Many consultants at top firms eventually leave the field to join industry (sometimes taking positions with clients whom they have served) or to become entrepreneurs. At McKinsey, which has been called "a leadership factory" by the business press, approximately one in five alumni start their own venture, and some 200 plus serve as CEOs of companies with revenues exceeding $1 billion. Many others have gone on to hold distinguished leadership positions in public and social sectors.

McKinsey alumni with life sciences backgrounds have gone on to become senior executives of major healthcare, pharmaceutical, and biomedical research companies as well as financial services companies and investment firms, such as private equity and venture capital funds. Their positions range from CEO, COO, or chief medical officer to business development officer or managing director. Other life scientist alumni have gone on to start their own businesses, consultancies, or major foundations.

The top management consulting firms offer life scientists a chance to supercharge their careers, helping them to build strengths with some of the best training, mentoring, and apprenticeships available anywhere. Working across the private, public, and social sectors to serve some of the most successful organizations in the world, management consulting can allow life scientists a chance to discover new knowledge and capabilities as well as new passions. Whether joining the field for a few years or for an entire career, life scientists who make the move can find greatly expanded professional networks and opportunity.

Box 1. My Experience

Before I entered management consulting, I studied natural sciences at the University of Cambridge and stayed to earn a PhD in molecular biology. I enjoyed the subject, but I realized that I did not want to remain in academic research long term.

Although I loved the big-picture questions in science and the challenge of designing experiments, I found the average day to be less intellectually stimulating than I wanted it to be, given the repetitive nature of scientific inquiry. I also worried about the importance of serendipity, the relatively solitary nature of the field, and the difficulty of having a meaningful impact when 90% of the scientists who ever lived are working today—making any one person a very small part of a very large endeavor.

So I began talking to biotech companies and those in the life sciences industry and related fields, such as venture capital. More than once, I heard from these professionals that although they thought their own jobs were interesting, in their view, management consultants were doing the most exciting work. Consulting sounded like an extension of the learning experience, and more than that, it also offered an accelerated way to learn.

My initial plan was to join a management consultancy for a few years and then go into biotech, and I discussed that openly with interviewers. With that in mind, I joined McKinsey's London office in 1995. For the next few years, I worked on a wide range of projects—from a pro bono engagement aimed at combating youth homelessness, to studying electricity deregulation for a utility, to developing a growth strategy for a fast food chain. But eventually, I found my way back to healthcare and to pharmaceutical research and development (R&D), which I was most passionate about. I was even lucky enough to serve a client that had licensed technology that I had worked on for my PhD (involving protein-RNA interactions in HIV). After approximately two years, I decided I wanted to see a different part of the world, and I moved to the United States. One of the nice things about a global firm such as McKinsey is that relocating is easy to do. Since I moved to New York, I have specialized in serving U. S. and global healthcare clients, which has taken me all over the world—from Brazil to India to Tokyo.

One of things I have most enjoyed, and that was facilitated by the intellectual freedom of the workplace, has been helping to found our R&D practice, within our healthcare practice. Together with like-minded people who also have a background in life sciences or medicine, I started to serve clients on R&D productivity issues. This was a lot of fun and grew to become a significant part of our healthcare work. It also allowed us to stay close to the broader life sciences world, including its reputable journals. Some of our work has been published in *Nature Reviews Drug Discovery* and other leading journals.

Along with intellectual freedom comes the potential for a tremendous breadth of work. Within life sciences, I have had a chance to work on issues involving R&D productivity, medical device launch diagnostics, personalized medicine, mergers and acquisition (M&A), organizational design, growth strategy, and other issues. I have also had an opportunity to move to the other side of healthcare and lead the Health Care Services Practice, which serves hospitals, healthcare systems, payers, pharmacy benefit managers, and the like, and which is an exciting and fast-growing component of what we do. As part of that, we have also had a significant role in helping the industry to prepare for U.S. healthcare reform, which has involved everything from thinking through how to improve operations in hospitals to considering how profit pools will shift—and what that means for companies—as well as how to help more people get access to insurance coverage.

Healthcare sits at the intersection of business, technology, clinical developments, and public policy, and consulting is one of the rare fields that provides a view into all of these domains. I feel very fortunate to have chosen to build a career here.

Box 2. Some Lessons Learned

In speaking with candidates who are considering the management consulting field, our recruiters and interviewers hear some questions frequently. Here are some responses to questions that I have gotten from candidates in the past. In this case, the interviewer was a McKinsey colleague.

Q. What are the most important lessons that you have learned?

A. Assuming the role of leader of McKinsey's New York and northeast offices recently has provided yet another perspective, reinforcing some themes and bringing others into full view. And one of the most exciting things to see up close is also one of the most established values of our firm: We are a talent organization. Across all industry and functional practices, we place huge importance on finding, developing, and mentoring the very best people. This is consistent at every tenure.

Another important lesson involves the consulting lifestyle. One thing everyone said about consulting is that we work really hard and that the travel burden is huge. It is true that we travel a lot, although that depends a bit on your client base. Still, I always thought that I would be okay with that early in my career, but not once I had children. Instead, I have found that I manage it quite well. My wife and I live happily on Manhattan's west side with three kids, and I have reasonably good control over my schedule. As I look at our clients, and other leaders in industry, I find that they are traveling just as much. Similarly, academics and scientists at leading institutions work just as hard. I do not believe that consultants work any harder than top people in these fields. Moreover, we have built increasing flexibility into our model. More than 1100 of our people have chosen to work part time, and 40 partners have been elected while working part time. The programs reflect different needs and can involve working fewer days a week, taking extended time off between engagements or job sharing.

These flexible programs reflect, in part, the great diversity of our people. And that is one of things I found most surprising as I entered this field. I thought that I would find a bunch of MBAs with firm handshakes and stiff shirts who read the The Wall Street Journal cover to cover everyday. Instead, there is a whole range of talented people in this profession, from PhDs and those with other advanced degrees, to journalists, entrepreneurs, and even people from the military. And there is incredible diversity in nationalities.

Q. What has surprised you about the management consulting field?

A. One surprise has been how careers in management consulting evolve over time. There is always something new. I rarely feel that I am considering the same question twice. For someone interested in "the life of the mind," it is a very rich field indeed.

Q. What do you wish you had known earlier?

A. Early on, it would have been great to have confidence that clear thinking, logic, and asking good questions could get you a long way. And another thing: It is not enough to solve the problem. You also have to understand the people with whom you are interacting, where they are coming from, and what it is going to take to change. It is important to think as much about how to get something done as what the right answer might be.

And that is an important difference in the work of a management consultant versus a scientist. You have to enjoy working with people and through others and helping your clients to become more successful. You also need a tolerance for ambiguity and an interest in business. And management consulting demands a different kind of creativity than the kind you need in a laboratory. So even though there are lots of similarities between the two fields, it is not for everyone.

Q. What best equips people for a consulting career?

A. Clear and analytical thinking, reasoning ability—not necessarily requiring a great facility with numbers—clarity of communication, an ability to understand and empathize with people, and taking initiative.

Q. What will be the most important skills for management consultants in the future?

A. All of those capabilities and an ability to maintain a broad perspective while having an increasing depth of knowledge in a specific functional area.

Q. How could you have better prepared for a management consulting career?

A. Once I knew I was interested in management consulting, I started to read business books and newspapers, and I found that somewhat helpful—but only somewhat. What is more helpful is talking with people who are in the profession or who have interacted with consultants.

Q. What do you look for in a candidate?

A. What excites me is meeting someone who has real passion and enthusiasm in addition to the intellectual skills. That gives you the confidence that they are going to bring a lot of leadership to what they do.

Q. If you were not in this career, what would you want to do?

A. I do not have a good answer to that. This is a great fit for me personally.

(Continued.)

Q. What will you tell your children about choosing the right path?

A. Do what you are excited and passionate about. When that is the case, you will be good at what you do. And do something that has variety. That will ensure that you stay excited about it for the long term.

12

Medical Communications:
The "Write" Career Path for You?

Yfke Hager

Articulate Science, of Nucleus Global, Manchester M3 4JL, United Kingdom

The pharmaceutical industry spends billions each year on the clinical development of new medicines. Getting those products to the patients who will benefit from them requires an ability to convey the results of extensive clinical research programs to regulatory authorities, physicians, and payers. Employed by medical communications agencies, contract research organizations, and pharmaceutical companies, medical writers distill and translate complex clinical and scientific data to develop documentation spanning the entire pharmaceutical-product life cycle, from clinical development to registration and marketing. Despite being a relatively new career, the market for medical communications professionals has doubled in recent years and future job prospects look promising.

Medical communications offers two distinct career trajectories: editorial and account management. The editorial track, which is the most common track for those with a scientific bent, includes editorial assistants, medical editors, and medical writers, who are responsible for the development of all editorial content. They produce and/or manage the production of a wide range of materials, including newsletters, slide decks, posters, manuscripts, conference booth materials, websites, and electronic applications. After gaining some experience at a company, a medical writer can move into a management position, become a freelance writer, or move to a related career. Those in the account management track support the editorial team to ensure that projects are delivered on time, on budget, and in compliance with stringent industry guidelines and regulations.

The career path of medical communications blends scientific expertise with a passion for communication. Successful medical writers are excellent communicators, fast learners, sticklers for detail, and have a service-oriented mind-set. If you recognize yourself in this description, then perhaps it is time to throw off that lab coat and launch your medical writing career.

Over the past half century, scientific and medical knowledge has increased exponentially—so rapidly, in fact, that the originators of that knowledge (including scientists and medical doctors) began to struggle to communicate it effectively. Submitting a new drug to regulatory authorities for marketing approval involves the painstaking preparation of scientific documents so detailed and numerous that, until electronic submissions became the norm, they could quite literally fill entire trucks. The proliferation of promising drug targets in recent decades led to a boom in regulatory submissions and a definite shortage of people with the required skills to prepare this documentation. Medical writers stepped into the breach, deftly taking up the challenge to accurately disseminate biomedical information to a variety of audiences, whether charting the clinical development of a new drug for submission to healthcare authorities, drafting a clinical-trial report for publication in a medical journal, or preparing a slide presentation for a symposium at a scientific conference.

Medical writing may be a relatively new career, but the market has spread so quickly that medical writers can now be found in an astonishing variety of organizations. Medical writers are most commonly employed by medical communications agencies (also known as medical education agencies), contract research organizations (also known as clinical research organizations [CROs]), and pharmaceutical and biotechnology companies. However, many also find gainful employment in advertising or public relations agencies, hospitals or university medical centers, nonprofit organizations, medical or scientific publishing companies, and government agencies. This diversity of employers reflects the broad array of tasks that medical writers are expected to perform—all of which makes medical writing an exciting and varied career choice. Because the vast majority of medical writers launch their careers at one of the three main employer types—medical communications agencies, CROs, and pharmaceutical companies—this chapter focuses on them.

These three most common employers generally focus on three categories of medical writing: marketing, educational, and regulatory. Medical communications agencies such as Adelphi Communications, Complete Medical Group Worldwide, KnowledgePoint360 Group, Nucleus Global, and Ogilvy Healthworld tend to specialize in marketing and educational materials. Marketing materials are promotional in nature and explain the benefits of newly launched medicines or therapeutic agents, diagnostics, and devices to healthcare professionals such as physicians, nurses, and pharmacists. Materials may include slide presentations for stand-alone promotional meetings, scientific websites, webcasts, summaries of key clinical manuscripts or clinical case studies, interactive conference booth materials, and sales aids for pharmaceutical sales representatives. Educational materials are intended to inform a variety of audiences about the latest clinical trial results; these could include training manuals and product monographs. But educational materials can also be aimed at healthcare professionals: newsletters for investigators involved in clinical trials; posters and oral presentations at medical conferences; presentations for satellite symposia at medical conferences, advisory boards, and preceptorships; clinical manuscripts; and programs for continuing medical education (CME) activities. The work in communications agencies tends to be more creative than that at a CRO or pharmaceutical company, and is likely to suit those with commercial acumen who are driven by business objectives.

Whereas writers in medical communication agencies focus mostly on materials related to marketed products, those in pharmaceutical companies and CROs prepare materials describing products that are still in clinical development. Pharmaceutical and biotechnology companies include Abbott Laboratories, Amgen, AstraZeneca, Bayer HealthCare, Bristol-Myers Squibb, Eli Lilly, F. Hoffmann-La Roche, GlaxoSmithKline, Johnson & Johnson, Merck & Co, Novartis, Pfizer, and Sanofi. In general, medical writers at pharmaceutical companies write the regulatory documents required to obtain product marketing approval from international regulatory authorities such as the Food and Drug Administration (FDA) and the European Medicines Agency (EMA), but they are also responsible for developing a variety of other clinical documents supporting the approval process. These materials include clinical study protocols, clinical study reports, investigator brochures, periodic safety update reports, briefing documents for regulatory authorities, and responses to queries from regulatory authorities. CROs such as Charles River Laboratories, Covance, Parexel, Pharmaceutical Product Development (PPD), and Quintiles conduct clinical studies and assist pharmaceutical companies with regulatory submissions. Medical writers in CROs tend to prepare clinical and regulatory documents, but may also write manuscripts for publication in medical journals.

Medical and scientific publishing is one of the fastest growing media sectors. Between 2003 and 2008, the medical writing market doubled from an estimated $345 million to $694 million, according to a CenterWatch report published in December 2008. Job prospects for technical writers, including medical writers, are expected to remain good in the coming years. According to the U.S. Bureau of Labor Statistics, employment of technical writers is expected to grow 17%, about as fast as the average for all occupations, from 2010 to 2020. The U.S. Bureau of Labor Statistics attributes the rise in job opportunities to the ever-increasing complexity of medical and scientific information, and to the fact that significant continued growth in online publications and services will spur demand for writers and editors with expertise and experience in electronic media. Medical writing is a desirable and specialized skill set, which can only be honed by experience. It may be difficult to get a foot in the door, but those who manage to gain relevant on-the-job experience will find that they are truly a sought-after commodity. There are simply not enough experienced medical writers to fill the number of editorial roles available. As a result, salaries are competitive and have increased steadily over the past several years.

JOBS

Most medical communications agencies and CROs offer two distinct job tracks: editorial and account management/client services. However, some employers offer roles that combine aspects of both of these tracks. To understand the full range of possibilities, you should speak to people in different jobs and different companies and think carefully about the mix of responsibilities that would suit you best.

Editorial Careers in Medical Communications Agencies and CROs

Within medical communications agencies and CROs several editorial career paths exist (see Fig. 1). Editorial assistants support the editorial team; they do not produce medical or scientific content themselves, but they proofread and edit all materials produced by medical writers to apply consistent editorial style, check manuscript layouts, and perform general administrative editorial tasks, such as the electronic submission of abstracts to medical conferences and manuscripts to medical journals. They also liaise closely with experts in other departments within the company (e.g., layout production

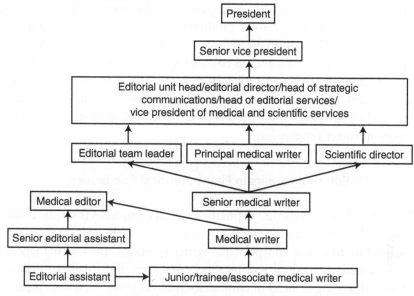

Figure 1. Typical editorial career structure.

artists, PowerPoint specialists, or electronic media specialists) to develop final print and electronic materials that meet client specifications. In larger companies, editorial assistants may have the opportunity to progress to the position of medical editor and senior medical editor. Medical editors are responsible for ensuring that all materials are completed to a high editorial standard in terms of both language and content. It is possible, although not very common, for editorial assistants to switch to medical writer positions, and for medical writers to switch to medical editor roles. Editorial assistants and medical writers can also transition to account management roles, although this is quite rare.

Most new recruits to the medical communications industry join as junior, trainee, or associate medical writers. Combining scientific knowledge and a flair for communication, medical writers translate the latest clinical trial results into language appropriate for a wide variety of audiences. They produce educational, promotional, and training materials for the healthcare industry and other end users. Although most of the work is office based, medical writing is not just a desk job. In medical communications agencies, some writers travel quite frequently to fine-tune slide decks for presentations by healthcare professionals at stand-alone or satellite meetings, or to take minutes at pharmaceutical industry meetings. More senior medical writers are expected to provide strategic input—for example, by developing annual communication plans or publication plans for specific products or business units. The editorial career path within agencies eventually leads to management positions, such as editorial unit head, vice president of medical and scientific services, or editorial director. Although the titles of these positions differ to reflect the naming conventions at individual companies, they tend to have similar duties, which are discussed in more detail in the section on career progression.

Editorial Careers in Pharmaceutical Companies

The editorial career structure in pharmaceutical companies is similar to that in medical communications agencies and CROs, with junior writers progressing first to senior and principal writer positions, then to managerial positions such as medical writing group manager, and finally to director of medical writing or head of clinical/scientific communications. At pharmaceutical companies, medical writers tend to work on complex regulatory documents, including clinical components of marketing authorization applications and briefing documents for interactions with healthcare authorities. At some pharmaceutical companies, medical writers also deliver study-level clinical documents such as clinical study protocols and clinical study reports.

Account Management Careers

A somewhat more linear career structure exists within account management (see Fig. 2). Project assistants provide general administrative support to project teams, often related to the logistics of event management such as satellite symposia at conferences, scientific preceptorship programs at hospitals, or advisory board meetings (at which pharmaceutical companies obtain advice on their clinical development programs from healthcare professionals who are recognized experts in their therapeutic area). Account executives, account managers, and account directors develop and manage client relationships for specific product accounts. They develop an understanding of client and product strategy and develop long-term communication plans to meet client needs. Next, they develop time lines, documents confirming the briefs received from clients, budget proposals and reconciliations, and are expected to maximize revenues and profitability within their accounts.

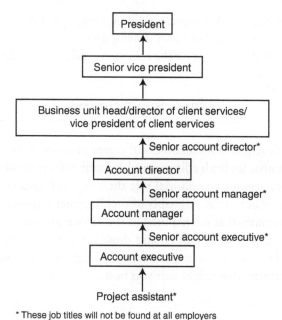

Figure 2. Typical account management career structure.

The account management team provides guidance and leadership to the editorial delivery team to ensure that each project in the plan is produced in compliance with industry guidelines, and is delivered on schedule and on budget. In most companies, both editorial and account management staff have direct contact with clients. As with the editorial career track, the precise titles of senior roles in account management vary depending on the company.

Executive Careers

Both editorial and account management tracks can lead to executive positions within medical communications agencies or CROs. Senior vice presidents are generally responsible for an entire section or division of the company, with accountability for a large number of product teams. Depending on the size of the company, senior vice presidents may specialize in certain therapeutic areas or might work across several therapeutic areas. Their work often involves complex client negotiations, client appraisals, and winning new business. Finally, the president of an organization is responsible for the overall strategic and commercial development of the company, which involves keeping abreast of industry developments, identifying new business opportunities and directions for the company, and generally driving growth.

SKILLS/QUALIFICATIONS

The core skills required for a successful career in medical communications are broadly similar for both editorial and account management career tracks, although of course for an editorial role there is much greater emphasis on writing and research skills. Arguably of much greater importance is the difference in attributes that are required in the service industry (medical communications agencies and CROs) and those needed in the pharmaceutical industry, and this section is structured accordingly to help you identify the work environment that might suit you best.

Core Attributes

Established scientific credentials are important, particularly for editorial positions. Most employers look for life science graduates (biological science, pharmacy, pharmacology, chemistry, or biochemistry), but a small number of medical writers have a background in journalism or technical writing. Although an advanced degree (MSc, PhD) or postdoctoral experience is certainly advantageous, it is not essential. Former medical professionals are also welcome additions to any medical writing team. For account management positions scientific credentials are usually less important but are certainly advantageous, particularly for career progression.

It goes without saying that you will need excellent writing skills for editorial positions, so be prepared to provide evidence of an ability to produce high-quality scientific materials. You should also demonstrate enthusiasm and a keen interest in medicine and medical science, as you will be expected to learn quickly about different therapeutic areas on the job. A willingness to learn and flexibility are also traits that characterize good medical writers. Excellent research skills are essential, as medical writers are expected to assimilate large volumes of data. Good numeracy skills are also important—you do not need to be a mathematical expert, but you will need to have a good understanding of the more common statistical approaches used in clinical development. A keen eye for detail is vital; if the documents that you produce do not represent the clinical data accurately, the consequences could be very serious indeed—errors could lead to compromised patient care, the rejection of a new drug application, lawsuits, or lost business for your company. In this field, being a pedant is a huge bonus.

Materials produced by medical writers must meet high ethical standards, so be prepared to learn about, and adhere to, strict industry regulations and guidelines. These include Good Publication Practice 2 (guidelines developed by the International Society for Medical Publication Professionals for responsible and ethical reporting of company-sponsored medical research) and the International Conference on Harmonization of Technical Requirements for Registration of Pharmaceuticals for Human Use (to ensure harmonized interpretation and application of technical guidelines and requirements for pharmaceutical-product registration). You will also be expected to undertake ongoing pharmaceutical-compliance training.

Finally, it helps to be thick skinned. At agencies and CROs, all work is subjected to quality control by senior editorial team members before going out the door, and then, it will be scrutinized by the clients. An ability to cope with and to use criticism to improve your work is absolutely essential.

Attributes of Particular Relevance to the Service Industry

How many medical writers does it take to change a lightbulb? If you answered "How many would the client like it to take?" you should give serious consideration to a job at an agency! It might sound obvious, but the single most important attribute for working in the service industry is a service-oriented mind-set. If you are considered an expert in your academic field and are accustomed to your opinion being valued, learning when to bite your tongue might be one of the most challenging aspects of your job. The scope and content of all projects are defined by your clients. Being a good listener and having an ability to interpret your client's requirements, instill confidence, and gain their trust is the key to a successful agency career.

The second most important attribute is outstanding time management skills. Sticking to budgeted time lines is of paramount importance in an agency—in fact, it is almost as important as the quality of the work itself. It will not matter that your project is perfectly crafted if it has taken twice as long to produce as your account manager has budgeted for. Closely linked to time management is the ability to multitask under pressure. If the thought of receiving dozens of emails and phone calls a day while trying to finalize a slide deck and negotiate with your production team to amend several posters in time for next week's medical conference terrifies you, working at an agency might not be for you. With experience, you will be expected to juggle multiple projects and reassess priorities on a daily basis.

Do not make the mistake of assuming that writers are loners stuck in a cubicle, tapping away at a keyboard all day. Depending on the agency and your role, you might be asked to travel extensively to medical congresses or to hospitals or hotels for stand-alone meetings. During these meetings, you will be expected to communicate confidently with senior healthcare professionals and pharmaceutical industry executives. Attending these meetings can certainly be exciting, but do not expect to get much sleep or to see much of the city where the event is being held. Be aware that promotional writing does not suit everyone. You will need to be familiar and comfortable with the commercial drivers behind the materials you produce. Agency life can be stressful, but the work is also fun, fast, and furious. It suits those who work best in teams, and you will find that the fast pace of the work also leads to a true sense of camaraderie within project teams, which can be quite rewarding. Finally, agency work is more creative and varied than clinical and regulatory writing—so if you get bored easily, an agency might be the right place for you.

Attributes of Particular Relevance to the Pharmaceutical Industry

When I moved from an agency to the pharmaceutical industry, I was initially surprised at the strong emphasis on leadership and project management skills during the interview process. But I soon discovered that a medical writing position within the pharmaceutical industry really is a leadership role. You are accountable for the timely delivery of large, complex clinical and regulatory documents that require input from people with a wide range of skill sets within the company, and you will be expected to lead cross-functional teams to deliver each project. That means working and negotiating with physicians, regulatory affairs managers, patient safety scientists, programmers, statisticians, pharmacometricians, and toxicology specialists. Due to the size and complexity of the documents, the pace of work is slower than that within agencies; each project can take months to complete, so strong project management skills are essential. Finally, problem-solving ability and decision-making skills are helpful attributes in this environment.

GETTING A FOOT IN THE DOOR

Ask any medical writer how they ended up working in this field and it is likely that serendipity will have featured at some point in their career path. But that does not mean that you cannot take proactive steps to forge a successful career in medical communications.

First, focus on activities that will help you demonstrate a passion for writing and communication in your job application. Join clubs or societies and volunteer for their communication or public relations (PR) positions. Submit articles to university newsletters, newspapers, or magazines. Enter science writing competitions. If all else fails, start a blog. Take advantage of opportunities to hone your oral presentation skills—offer to lead a journal club or give a seminar in your department. Confident public speaking skills are a key requirement for many aspects of a medical writer's duties, including presenting to existing clients, pitching for new business, and negotiating with healthcare professionals. If you are willing to invest the time and money, consider enrolling for a journalism or science communication qualification. Not only will this help you stand out from the crowd and demonstrate that you are serious about pursuing a new career path, it will also help you determine whether you have the aptitude for a writing career. Some dedicated postgraduate courses are available, including one in biomedical writing at the University of the Sciences in Philadelphia and one in medical communications at the University of Worcester, United Kingdom. Finally, having any practical experience is of course an important asset, so consider contacting medical communications agencies or editorial/publishing houses to ask about internship opportunities.

Next, start identifying and researching possible employers and job vacancies. Use LinkedIn or other social networking sites to expand your professional network; try to connect with people working in medical communications and arrange informational interviews to learn about different roles and employers. Join relevant groups on LinkedIn (such as the MedComms Forum, Professional Medical/Scientific Writers, Science Writers, and The Publication Plan) and sign up to receive digests of discussions and jobs posted to these groups. This will help you build an awareness of relevant issues in the field. Because medical writers need to keep abreast of developments in medicine and medical communications, you can make a good impression in interviews by demonstrating an awareness of recent issues. Join the American Medical Writers Association (AMWA) or the European

Medical Writers Association (EMWA) and attend their conferences—these offer excellent networking and educational opportunities, including workshops that will teach you valuable practical skills. Their member magazines and job listings are also useful resources. Finally, consider registering with specialist healthcare recruitment agencies. A good recruitment agent can educate you about the industry, match you to suitable companies, and support you through each step of the job application process.

Once you have decided to apply for a position, there are pitfalls to be avoided. Remember that your curriculum vitae (CV) will be screened by a panel of editors and writers, so any typos or grammatical errors in your CV will end your medical writing career before it has even started. Do some background research so you can ask knowledgeable questions; before an interview at a pharmaceutical company, find out about their research pipeline, and before an interview at an agency, make sure you know something about their therapeutic niche in the industry. It is very common for job applicants to be sent a writing test as part of the interview process, particularly those who are new to the field of medical communications. These tests can take various forms: you might be sent a medical poster or clinical manuscript and asked to draft the missing abstract, or you might receive a slide deck and be asked to select three to five key slides to print in an abstract book. Some employers might ask you to prepare a presentation on a given topic and deliver it to a small audience at your interview. There may also be an editing component to the test. The key to successfully completing any writing or editing test is to remember that you are not being assessed on your medical knowledge, but rather on your attention to detail, ability to follow a brief, and ability to construct a coherent and logical story.

Breaking into this world may well require some serendipity, but more importantly, it requires an ability to identify and sell your transferable skills to prospective employers. Many employers use behavioral interviewing techniques, where the job applicant is asked to describe situations in which they demonstrated particular qualities or attributes. You can prepare for these questions by considering detailed examples from your academic career, focusing on how your behavior and actions led to particular achievements. As examples of written and oral communication skill, consider your doctoral thesis, publications, conference presentations, and grant applications. To demonstrate project management skills, mention field courses you have led or student-club events you have organized. Teaching and tutoring duties might be a good source of examples of mentoring and people management skills, whereas any multilaboratory research collaborations can provide evidence of teamwork. Experience running a laboratory will also be valuable when you are asked about leadership qualities. Finally, almost any research project should provide excellent examples of problem-solving skills.

CAREER PROGRESSION

With about five to seven years of experience as an in-house writer with a given employer, a medical writer can progress by becoming a line manager, specializing in a particular therapeutic area, becoming a freelance writer, or making a lateral move to a different career track related to medical communications.

Associate medical writers generally progress to medical writer and then senior medical writer positions. At this point, there are usually three possible routes depending on whether the writer is interested in line management responsibility: principal medical writer, scientific director, or editorial team leader (see Fig. 1). Principal medical writers continue to focus on the delivery of editorial material, applying their extensive therapeutic area expertise to complex projects. Scientific directors are also involved in the development of editorial material, but they have a greater responsibility to provide strategic input and tend to specialize in a specific therapeutic area. Editorial team leaders have line management responsibilities, and are accountable for the quality of all editorial materials produced by a team of medical writers. Senior medical writers should try to gain experience mentoring junior writers to determine whether they have the right skill set and attributes for line management. Good editorial team leaders are extremely valuable to the company, and are always sought after.

With career progression into more senior positions, the boundaries between the editorial and account management career tracks become increasingly blurred, as tasks and responsibilities begin to overlap. Those in the editorial career track will be expected to increase their understanding of the financial aspects of the business, while those in account management will need to contribute to higher level discussions with clients and health-care professionals, demonstrating a grasp of the scientific background and medical data underpinning the business strategy. Those in senior roles in both career tracks will prepare for and attend pitches to potential new clients, selling medical writing as a service to win new business for their company. They will be involved in annual strategic communication planning for each product, project pricing and negotiation, writing proposals, as well as having financial responsibilities such as predicting revenues, meeting budget targets, and measuring team productivity. In addition to these project management duties, senior team members will also be expected to manage teams, which includes mentoring and guiding junior team members and conducting annual performance planning and reviews.

Working at a pharmaceutical company has a number of advantages when it comes to career progression. Because medical writing allows you to develop leadership skills and a detailed understanding of the entire clinical development process, it is an excellent gateway to other careers in the pharmaceutical industry, including positions in regulatory affairs, clinical research, medical information, document management, competitor intelligence, patient safety, and medical affairs. Most pharmaceutical companies encourage career progression within the business and are large enough to offer a range of different roles and internal transfer opportunities.

Not all writers are keen to move into management positions or remain at a company, working a typical 9-to-5 job. Becoming a freelance writer is a relatively common career choice, not only because it can be surprisingly lucrative, but also because it offers greater flexibility when it comes to work/life balance and the ability to choose your projects. However, a word of caution for new recruits hoping to break into medical writing as a freelancer: Clients will rarely, if ever, commission unknown or inexperienced freelance writers. For this reason, it is strongly advisable to gain significant experience (5–10 years) as an in-house writer at an agency, CRO, or pharmaceutical company before embarking on a freelance career. Those years spent learning the craft of medical writing are invaluable, allowing you to gain knowledge of different therapeutic areas, experience of developing a wide variety of materials, and an understanding of the financial aspects of the medical writing business. But most importantly, you will build a reliable network of healthcare professionals, pharmaceutical executives, and medical communications employees, essential for developing a strong client base for any freelance business. Successful freelance writers with entrepreneurial spirit might even consider starting up their own medical communications agency by employing other writers.

WAY OUT

Although most of this chapter is devoted to "traditional" medical communications, medical writers and account managers can use their specialist skill sets in a number of closely related areas. Making a lateral move is advisable when you feel that your current position no longer challenges you, or when you have identified an aspect of medical communications that you enjoy most and want to find a job that offers greater focus on that particular aspect of work.

For example, if you find preparing for and attending conferences and stand-alone meetings one of the most enjoyable aspects of your job, you could consider moving to an event management company, which specialize in logistical support for meetings and events. Lateral moves to companies specializing in PR or medical advertising might appeal to those who enjoy devising promotional campaigns and are less keen on writing data-heavy documents. Writers with a background or strong interest in economics and finance might wish to consider jobs at agencies specializing in health economics and outcomes research (HEOR), which involve the development of reimbursement strategies to demonstrate the clinical and economic value of pharmaceutical products.

For those who are interested in journal production or wish to focus on clinical publications (a term encompassing manuscripts, abstracts, posters, and oral presentations for conferences), medical or scientific publishing companies such as Elsevier or Wolters Kluwer Health offer related careers such as journal editor, production editor, or editorial director. Similarly, scientific publication managers working either in the pharmaceutical industry or at specialist companies are responsible for developing and delivering global publication plans to communicate the benefits of pharmaceutical products to healthcare professionals.

Gaining expertise across a range of therapeutic areas and experience with different types of medical writing are important if you want to remain competitive in the medical communications job market. So whatever role you are in and whatever employer you work for, make sure that your personal career development plan encompasses sufficient diversity to ensure career progression in this exciting and diverse field.

Box 1. My Experience

Having completed a BA in Natural Sciences (Zoology) at the University of Cambridge, United Kingdom, I was full of enthusiasm about an academic career. I was lucky enough to gain the support of an excellent PhD supervisor

(Continued.)

who helped me navigate the maze of grants and bursaries available to European Union students at Cambridge (I am of Dutch/Belgian extraction). Because I had always enjoyed science communication, I spent a considerable amount of time traveling to schools and outdoor festivals to perform interactive science demonstrations for children as a volunteer for National Science Week and Cambridge Hands-On Science, a student-run group with the apt acronym CHaOS. I also started writing for the science page of Varsity, the student newspaper at Cambridge, where I discovered that I really enjoyed listening to scientists enthuse about their latest research.

Then a chance email changed the course of my career. While I was writing my PhD thesis, a bursary was advertised on a science communication mailing list. The winner would hold a temporary position as press officer for the Society for Experimental Biology (SEB), interviewing scientists and writing press releases for the SEB's annual main meeting. I won the bursary, and managed to convince my supervisor that this would be a month well spent. At the SEB conference, I met the news and views editor of the Journal of Experimental Biology (JEB), a scientific journal focused on comparative animal physiology. Using my SEB press releases to showcase my writing expertise, I persuaded the editor to commission me to write some freelance articles for the journal. This subsequently led to a position covering her maternity leave for a year, the start of which happily coincided with the submission of my PhD thesis. As the year was coming to an end I entered and won the Daily Telegraph Science Writer Award, a prestigious national science writing competition in the United Kingdom, which boosted my confidence and confirmed that I had chosen the right career path.

When my contract at the JEB ended, I moved to the North West of the United Kingdom to join my husband, who had started postdoctoral research at the University of Manchester. Through a contact from my SEB placement, I discovered that Cheshire is a hot spot for medical communications agencies, and successfully applied for a position as a trainee medical writer at a global medical communications agency. Some years later, I learned that it was the combination of my scientific background, experience at a scientific journal, and the Science Writer Award that helped me secure an interview and subsequently the job offer—it can be difficult to convince employers to take a chance on new recruits with no prior medical writing experience. The focus of the work was the delivery of educational and marketing materials for a blockbuster oncology drug. It was a steep learning curve, the work was varied and fun, and I enjoyed building good relationships with my colleagues, clients, and healthcare professionals.

After five and a half years, I decided that it was time to broaden my medical communications expertise beyond commercial writing. When a global biopharmaceutical company based in Cheshire advertised a vacancy in their medical communications department, I spoke to several LinkedIn connections about their experiences in clinical and regulatory writing and decided to apply. Regulatory writing certainly broadened my perspective; during the first year, I worked on products in three different therapeutic areas. After two years, the company announced the imminent closure of its Cheshire site, so I moved back to a medical communications agency. I am confident that medical communications will continue to offer sufficient challenges for a long and happy career!

Box 2. Ten Dos and Don'ts

1. Do not submit a CV with typos or grammatical errors.

2. Do join the European Medical Writers Association (EMWA) or American Medical Writers Association (AMWA) and attend their conferences/workshops.

3. Do not give up too soon if you struggle to get a foot in the door; persevere and try to find an employer who is willing to train new recruits.

4. Do expand your network of contacts. Use LinkedIn or other social networking sites to connect with people working in medical communications and join relevant discussion groups.

5. Do not forget to add scientific publications and conference presentations to your CV—they provide evidence of communications expertise.

6. Do arrange informational interviews with new contacts to find out more about specific companies and/or job roles.

7. Do not rule out companies based on location alone; some employers offer the possibility of working remotely.

8. Do send your CV to specialist healthcare recruitment agencies and ask for advice.

9. Do not be afraid to send speculative letters to potential employers and attempt writing tests to determine whether you have an aptitude for the job.

10. Do consider taking a writing or journalism course to gain experience, boost your CV, and demonstrate your commitment to a writing career.

13

Science Journalism and Writing

Helen Pearson

Chief Features Editor, Nature, *London N1 9XW, United Kingdom*

Science journalists cover some of the most complex, exciting, and important issues of our day, ranging from the impacts of climate change to emerging infectious diseases. They use words, sounds, images, and graphics to create compelling stories about science that appear in newspapers and magazines, online, on the radio and TV, and in podcasts and videos. The field is undergoing rapid change, which presents both challenges and opportunities. The migration of readers and advertising to the internet and digital platforms has led to declining sales of newspapers and magazines. This means that jobs are now scarce in traditional print media, but that there are growing opportunities to produce content online.

Science journalism as a career is hard work and is unlikely to make you rich; it is also varied, fascinating, and rewarding. It combines the creativity of writing and media with the intellectual fascination of the scientific field. It is very satisfying to have your story read or watched by perhaps tens of thousands of people, and even—at its widest reach—have an influence on policy or on society at large. It is also an important profession, because it involves investigating, analyzing, and communicating issues that are crucial to society, such as pollution and human health. There is arguably an urgent need for outstanding science journalists and communicators who can help translate and analyze these issues, as well as hold science and scientists to account.

If all of this sounds appealing, then the best way to take a step into science journalism is to have a go at it. Write something, record some audio, and shoot some video. Although there is no set route into the field, many people in the United States do attend science journalism programs, which can help build skills, establish contacts, and open doors. It is competitive, but very talented people can find a unique and highly rewarding career in science journalism.

What Is Science Journalism?

Science journalists and writers cover subjects ranging from contentious developments in embryonic stem cell medicine, to the discovery of planets in remote solar systems, to arcane advances in quantum physics and gene regulation. Science journalists also provide analysis, context, and perspective by, for example, exploring a discovery's social and political implications.

Science journalism serves as a major route by which sometimes-complex scientific issues are communicated to a broad audience. Journalists cover issues in which science impacts on society and policy, such as climate change, energy, pollution, genetically modified crops, medicine, nuclear proliferation, and natural disasters. Journalists also hold scientists and the scientific process up to scrutiny. They examine questionable statistics or overinflated claims; they investigate scientific misconduct, conflicts of interest, and ethical breaches. At their best, they can be cool, objective critics of science.

In many ways, science journalism is very similar to research. Journalists, like scientists, find an aspect of science that fascinates them and that they may know little about. Journalists ask questions and look to evidence to provide answers. But rather than dedicating several months or years to researching a question, a news journalist spends somewhere between two hours and two weeks—depending on the deadline—researching it and turning it into a story using writing, sound, or video. Then—unlike some academic science—the story is quickly published or broadcast and, with any luck, a significant number of people read or watch it. Some of those people may comment that they like it or hate it, or that it had an impact on their thinking, or even on their life or on science policy. (By then, of course, our news journalist will be researching and writing about something else.)

For the journalist, all this makes for an endlessly fascinating, constantly changing, and intellectually stretching profession. For the audience, it hopefully makes for an enlightening, stimulating, informative, influential, and entertaining article or program.

The Spectrum of Science Communication

There is a wide range of careers involving science writing and communication. Within that, many people in the profession make a distinction between straight science journalists and those who communicate science for the purpose of publicity. Those in the latter category might call themselves science writers, science communicators, science publicists, or public information officers (PIOs). This chapter uses the term science publicists.

Science publicists typically work for universities, research institutes, museums, government agencies, charitable bodies, or private foundations—any organization with an interest in science. They typically write, or produce other media content, about the science and scientists being supported by the organization for which they work. This work may appear on the institution's website and in its print publications, or form part of a press release sent out to the media. This is largely done to promote the organization and its work.

Science journalists, by contrast, typically work for newspapers, magazines, TV and radio stations, news websites, and other commercial or not-for-profit media organizations. They conventionally do more reporting, critique, and analysis of the subject for their readers than a science publicist.

The following example illustrates the difference. Imagine that scientists at Prestige University (PU) are about to publish a paper in a top-tier journal reporting a link between a type of cancer and a common viral infection. Science writers in the communication office of PU put together a press release summarizing the work and send it out to various media. They also interview the scientists and write a story about the paper and its potential implications, which is then published on PU's news website. The aim is to increase the profile of PU and communicate its findings widely.

The journalist who wants to cover the story, however, typically digs a bit deeper. They call the scientists who did the work, as well as a handful of other researchers in the field, including the author's main competitor, and a patient advocacy group. (Is the link plausible? Do the data look sound? Is the interpretation reasonable? Who funded the work? How far is it from being clinically useful?) The journalist might end up writing an article saying that the work is being embraced by patient communities but raising eyebrows among scientists, who question the rigor of the data and analysis. The journalist is writing about the same paper as the science publicist, but it is reported and analytical.

Some people view science publicity as a different—and even slightly lesser—pursuit than science journalism because it can have less depth of analysis and the author has less freedom to write objectively. ("You don't own your story," says writer and author Ann Finkbeiner, who served as Director of the science-medical writing graduate program at Johns Hopkins

University.) The boundaries between journalism and publicity are increasingly blurred, but it is still worth having an appreciation of the difference. In this chapter, however, the terms science journalist and writer are used fairly interchangeably to cover the spectrum of science journalism, publicity, and communication.

This chapter attempts to outline a few important things to know before taking the leap into science journalism as a career: what science journalists do, how to dip a toe in the water, and what qualities and skills it takes to succeed. It focuses on writing about science, because that is the area that I know best; it also focuses on the United States, although much of the content is also relevant to those elsewhere in the world. In researching this chapter, I interviewed the leaders or directors of several major science journalism and writing programs in the United States: at the Massachusetts Institute of Technology (MIT), University of California–Santa Cruz, Johns Hopkins University, Boston University, New York University, and the University of Wisconsin–Madison, as well as a handful of other experts in the field.

The Changing Ecosystem of Science Journalism

Journalism is in a state of rapid transition—a bust following a boom. In 1978, the launch of *The New York Times* science section kicked off a decade-long expansion of science journalism. Many other newspapers followed suit, and several popular science news magazines, such as *Discover*, started up.

Today, the landscape is different and in flux. *The New York Times* and *The Washington Post* are unusual in maintaining a weekly section dedicated to science, although other major national and regional papers still use reporters devoted to covering science, health, technology, or the environment. A cluster of major science news magazines caters to the science-interested public, but they are increasingly focused on digital content. These include *Scientific American*, *Science News*, *New Scientist*, *Wired*, *Technology Review*, *National Geographic*, *Popular Science*, *Popular Mechanics*, and *Discover*. There are also well-known specialist publications that maintain news sections and whose main audience is working scientists and engineers, such as *Science*, *Nature*, *The Scientist*, *IEEE Spectrum*, and *Chemical and Engineering News*.

The reason for changes in science media lies in the internet and digital publishing platforms, which are causing a profound and rapid change in the media as a whole. A 2013 report by the Pew Research Center showed that in

2004, 24% of people surveyed had consumed the previous day's news from the internet; by 2012, that figure had risen to 39% and some 50% had consumed news from some kind of digital source. Users of social media such as Facebook and Twitter are increasingly relying on these sources for news. The "old" media—including newspapers, magazines, books, TV, radio, and anything else predating the internet—is sometimes referred to as legacy media.

All of this means that print circulations of newspapers and magazines are decreasing as readers migrate to the internet and mobile devices to consume their news; at the same time, print advertising revenues have dropped. With readers and income decreasing, many print outlets for science journalism have shrunk, or closed. According to one analysis, the number of U.S. newspapers with a science section dropped from 95 to 34 between 1989 and 2005. Of the roughly 2300 members of the National Association for Science Writers (NASW), the professional body for science writers and journalists in the United States, only 3% were staff newspaper reporters in 2011. (In Europe, decreasing circulations are also creating problems, but the situation is not quite as dire; in the United Kingdom, for example, there has been a slight decrease in the number of science journalists since 2005.)

The internet and other forms of "new" digital media are also leading to a proliferation of new outlets for science news. There is a growing ecosystem of specialist science news websites. The internet also partly explains the expansion of science media and communication offices run by research agencies (such as the National Institutes of Health or NASA), universities, research foundations (such as the Michael J. Fox Foundation, Simons Foundation, and others mentioned in this book), and other science-related organizations (such as the American Geophysical Union, American Chemical Society, and Society for Neuroscience, to name just a few). Rather than writing news releases, as they might have done in the past, these organizations reach their audience directly by writing and publishing their own material. Some nonprofit organizations are running science news outlets in their own right.

Meanwhile, the broadcast media have been more stable. Several established outlets such as Public Broadcasting Service (PBS) and National Public Radio (NPR) produce science news and programs, as do smaller production companies. There is also a diverse, thriving world of science podcasts. Some of these are produced by scientists; some are spin-offs from other media; many break with the model of standard science journalism and are trying innovative forms of communication, exemplified by NPR's *Radiolab*. Newspapers and magazines are increasingly producing podcasts or short videos, creating another hybrid between old and new media.

JOBS: WHAT DO SCIENCE JOURNALISTS DO?

Reporter, Editor, Staffer, Freelancer, Author

Many people in journalism today started out as reporters. Reporters find stories, interview sources, and then write them up for publication in a newspaper, magazine, or online outlet. They write short news stories over a period of hours or days—and longer features, which can take weeks or months to report and write. Most journalists have a specialty, or "beat," such as biomedicine or physical sciences. Broadcast journalists tell the same stories using scripts, audio, and video.

Staff reporters are typically employed full time by a media organization. Freelancers, by contrast, effectively run their own business, writing or producing content for many outlets. Staff positions provide a steady wage and benefits and can be relatively secure (depending on the financial health of the employer, of course); on the other hand, staff reporters answer to editors who can tell them to drop everything at 6:00 p.m. and cover a breaking story. Freelancers have more autonomy to pursue stories that interest them and to manage their own time, but they often have less financial security and may have to work harder to get the attention of an editor. There is a thriving community of freelance science journalists and writers.

Editors oversee the process. They typically commission stories from staff and freelance reporters. They might commission stories they have identified, or ones the reporters have "pitched" to them. A print editor will edit the story, which might involve anything from tweaking a few words to rewriting most of the piece. They also oversee the printed pages or the website, coordinate pictures and graphics, and plan special issues—themed around exoplanets, autism, or GM crops, to point to a few examples from *Nature*. Copy editors check stories for accuracy and grammar, after editing and before publication. Online news editors typically oversee the posting of stories, blogs, and other media and curate the site; they might also be dealing with the news organization's online commenting, Twitter stream, and other social media.

A communication office at a university might have a similar structure, made up of science writers and editors, overseen by a head of communications. These often have the advantage of being secure, relatively well-paid jobs.

Salaries for journalism and writing positions vary enormously: A junior reporter might earn $20,000–$50,000 per year; a senior reporter at a national newspaper or a senior magazine editor could earn more than $100,000 per year. Freelancers typically earn a minimum of $1 per word, but word rates can be considerably more and depend on the publication and on a writer's experience.

A Word on Blogging and Social Media

The last decade has seen a rapid proliferation of science blogs, some of which are now part of major blogging networks—such as those hosted by *Scientific American* (see http://blogs.scientificamerican.com/), *Wired* (see http://www.wired.com/blogs/), and *National Geographic* (see http://phenomena.nationalgeographic.com). The blogging ecosystem is a diverse, interesting mix between old and new media. Scientists are blogging for themselves and on newspaper or magazine websites, and blogs are also helping to develop and launch a new generation of science journalists.

Bloggers write online about what interests them, without having to answer to bossy editors or stick to word limits. Easy-to-use platforms such as WordPress mean that anyone can quickly start a blog. Some bloggers report their entries and write much like a journalist; others are known for opinionated commentary. Some blogs are very high quality and build major followings; others are uninformed rants.

Twitter has become an integral part of many science journalists' toolbox as they find it an invaluable way to communicate directly with their audience. Some journalists tweet prolifically, build up a huge following, and use the medium to help establish a reputation and increase their readership. Most news sites run a Twitter feed to discuss and promote their content. There are all kinds of other experiments in digital science media going on all the time, and the annual ScienceOnline meeting is becoming a popular meeting place for people who inhabit this world.

However, it's almost impossible to make a living from blogging and tweeting alone. Most writers blog for free because they love to write, it helps to build a reputation and online presence, and because it allows them to interact closely with their readers. Some bloggers who are part of the big science blogging networks are paid a small amount, such as $25 for 10,000 page views.

The Multifunctional, Multimedia Journalist

The boundaries between different roles in journalism are blurred and people move from one to another. A freelance writer might run his or her own blog, Tweet avidly, write for newspapers and magazines, and also pen books. A video journalist might record a story, and then produce a written version to accompany it on the web. When considering a story, editors increasingly decide whether it makes most sense to cover it as print news, a blog, or using video or audio. All of this is leading to a demand for "multimedia" journalists who are comfortable producing content using text, graphics, digital media audio, and video—although most journalists end up specializing in the end.

The Good, Bad, and Ugly of Working in Science Journalism

Science journalism is never dull, because journalists move onto new stories quickly and are always learning. It is exciting to be writing about the frontiers of research and to see the big questions. It can also be very satisfying to work hard on something and know that many people will read or watch it, and perhaps be influenced by it or respond to it. Many journalists build name recognition and a reputation among their readers. Some journalists, presenters, and book authors achieve more widespread fame: for example, Rebecca Skloot, whose book *The Immortal Life of Henrietta Lacks* topped the *The New York Times* bestseller list, and freelancer Carl Zimmer, who writes regularly for *The New York Times*, has written a string of books and has built an extensive following on social media.

On the downside, journalism can be stressful. Journalists work to constant, immovable deadlines. They may have as little as an hour to write a story. They have to quickly get to grips with complex subjects about which they may know very little, and translate those into more accessible language. They have to file well-written copy, on time, having interviewed sources and double-checked the facts. "The day by day journalism is to get it out quick, and get it out fast," says Marcia Bartusiak, Professor of the Practice of the Graduate Program in Science Writing at MIT.

Many journalists who have held onto their jobs during the recent hard times are also facing increasing workloads. In a survey of science journalists for *Nature* in 2009, 59% of science journalists said the number of pieces they worked on in a week had increased in the last five years (Brumfiel 2009). Journalists who were once dedicated to print are now asked to produce content for online news, podcasts, and blogs. A 2009 report on the state of science journalists in the UK found that, faced with limited time, journalists were becoming overreliant on easy-to-digest press releases written by science publicists at journals, universities, and other organizations (see http://cf.ac.uk/jomec/resources/Mapping_Science_Journalism_Final_Report_2003-11-09.pdf). They can find it hard to carve out time to pursue an exclusive, investigative story or feature. "The critical nature of science journalism is blunted," says Andrew Williams at Cardiff University, UK, who wrote the report and studies science media. "There is a corrosive dependency on sources because of the availability of well-crafted PR," he says.

SKILLS AND QUALIFICATIONS

There is no set route into science journalism. Some people in the field today attended a journalism program, and later specialized in science. Many others went from science to journalism. A fair few gave up on their PhD partway through when they realized that writing was for them, and never looked back. (Writer and blogger Ed Yong has an excellent collection of minibiographies from science writers about how they got into the field (see http://blogs.discovermagazine.com/notrocketscience/2010/07/29/on-the-origin-of-science-writers/). At *Nature*, the news team contains a mix of people with all these backgrounds.

In the past, many journalists entered the profession by finding a junior reporter position at a newspaper or other media organization. They learned their skills on the job and worked their way up. (That is what I did.) A few people still get in this way, but the contraction of so many media organizations means that those entry-level positions are highly competitive and hard to come by.

Many people coming into the field today have attended a science writing or journalism course. There are more than 50 courses in the United States that train students in communicating science to the public (see http://dsc.journalism.wisc.edu/index.html) and a growing number in other countries. A subset of these is focused on professional science journalism, in which students learn essential skills such as finding stories and reporting, and gain experience in a range of media, from writing a lengthy feature article to reporting, shooting, and producing a short documentary. "You learn the field systematically and get all the tools at the outset," says Douglas Starr, codirector of the science journalism program at Boston University.

Is It Necessary to Take a Science Journalism Course?

It is not essential to have completed a science journalism course, but it can ease your way into a competitive field.

Course directors acknowledge that some people have no need for a post-graduate course. These include highly motivated students who have some hands-on experience in science and are ambitious enough to have secured science journalism internships, people who start out blogging and establish a reputation and a writing career on the back of their blog, and a handful of working scientists who are also lucky enough to be highly gifted writers. These people can skip further training.

For everyone else—scientists without any "clippings" of their written or recorded work, for example—a science journalism course has advantages. As well as building skills and confidence, a course helps open up a network of contacts. For example, many science journalism programs have established links with science media organizations and help set up internships there. (*Nature* has found a string of talented interns from the University of California–Santa Cruz [UC Santa Cruz] program and others; graduates from the Science, Health, and Environmental Reporting Program (SHERP) at New York University [NYU] tend to dominate the internships in New York.) These help to make contacts for future freelancing and open the door to jobs.

The disadvantages of a science journalism course are the time, commitment, and expense. SHERP costs around $60,000 tuition alone for 16 months; an in-state student attending the University of Wisconsin–Madison pays about $20,000. The course directors strongly recommend that prospective students carefully research the program and examine whether and where recent graduates have landed jobs. "Find one that reflects the reality of the marketplace that exists now and 10 to 20 years from now," says Dan Fagin, who heads SHERP. Competition for the top science journalism courses is also stiff: The MIT program, for example, gets some 70–80 applications for eight places.

Do You Need a PhD?

No. It is more important to be a talented reporter or writer (see discussion of skills and qualities, below) than to have a PhD or postdoctoral experience. But having one will not do you any harm, and in some cases might help.

Some of the top science journalism courses do look for in-depth experience in science. Entry to the UC–Santa Cruz program requires at least six months research or professional experience and about two-thirds of those entering the program have a master's or PhD. NYU likes to see significant experience in science, such as a science major or a master's degree, in students wanting to attend SHERP.

Having research experience can provide you with expertise in a particular field. This could give you confidence interviewing scientists—and having a niche, such as infectious diseases or genomics, can be an advantage when editors are looking to assign a story. "It's really important to establish yourself as a source of information that can't be easily obtained elsewhere," says Fagin. "Make yourself the go-to person in a particular subject." Research experience can also give you insight into the research process and community that you will be writing about.

On the other hand, a PhD is often no help at all. Many of the best science journalists have little to no research experience. The research from a PhD quickly becomes out of date. (My PhD in developmental biology was of little help when writing about the science leadership of Harvard University, for example). I hardly ever advertise my PhD to people that I interview, because it is usually irrelevant to the topic I am writing about. It can also cause them to assume I know more than I do, when I actually need them to explain their work to me from scratch.

What Skills and Qualities Do You Need?

To be successful in science journalism, there are many qualities that are more important than any qualification. When I receive a story "pitch"—a note from a freelance journalist outlining a story they would like to write for *Nature*—I do not look at the writer's resume or academic qualifications. I read the pitch to see if it is a great idea, well written and researched, and of interest to *Nature*'s readers. I also look to see if the author has written outstanding feature stories that demonstrate that he or she can carry out high-quality reporting and writing.

The directors of the science journalism courses—experts at screening through applications—say that they look for some of the following skills and attributes in aspiring science journalists.

1. A talent for writing, with an appreciation of the difference between academic and science writing. When course directors read application letters, essays, and clippings they look for a spark that makes the writing stand out. "I look for that flair of voice," says Robert Irion, whose course at UC–Santa Cruz graduates about 10 students a year. "It might be raw and untamed but there needs to be a spark—rather than a dry academic voice."

2. Evidence that an applicant has tried writing or journalism by, for example, blogging; writing for an institutional newsletter, website, or local newspaper; or taking a class (see next section, Getting a Foot in the Door).

3. Evidence that a candidate has carefully studied the field and is committed to a career in it. "We want people who have done their research and feel certain that this is really what they want to do," says Fagin.

4. Some life experience. Many course directors say they prefer students who have done more than trodden the straight and narrow academic path. "If they've lived and experienced the world then it leads to better journalism," says Irion, who says that most of his students have had challenging jobs or traveled abroad.

5. Other qualities that make a good reporter and writer: a sense of what makes a science story; a fearlessness in talking to new people (journalists have to cold call the people they want to interview); the ability to quickly read and synthesize a mass of scientific information; a healthy skepticism; and the ability to chase a story down. "They need a certain type of sharkiness, to go after a story and get it," Finkbeiner says.

GETTING A FOOT IN THE DOOR

Is Science Journalism for You?

You may already have a strong feeling that science writing or journalism is for you. It is fairly common to meet science journalists who started out doing a PhD or studying science in some capacity, but felt that they were out of place, lacked a passion for bench research, or found (as I did) the focus on one sliver of science unsatisfying. "When our class gets in the room for the first time and look at each other, there is this spark of recognition—you too?" says Starr. "When they find us there is sometimes a sense of relief: at last I can be me." Irion says that another sign of a wannabe journalist is an insatiable appetite for news. "If you pick up *Nature* and *Science* and scan the front of the magazine before the back, it's a good sign you want to communicate."

However, few people feel comfortable making major career choices on the basis of intuition alone. There are many other ways to communicate science, such as teaching, which might suit you better. So the best way to work out if science writing or journalism is a good career choice is simply to try it. Take small, practical steps that allow you to try out a little writing, or other media, without sucking up all your time. You could start a blog. You might ask at your institution's communication office if you could write for them, or record an interview. You might write for the university magazine, newspaper or website, or volunteer to write for a newspaper in your town. Perhaps you could sign up for an evening class in nonfiction writing. Any of these activities can help you get a feel for what is involved and help you work out whether you like it. Whether you end up applying to a science journalism course or for a job, these will also demonstrate your commitment and provide you with some work to show.

Aside from this, there are other ways to start informing yourself about the industry, and integrating yourself into it. Read newspapers, magazines, news sites, and blogs voraciously; consume radio, TV, podcasts, and videocasts. Research the field, by talking to people who are already working in it about how they started out, and what it is like. Most science journalists love what they do, and are happy to talk to others about it.

Getting Started through Blogging and Social Media

There is a thriving community of scientists, science communicators, journalists, and others passionate about science that is very active online, and integrating yourself into this community through blogging and social media is an excellent doorway into the field. Twitter and other social media encourage anyone to join the conversation and establish a presence for themselves online, if they have something interesting to say.

At the minimum, you should get online, read science blogs, become familiar with the community and the blogging networks, and start experimenting with Twitter, Facebook, Reddit, and other social media if you are not already. Starting your own blog or offering to guest post on someone else's helps a writer practice and find their interests and writing style. On the other hand, it's not obligatory to start a blog in order to get into the field.

Internships

Science journalism and writing internships, which are offered by many science media organizations, are an excellent way to gain experience and contacts. Some of these are advertised on the NASW jobs list. Competition for some of the most prized internships can be stiff, however, and you may be up against top candidates coming out of science journalism programs. The annual meeting of the American Association for the Advancement of Science (AAAS)—one of the big professional get-togethers for science writers—hosts an internship fair for recruiters and those seeking internships who are members of the NASW. There is also a mentoring program at the meeting which pairs up students with working journalists or science publicists.

There are other opportunities to get a taste of the media. The AAAS Mass Media Science & Engineering Fellows Program offers 10-week summer placements at media organizations for graduate and postgraduate science students (see http://www.aaas.org/programs/education/MassMedia/). In the U.K., the British Science Association Media Fellowships provide similar opportunities (see http://www.britishscienceassociation.org/science-society/media-fellowships).

Does the World Need More Science Journalists?

No one really knows, particularly with such rapid change in the way news is being consumed. With so many U.S. science writing programs but a contracting workforce in legacy media, some science journalists do worry that the job market is saturated or heading that way. Even so, many course directors say that the majority of their graduates are going on to get good jobs within months of graduating. The best science journalism courses are transparent about exactly where all of their graduates are working, so make sure that you do your research.

CAREER PROGRESSION AND THE WAY OUT

The career choices and paths of recent graduates from science journalism programs reveal where the employment opportunities now lie. (You can get a more detailed picture of this by looking at the course websites, many of which show the paths of their alumni.)

According to the course leaders, only a small fraction of graduates are now finding work as science journalists in newspapers. "You can count on one hand the number of jobs available at newspapers for students," says Irion. (Employment at magazines, TV, and radio has been more stable.) The shortfall from print, says Irion, is made up by online news sources. Some are writing for the online news operations of established magazines such as *New Scientist* or *Scientific American*; others are finding jobs in smaller, more specialized news websites.

Most course leaders said that around half of their graduates find work in science publicist positions in universities, research institutions, and science-related organizations. And a substantial fraction of graduates are making it as

---

Box 1. My Experience

When I was about 15 years old and at British high school, I completed a career questionnaire. I filled in answers to numerous questions about my likes and dislikes, which were sent off and plugged into a computer. About a week later, my ideal career came back: quarry manager. (Yes, that is someone who manages quarries.)

This did not quite jibe, so instead I took a pretty conventional path into science. I went to the University of Cambridge to study Natural Sciences, and specialized in genetics. Toward the end of the course, I still did not know what to do. I had an interview with MI5, the British Intelligence Agency, but I cannot tell you much about that. I took a year off, continuing my Cambridge undergraduate laboratory project for a few months and then traveled in Central America. Then I started a PhD in developmental genetics at the University of Edinburgh, an amazing city with grim weather.

(Continued.)

It is no reflection on my excellent supervisors, but I did not have the passion that it really takes to succeed in research. I had to hold the edges of my chair to keep from running out of seminars. I had wondered whether writing or some other form of science communication was for me—but, lucky for me, my PhD studies and living expenses were fully funded by the UK's Medical Research Council, and I figured having a PhD would not hurt if I eventually took a different route.

And that is what I did. Toward the end of my PhD I was offered an internship at *New Scientist* magazine. (I had to write a trial article and I swotted up like crazy before my interview so that I was armed with story ideas.) But I was told that I had to start the internship immediately, before I had finished writing up my PhD, so I turned it down. Instead, I wrote the thesis and joined London's Science Museum, where I wrote educational materials and eventually got to work on a fast-turnaround "science news" exhibition. Meanwhile, I had also developed the confidence to pitch and write a few freelance news stories for *New Scientist*.

Those clippings were enough to get me a position as an online reporter at *Nature* in 2001, when it was just looking to expand its online news team. I was thrilled and terrified to get the job. The deadlines were relentless and I lived on adrenaline for at least a year. (On the other hand, I could now walk out of a dull conference seminar without looking back.) After 18 months, I moved to *Nature*'s New York office, to continue reporting there.

I went to New York for what I expected to be two years, and came back to London after eight years, with two children and running the features section of *Nature*. This means that I commission, edit, and oversee the feature-length stories in the magazine. I will be honest; editing features for a weekly magazine is more compatible with family life than writing news to daily deadlines. But I have also come to love writing and editing longer-form stories because they allow me to explore subjects and people in depth, and spend more time crafting the words. I have been fortunate enough to pick up a few journalism awards for my own writing, and I'm now finishing a book that spun off from one of my *Nature* features.

As an editor, I have the advantage of seeing the bigger picture: commissioning stories that cover all areas of science research, science policy, and the scientific community. At *Nature*, I am also surrounded by an incredible brain trust of people who know science inside out. It is never less than really hard work, and never dull. But like many editors, I struggle to find time to write. I am really happiest when I have finished reporting a story, close my notes, and sit down to write it. However, it is possible I would have loved managing a quarry more. You never know.

freelance writers, by producing material for established science news providers and the many online outlets. Of graduates from the MIT science writing program since 2003, approximately half are supporting themselves as freelancers.

Box 2. Ten Dos and Don'ts

Some condensed tips for those wanting to enter the profession.

1. Do get some practical experience in science journalism and writing: Start a blog, write for your institution's communication office, take an evening class.

2. Do research the field, the job prospects, and the challenges, so that you have an accurate idea of what you are getting into, before quitting science. And do research graduate schools, if you decide to take a course.

3. Do not read a science article and assume that writing it was easy. You do not know what went into reporting that story—sometimes many months of work.

4. Do read voraciously. Work out your favorite science writers, magazines, blogs, and media outlets.

5. Do join the NASW. This active professional society of science journalists and communicators has lots of excellent information, resources, an annual meeting, discussions lists, and a great jobs list that includes internships. Other excellent groups include the Society of Environmental Journalists and the Association of Health Care Journalists.

6. Do not assume you need a PhD, a Master's, or specialist training in science. Talent and hard work are more important.

7. Do get online and use social media to become familiar with the community.

8. If you apply to a science journalism course, do write a beautifully worded application and check it carefully for accuracy. Sloppiness or spelling mistakes will not do. Do not send in a research paper or anything written for academic colleagues.

9. Do not assume you are going to educate people about science, or that you are a cheerleader for science.

10. Do persevere, if this is what you really want to do.

Like entry points, career paths in science journalism vary. My news colleagues from *Nature* have gone on to diverse positions in TV, radio, national newspapers, and research foundations, and several have become excellent book authors and successful freelance writers. Science journalists who are looking for variety during their career can take on freelance work or write books on the side. Some also take up journalism fellowships, which allow them paid time off to pursue in-depth projects.

The traditional divide between promotional and journalistic writing can be hard to cross, however. Someone in a promotional position could well find it hard to do freelance journalism on the side, as there is a perceived conflict of interest in, for example, reporting on the type of science that is being carried out at the institution that is paying your salary. Finkbeiner warns those who choose a science publicist position to only remain in it for a short while if they are interested in returning to journalism. In Finkbeiner's experience, "anyone who stays there for more than a few years stays there for good."

An individual with a broad understanding of science who can also write or speak lucidly about it, has skills that can prove valuable in many career paths, including others outlined in this book. In fact, these are some of the qualities that make for an outstanding researcher—should you decide to return to the bench. "There's nothing lost—a scientist who learns to be a communicator is a good thing," says Deborah Blum, a Pulitzer Prize–winning journalist and professor of journalism at the University of Wisconsin–Madison.

ACKNOWLEDGMENTS

Thanks to Alexandra Witze and Dan Fagin for their helpful comments on the draft.

REFERENCE

Brumfiel G. 2009. Science journalism: Supplanting the old media? *Nature* 458: 274–277. http://www.nature.com/news/2009/090318/full/458274a.html.

ADDITIONAL RESOURCES

Blum D, Knudson M, eds. 2005. *A field guide for science writers: The official guide of the National Association of Science Writers*, 2nd ed. Oxford University Press, New York.

Hayden T, Nijhuis M, eds. 2013. *The science writers' handbook: Everything you need to know to pitch, publish, and prosper in the digital age.* Da Capo Press, Cambridge, Massachusetts.

WWW RESOURCES

http://blogs.discovermagazine.com/notrocketscience/2010/07/29/on-the-origin-of-science-writers   Yong E. 2010. On the origin of science writers.

http://casw.org/casw/guide-careers-science-writing   Council for the Advancement of Science Writing: A guide to careers in science writing.

http://dsc.journalism.wisc.edu/index.html   Directory of science communication courses and programs, University of Wisconsin.

http://theopennotebook.com   The Open Notebook: Tools and resources for science journalists at all experience levels.

http://www.nasw.org/faq-new-and-aspiring-science-writers   NASW: FAQs for new and aspiring science writers.

14

Careers in Science Publishing

John R. Inglis

Cold Spring Harbor Laboratory Press, Cold Spring Harbor, New York 11724

Publishing, particularly journal publishing, offers the chance to stay in contact with science and scientists and so appeals to people considering leaving the laboratory for another career. Professional editors of research journals review and select manuscripts for publication, negotiating as needed with authors and referees. Review journal editors commission articles on suitable topics and work with authors to shape manuscripts appropriately for the readership. Experienced individuals may advance to become a Managing Editor and further to a Publisher/Publishing Director position within a company or a not-for-profit organization, with responsibility for the business aspects of a publishing program. Would-be editors must be prepared to broaden their scientific knowledge, engage in person with community members, be tactful but firm in decision making, and work happily in the background. Evidence of a genuine interest in the communication of science beyond the usual writing and publishing of papers is necessary to compete successfully for entry positions.

No one reaches postgraduate level in science without reading and usually contributing to the professional literature. So it is not surprising that publishing comes readily to mind when postgrads or postdocs in the life sciences consider leaving the laboratory for another career. Editorial work, and the chance to stay in contact with science and scientists, is an appealing option.

The STM (science, technical, and medical) publishing industry produces journals, books, technical information and standards, databases and tools, and newsletters. Here, I pay particular attention to journal publishing because most scientists trained to doctoral level find employment in that sector. I do not discuss the better known businesses of publishing books on popular science or undergraduate textbooks, because these are usually the responsibility of people with sales and marketing expertise, not postgraduate science degrees. For the same reason, my focus here is on editorial work rather than jobs in composition, production, marketing, or IT support.

Journals are arguably as essential to the progress of science as the experiments they describe. Journals communicate information but also register the precedence of an author's research, ensure quality through peer review, maintain archives for future scholarship, and provide navigation through the ever-increasing volume of published material. From their origins in 1665, with *Journal des Scavons* and *Philosophical Transactions of the Royal Society*, STM journals have become the product of a global industry of 5000–10,000 organizations, which publish around 30,000 journals with a collective output of 1.8–1.9 million articles a year and employ 110,000 people (not counting freelancers and the hundreds of thousands of unpaid referees). The number of journals and their output has grown steadily for more than two centuries by about 3% per year, driven by an equally steady 3% annual expansion in the number of research scientists. The United States produces the largest share of published articles (~21%) but the most dramatic recent growth has been in China, which now has 10% of global output, followed by the United Kingdom (7%), Japan (6%), Germany (6%), and France (4%). Looking ahead, India's research productivity is predicted to overtake that of most G8 nations by 2020.[1]

The number of English language STM publishers is estimated at around 650. Of these, 27% are commercial companies and the others not-for-profit organizations such as scientific societies and university presses. However, 64% of the articles come from commercial publishers (this includes many journals published on behalf of scientific societies), 30% from societies that publish for themselves, and the remaining 6% from university presses and others.[2] The five largest companies publish nearly 35% of all journals, three of them (Elsevier, Springer, and Wiley-Blackwell) producing well over 2000 titles each.

Most journals are sold to institutions and researchers on a subscription basis. The STM market as a whole has had growth rates of 4%–5% since 2007, and it is projected to continue growing at around this rate in the short-to-medium term, despite concerns about a leveling off of institutional library budgets. The drivers of this growth are emerging regions such as Asia,

---

[1] *The STM Report*, by Mark Ware and Michael Mabe, 2012.
[2] Thomson-Reuters Journal Citation Database, 2011.

India, and Brazil and the release of new titles, as well as traditional annual price increases.

The shift to web delivery of journal content, allied with concerns about increases in the price of some subscription journals, has prompted exploration of alternatives to the traditional journal subscription business model. Now an open access-publishing model in which authors or funders pay to publish a research paper that can be read free of charge online has firmly established itself. The recognition of the revenue that can be generated by an open access journal when it publishes a large volume of manuscripts has fueled a wave of new publishers in the past decade and the launch of open access journals by both commercial companies and not-for-profits. The Directory of Open Access Journals now lists more than 9000 scholarly titles, a substantial proportion in STM.

The digital transformation of STM journal publishing in the past 20 years has opened other avenues for change. Anonymous peer review, for example, is under particular scrutiny. Some believe it can be improved by greater transparency, with publication of referees' reports alongside the paper, ideally signed by the referees concerned. Others consider that the selection of papers for novelty or importance is wrong and that peer review should be confined to the assessment of scientific validity rather than the "importance" of the findings. Yet others think the peer-review system is irretrievably broken and advocate instead for replacing it with postpublication, public commentary. There is also growing enthusiasm for the distribution of unrefereed preprints of research papers on sites such as arXiv and bioRxiv that allow authors to communicate findings more rapidly and get feedback before submission to a journal.

Anyone considering science publishing as a career today, therefore, should be aware that the industry has been in transition over the past decade. There has been a dramatic increase in start-up ventures intent on catalyzing and capitalizing on this disruption. The impact of digital technologies is the primary cause but in addition, the academic community, supported by some science funders, is pushing back against the established publishing ecosystem, concerned that large commercial companies are deriving excessive profit margins from the shrinking pool of public funds for research.

JOBS

Publishing organizations are diverse in structure and function, particularly with respect to titles and responsibilities. What follows is a general view and should be checked against the particulars of any organization in which a prospective recruit is interested. A generalized career path in publishing for individuals with a science PhD is shown in Figure 1.

Regardless of the output (a book, a reference work, a review journal, or a research journal), the editorial department is always responsible for interactions with authors and the selection, and if necessary the reshaping, of manuscripts that accord with the desired scope, audience, and quality standard. The selection process usually requires some form of peer review, more often than not involving practicing scientists who specialize in that particular field. When a manuscript is accepted, it may undergo further editing for scientific content by a science editor. The production department then copyedits it, correcting spelling and grammar and imposing house style and design elements, and then works with a compositor to transform it into file formats that can be published online (HTML) or as an e-book (ePub), printed (PDF), or conveyed to repositories and indexing services such as PubMed Central (XML). If advertisements or commercial sponsorship of content is appropriate and can be secured, a specific department is responsible for their

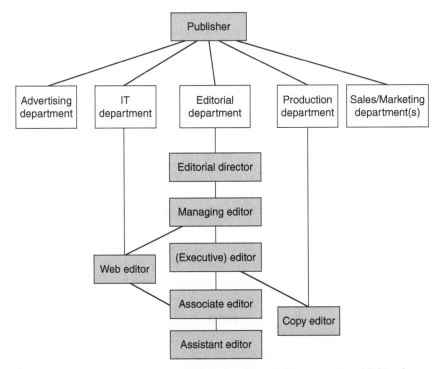

Figure 1. A typical career path for a science graduate within a generic publishing house. For clarity only positions that usually require a PhD are shown.

acquisition. Marketing and sales departments promote the publication to researchers (as both authors and readers), clinch the purchase and the renewal of subscriptions if that is the journal's business model, and provide customer service. A finance department ensures appropriate record-keeping, analysis, reporting, and projections. In some organizations, responsibility for online functionality rests with a specific department. In others, this is handled by a hosting service. As emphasized above, however, editorial is the department most likely to contain the people with science qualifications.

Journal Editors

Journals are thriving in the digital world. Many types of publication are loosely referred to as "journals" but here the term "research journal" is used to denote a periodical that publishes accounts of research written by the investigators themselves that have been subjected to a peer-review process (see Fig. 2).

A "review journal" is a periodical that publishes reviews or surveys of current research and commentaries rather than original data. A handful of publications, most notably *Nature* and *Science*, combine research papers with reviews, commentary, opinion pieces, features, and news, and are referred to in this chapter as "magazines."

Research Journal Editors

At a research journal, submitted manuscripts are evaluated, accepted, or rejected by an editorial team that will vary in size, depending on the journal. The Editor (or Executive Editor or Chief Editor or Editor-in-Chief) has ultimate responsibility for everything that appears in the journal, which includes the selection of articles, scientific scope of the content, the styles of article, and their relative balance within the journal. The Editor is ultimately responsible to the Publisher for the success, or failure, of the journal in terms of its reputation or value within the community it serves. Although most STM journals are edited by academics who do the editor's job on a part-time basis, a number of journals have scientifically qualified editors who are paid employees of the publisher. Most review journals are staffed this way, as are many of the most prominent research journals and magazines in the life sciences. Because these "professional editors" are encouraged to visit research centers and attend conferences, of all the scientifically qualified

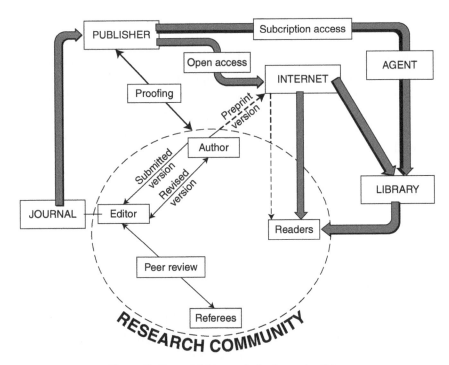

Figure 2. The publishing cycle for journal articles.

individuals who work in publishing, they are the most visible to the research community. When scientists express interest in a publishing career, this is the job they most frequently imagine having and where those exiting academia most often get their start in editorial work.

There is a hierarchy of positions within professional editorial teams. An entry-level position is most likely that of Assistant Editor, with advancement possible to Associate Editor or Senior Editor. The Chief Editor or Executive Editor in a professional team has the broad-ranging responsibilities outlined above, and a more senior Managing Editor may have overall responsibility for more than one journal (see below). But the consuming task of all the professional editors of a research journal is the selection of a small number of manuscripts from among the thousands submitted each year. The editors must have training and expertise in relevant subject matter and a general magazine such as *Nature* or *Science* will have a large number of editors with different scientific backgrounds. Because their task is to identify the most significant research papers for publication, they must read all the submitted manuscripts in their subject area and employ their critical judgment to select only a portion of them for peer review, declining the rest with a regretful letter to the authors. The editors must then engage appropriate reviewers for each paper, usually three, bearing in mind the special technical expertise that may be required and any factors that might influence the objectivity of the opinion expressed. Having assembled the reviews, the editor must then make a decision on the paper: an unqualified yes or no, or— frequently—"revise," the initiation of a conversation with the authors about current inadequacies that would be removed if certain changes were made. Some of these changes may require additional data or experiments. The conversation with authors is often lengthy and occasionally testy. Every scientific paper is the product of intense and challenging work and editors must be prepared to deal with authors who are passionate in their defense against criticism, however well-intentioned or necessary.

For journals that have academic editors who do the job on a part-time basis (such as many commercial journals and journals owned by scientific societies), responsibility for managing the journal and relationships with its academic editors (and if applicable its client society) usually lies with a managing editor. That person may be trained to postdoc level in one scientific specialty but will often manage a list of journals in several different subject areas. The duties of the managing editor depend on the ownership of the journal. If the owner is a society, defining the journal's scope and assessing editorial functions such as manuscript flow and acceptance rate are the responsibility of the society's publications committee, although the managing editor's views on weaknesses and improvements may be valued. In general, the managing editor is responsible for the negotiation, maintenance, and renewal of the contract that binds the society and the publisher and for reporting to the society on the business functions of the journal, including financial performance, subscription and advertising sales dynamics, market position, and usage metrics. For journals owned directly by a commercial publisher, the managing editor has similar business responsibilities but an additional obligation to assess the performance of the academic editors and the journal's competitive position, and take action to improve things if necessary. Managing editors are often science graduates but not always, particularly in some organizations in which the role is primarily administrative.

Some journals with academic editors also employ professional editors, sometimes called "staff editors" or "executive editors," to help with manuscript triage and oversee the peer-review process and administrative staff. These positions are occasionally filled by scientists fresh from research positions but more often by professional editors trained at the kind of journal described above. These individuals often combine the role of managing editor and research manuscript editor, bringing valuable publishing experience that permits the academic editors to focus primarily on manuscript selection.

Review Journal Editors

Review journals primarily publish articles that are commissioned and subsequently edited by professional editors. These individuals have the task of filling their issues with articles commissioned from groups of expert authors. Although there may be some volunteered articles, most of the time this responsibility requires a close eye on the progress of science in the journal's area and the generation of ideas for articles that summarize important new directions, concepts, or technologies. Suitable authors then have to be identified and persuaded to take on the task, with an agreed deadline. Because those deadlines are seldom met, prudent planning is required to ensure that issues of the journal can be published on time with sufficient content to satisfy the readership. Whereas the editors of research journals are usually dealing with an oversupply of papers, review editors have the constant challenge of filling the article pipeline with high-quality material and keeping it full.

As well as choosing referees and overseeing peer review of commissioned articles, review journal editors also "developmentally edit" the manuscript to make it accessible even to readers who do not work in the same field. This may involve rewriting parts of the manuscript, simplifying language used, and frequently querying aspects of the science. There can be much discussion with the author and it is critical that the editor has confidence in his/her opinions but deals tactfully with authors when asking for revision to a manuscript.

Web Editors and Science 2.0

Although many journals retain print editions for various reasons, all science journals are now published online, a transition from print-only that began in the mid-1990s. For the first decade of the transition, journal content had the same look and feel online as in print and the impact of the change was felt more by production, marketing, and sales staff than by editors. Now the online journal, with its wealth of features and functions, is the primary focus for most publishers, and editors and publishers have a multitude of new and emerging creative opportunities. This can involve web-only material, as well as new initiatives outside the traditional journal format, such as portals, knowledge environments, and social-media sites aimed at scientists. Some of these are initiated by publishers, but many are start-ups. There are jobs for web editors who maintain this type of content in many larger publishers, and an increasing number of scientists are moving into start-ups in this area straight from, or even while at, the bench.

Book Editors

For books for professional use or reference works, editorial activities are usually divided up into "acquisition" and "development." A book acquisition editor is responsible for the maintenance and expansion of a list of books in topic areas that the publisher has targeted for business reasons, and does so by finding and engaging with authors and editors who can create appropriate titles. In this respect the job resembles that of a review journal editor. Prospective authors may volunteer manuscripts but in science publishing, this is rare. Usually an acquisition editor, through reading or networking in the communities concerned, must instead come up with ideas for books that would be commercially attractive. These ideas must be validated by experts, before academic authors or editors able to create the manuscript are sought out. Not all ideas may be judged viable and not all projects may find willing participants.

When the manuscript arrives, it must be assessed. If it is not judged suitable for its intended purpose or audience, the acquisition editor may request changes from the author and/or engage the services of a developmental editor. Developmental editors edit the book manuscript in much the same way a review journal editor would edit a review article. To work effectively, they need a background in the subject matter, usually at postgraduate level, together with the editing skills required to adjust the manuscript's content, scope, or style for its intended market.

Developmental editors are usually freelancers who are engaged for a fee to work on a project-by-project basis and many scientifically qualified people take on such work in their specialties as an adjunct to other activities. Book acquisition editors, on the other hand, are full-time employees who are judged in part on the numbers of titles they commission and the sales of those books in relation to the publisher's total output and to competing books from other houses. Sales of print books in STM are declining in response to the availability of online information and the increasing share of shrinking library budgets being taken up by journals. Publishers with large book lists now often convert them to electronic formats and offer them for sale in bundles to libraries. However, as a medium for current scientific information, the book format is no longer as influential, or as profitable for publishers, as it once was.

Publisher

This position, the most senior in a publishing company, is also often filled by a science graduate. The Publisher is responsible for overall management and for meeting business goals and is involved in functions such as finance and personnel management and the fulfillment of legal obligations and ethical requirements. The Publisher's key responsibility is strategic planning in accord with the mission and standards of the owner, whether that is a commercial company or a not-for-profit. If entrepreneurial zeal for the development of new publications and services is expected or encouraged by the owner, it will be driven by the Publisher, although the novel ideas themselves may percolate from other parts of the organization, such as editorial and marketing. Publishers are often, but not always, drawn from the editorial track and larger organizations frequently have intermediate positions such as Publishing Manager or Assistant Publisher that are stepping-stones to this role editors can take.

SKILLS AND QUALIFICATIONS

To get a job as a professional editor, a PhD and some postdoc experience in a relevant science discipline is generally required. This ensures that the candidate has an understanding of the values and functions of the research community the journal serves. An ability to critically assess research manuscripts within the scope of the journal is essential. Would-be editors must be able to show they are familiar with and can discuss the key advances in any area they hope to cover. They must also be comfortable with discussing and rapidly coming to grips with subjects they have not worked on and are less familiar with. An eye for detail is important and, for review editors in particular, excellent written English and the ability to write about science clearly and concisely are required. All of these are skills candidates must demonstrate in formal tests that are set before and/or during the interviews for new positions.

The ability to build and maintain strong personal relationships with scientists is essential for any editor and this requires diplomacy, effective negotiation and problem-solving skills, and an ability to stand firm on decisions when required, even in response to angry authors, who can often be very senior and take exception to the judgments of an editor who may be younger and have much less research experience. Similarly, an editor may occasionally have to justify a decision to referees who feel their views have been too easily dismissed. Authors and referees, and sometimes referees of the same paper, all too often have starkly contrasting views of the merits of a particular paper, and it is the editor who ultimately has to make a decision. It is not a job for the faint hearted and editors must be able to deal calmly and tactfully with such situations.

Editorial positions require the juggling of multiple tasks often within strict deadlines, so excellent organizational skills are required, plus an ability to preserve them under pressure. Journals run to tight production schedules that must be maintained despite the ebbs and flows of manuscript submissions and revisions and referee delays. The ability to work in teams is vital, because publishing is a collaborative activity involving individuals with complementary skills. Many of them will not be scientists but professionals who have followed very different career paths. An editor must be able to interact well with people in production, marketing, and other departments, including those who do not consider that having a PhD warrants special treatment.

An important consideration for a scientist considering transition from research to a publishing position is the recognition that one is giving up the goal of being deeply conversant with one particular aspect of science for the requirement to be broadly informed across a discipline. It helps to be curious and excited by new ideas and approaches and to have the self-confidence to go alone to conferences and take part in conversations in which your companions know much more about the details of a topic than you do. Being comfortable in such situations and enjoying discussing science in person is essential. If you would rather e-mail someone a response than talk in person, a job as a journal editor is not for you. Similarly, it is important to remember that the editor is not the star of the show. Your best work will go unnoticed by most readers and you must be content that others—the authors who did the research—have center stage. The rewards of editorial work may be quiet but it can be satisfying to get the first glimpses of emerging concepts, novel technologies, or rising stars and have the opportunity and the means to bring them the focus and attention you think they deserve.

Finally, it is important for would-be editors to understand that STM publishing is a business that is going through the most significant shift in communication since the invention of the printing press. The internet, mobile devices, and their associated technologies are reshaping publishing. The blog "The Scholarly Kitchen," run by the Society for Scholarly Publishing, is an often lively forum for discussion of the trends, threats, and opportunities that preoccupy professional publishers. Scientists entering publishing should bring—or be prepared to quickly acquire—skills and awareness beyond their research specialty. Business modeling, technology development, design, social-media engagement, and marketing and sales strategies are all functions that are becoming ever more integrated with editorial work as the digital landscape evolves.

GETTING A FOOT IN THE DOOR

Every advertised editorial position attracts hundreds of applications from people with a PhD. Some say frankly that they are having difficulty staying in research and are looking to enter publishing to stay in touch with science. Such honesty, although perhaps commendable, is not recommended. Recruiters are looking for applicants for whom publishing is an active choice, not a fallback. What is needed is evidence of an intrinsic interest in the process of science communication that will make an application stand out from the rest, and the usual experience of writing papers based on your own research and publishing them is not enough. Any prior experience of science writing or editorial work should be emphasized. There are several things you might do to gain such experience and demonstrate a genuine interest in publishing.

One approach might include a track record of editing other scientists' manuscripts before they are submitted for publication, especially if the applicant's help is acknowledged. Some large publishers offer internships for postdocs to gain experience in editing and these are a good way to test the water and make contacts in the industry. There are also companies such as Edanz, American Journal Experts, and others who employ working scientists to help authors of papers whose first language is not English. Other noticeable experience might include reviewing manuscripts for journals, either as designated referee or as a principal investigator's proxy. You should include any evidence you can provide in your application and list the journals.

To build a collection or portfolio of your own writing, seek out prospects for communicating science in your community, for example, by working on an undergraduate or graduate student magazine or the college newspaper. Development or public affairs/communications offices at your institution may provide possibilities and welcome independent proposals. You might offer to interview and write a profile of a faculty member, describing research that has attracted interest in the community. Consider participating in or organizing a student journal; the *Yale Journal of Biology and Medicine* is an example of a student-run journal that gives students experience in science writing and publishing. Establish an online presence by writing a science-themed blog. An active Twitter account used for commentary on research results might also catch a recruiter's eye, as might posting comments on published papers on journal websites, preprint servers or blogs, or sites such as PubMed Commons. In all such endeavors, particularly longer-form writing such as personal or bylined blog posts, work should be carefully crafted and proofread. These efforts can become writing samples that influence how the author is perceived by potential employers.

Evidence of such activities and enthusiasm may be sufficient to get an applicant shortlisted for the position. At that point, journals may send out written tests or exercises to candidates, which are often followed by further tests at an interview. A research journal will typically ask a candidate to provide a critical assessment and recommendation for unpublished manuscripts that have already been decided on and then justify their recommendation to the in-house team. A review journal will usually give candidates a poorly written manuscript and ask them to improve it and draft a letter to the author detailing the revisions that are necessary.

Finally, be sure to look at papers published in the journal before you apply. Familiarity with them will impress interviewers, who will often ask your opinion about papers that have been published and whether, in your view, they should have been accepted.

CAREER PROGRESSION

Advancement in editorial positions is based on experience as well as competence. Assistant Editors can advance to Associate Editor and then to Senior Editor. In larger editorial teams there may be the opportunity to become a Deputy Editor and eventually Editor. At each stage of advancement, there is more and more diverse responsibility. Some promoted positions may offer the opportunity of commissioning articles for specific purposes or writing editorials. There is a growing trend for conferences to be sponsored by journals and in many cases, the more experienced editors at the journal are engaged in devising the program, inviting the speakers, and representing the journal at the meeting.

At some publishers, there is also the opportunity to launch new journals. This can be an exciting challenge, allowing an editor to shape something new rather than assume the reins of an existing project. As the online activities of science publishers continue to diversify, this opportunity may extend to other publishing projects, not just journals. In larger organizations, editors may have the opportunity to move into an Assistant or Associate Publisher position in which they become more engaged with the business functions of one or more journals and have a different career progression. Such advancement might be helped by acquisition of professional qualifications such as an MBA that can be earned part-time.

An additional potential career fork for people on an editorial track is the opportunity to become a managing editor for a suite of journals and their editorial functions. This may in time lead to advancement to a Publisher's position in the commercial sector in which the responsibilities are more business oriented. Another transition within the industry is into the role of acquisition editor for books and reference works (as described above), a position that benefits from extensive knowledge of research communities and their makeup.

Although I refer here almost exclusively to opportunities in English language publishing, research communities in Asia and other regions of the world have many established publications in local languages. As these communities have prospered through government investment in science, and their research output has increased, Western publishers have begun to pay attention. Many have established publishing partnerships with societies in Asia and are exploring ways of raising the profile of journals based there. The Middle East and South America are other potential growth areas. As these connections deepen, scientifically qualified people who have editorial skills but can also speak languages such as Mandarin, Arabic, Spanish, or Portuguese may have additional opportunities.

THE WAY OUT

STM publishing is a global industry with both commercial and not-for-profit employment sectors. There are extensive opportunities to move within the industry, especially for those with the freedom to change location, particularly internationally. Publishing, and in particular editorial work, gives scientifically qualified people an opportunity to gain a deep awareness of knowledge creation in major scientific disciplines such as neuroscience, stem cell biology, genetics, cancer biology, or immunology. They also acquire an extensive network of connections with prominent scientists in the field and a mutual degree of trust and confidence in their interactions with these individuals. These qualities, along with strong organizational skills and a well-developed capacity for critical thinking, may lead editorially experienced people back into academic life. The opportunities are many, for example, becoming administrative director for a university-based research institute or chief of staff for the president of a center for science and medicine. Additional avenues for individuals with publishing skills include organizing conferences, working with scientific societies and foundations, government jobs, and various other rewarding career options described elsewhere in this book.

Box 1. My Experience

My research experience at the University of Edinburgh, first at the veterinary school as a Research Associate, then at the medical school as a PhD student in immunology, was fun and productive but largely self-directed and susceptible to new ideas. I graduated knowing there were many more exciting things happening in medical research than could be engaged in as a postdoc. So I was fortunate to get the chance to become an Assistant Editor at the distinguished journal *The Lancet* in London and learn from its brilliantly and broadly erudite staff.

Nearly three years later, after a chance meeting with directors of Elsevier Biomedical Press, I was given the privilege to create and edit the journal *Immunology Today* (now *Trends in Immunology*) in Cambridge. Its timing captured an extraordinary wave of discoveries in the field—T-cell recognition, immunoglobulin structure, monoclonal antibodies, the HIVs—and it quickly caught on. Its success created the opportunity to launch *Parasitology Today* (now *Trends in Parasitology*) and begin laying the groundwork for future titles. I also contributed some articles on science to daily newspapers.

However, at this time, after 7 years in Cambridge, I was invited to meet Jim Watson, whose Nobel Prize–winning discovery of the structure of DNA with Francis Crick at the age of 24 was the first step in a remarkable career as a scientist, a teacher, an impresario of research, and the author of best-selling

(Continued.)

textbooks and the classic memoir *The Double Helix*. The Director of Cold Spring Harbor Laboratory in New York since 1968, Jim had personally built a small but highly regarded book publishing program at the laboratory that had just launched a research journal, *Genes & Development*. He extended an invitation to come to Cold Spring Harbor and develop from this foundation a fully fledged publishing house that could extend the name and reputation of Cold Spring Harbor Laboratory and contribute to its economic well-being.

Cold Spring Harbor Laboratory Press (www.cshlpress.org) is now one of five education divisions of the laboratory, one of the world's leading research institutions with programs in cancer, neuroscience, genomics, plant science, and quantitative biology. The Press has 44 staff members, including 10 talented people with postdoctoral qualifications in a variety of editorial positions. Its publications are sold through marketing and sales agents worldwide. I am the Executive Director of the Press and have been the Publisher of *Genes & Development* and *Genome Research* as they became two of the most successful and respected journals in molecular biology and genetics, as well as the more specialized research journals *Learning & Memory* and *RNA*. In recent years, I conceived and launched three review journals, *Cold Spring Harbor Protocols*, *Cold Spring Harbor Perspectives in Biology*, and *Cold Spring Harbor Perspectives in Medicine*. More new journals are planned. I have also commissioned and published several hundred books and manuals, including titles such as *Molecular Cloning* and *At the Bench* that have become essential resources for laboratories worldwide. At the dawn of the World Wide Web, I founded a venture-capital-funded start-up, BioSupply-Net.com, and more recently, cofounded the laboratory's preprint service for the life sciences, bioRχiv. Since Cold Spring Harbor Laboratory's graduate school began, I have been the academic mentor for 10 PhD students.

Box 2. Ten Dos and Don'ts

---

1. Do not go into science publishing if you are determined to remain as specialized as you were in research.

2. Do remember that publishing is a business, even within a not-for-profit organization.

3. Do make yourself aware of what trends, threats, and opportunities preoccupy publishers.

4. Do not say "I want to get into science publishing because I want/have to leave bench science."

5. Do not think you know about science publishing just because you have written some papers and had them published.

6. Do not say "I have always been interested in science publishing" unless you can back that up with evidence.

7. Do get some real experience in the communication and assessment of science, such as writing about research in blogs on magazines or posting commentary on research papers on appropriate websites.

8. Do be honest with yourself about how comfortable you are in social and professional interactions with other scientists whose field is not yours.

9. Do remember that editors work in the wings, not on center stage.

10. Do not go into science publishing because you think you will be better off financially than by staying in research.

ACKNOWLEDGMENTS

I am indebted to the 2012 edition of *The STM Report*, by Mark Ware and Michael Mabe, for much of the industry data quoted in this article and for the original version of Figure 2, and to Wayne Manos for helpful comments on an earlier draft.

REFERENCES

Morris S, Barnas E, LaFrenier D, Reich M. 2013. *The handbook of journal publishing*. Cambridge University Press, Cambridge.

Ware M, Mabe M. 2012. *The STM report*. International Association of Scientific, Technical and Medical Publishers, The Netherlands.

WWW RESOURCES

http://www.cambridge.org/us/academic/subjects/arts-theatre-culture/editing/handbook-journal-publishing Morris S, Barnas E, LaFrenier D, Reich M. 2013. *The handbook of journal publishing*. Cambridge University Press, Cambridge.

http://scholarlykitchen.sspnet.org The Scholarly Kitchen.

http://www.stm-assoc.org/industry-statistics/the-stm-report *The STM report.* International Association of Scientific, Technical and Medical Publishers, The Netherlands.

http://wokinfo.com/products_tools/analytical/jcr Thomson-Reuters Journal Citation Report.

Index

Page numbers followed by an *f* indicate a figure.

A

AAAS (American Association for the Advancement of Science), 101, 102, 190
ABRF (Association of Biomolecular Resource Facilities), 34, 35
Academic administration
  assistant department chair, 52
  career progression, 54–55, 55*f*
  categories of postsecondary institutions, 43–44
  components of institutions, 45*f*
  core director, 48, 50–51
  dean, 49
  department chair, 48
  diversity positions, 52
  dos and don'ts of jobs in, 57
  executive positions, 45–48, 47*f*
  financial acumen and, 53–54
  grants management, 51
  laboratory manager, 50
  nonexecutive positions, 50–52, 55*f*
  online resources, 43, 57
  organization chart, 46*f*
  a personal experience, 56–57
  positions overview, 43, 44
  president, 50
  provost, 49–50
  research subjects protection, 51
  safety office, 52
  senior research officer, 49
  skills and qualifications, 52–54
  technology transfer, 51
Account management careers, 164–165, 165*f*
Acquisition editors, 205
Administration jobs
  jobs available in universities (*see* Academic administration)
  small liberal arts colleges, 8–9
Advanced technician specialist, 28, 32
American Association for the Advancement of Science (AAAS), 101, 102, 190
American Journal Experts, 208
American Management Association (AMA), 54
American Medical Writers Association (AMWA), 169
American Physiological Society (APS), 93
  director of communication's duties, 97
  history of, 106–107
  organization chart, 95*f*
  outreach program, 102
  a personal experience, 105
  policy committees, 96
  positions in, 94
American Society for Biochemistry and Molecular Biology, 99
American Society of Association Executives (ASAE), 93
AMWA (American Medical Writers Association), 169

Angel Investor Forum, 144
APS. *See* American Physiological Society
arXiv, 199
ASBMB Today, 99
ASD (autism spectrum disorder), 117
Assistant department chair, 52
Assistant professor, 14
Associate dean of shared resources, 30
Associate professor, 15
Association of Biomolecular Resource
  Facilities (ABRF), 34, 35
Association of Health Care Journalists,
  193
Autism, 111
Autism spectrum disorder (ASD), 117

B

At the Bench, 212
Biomedical career options. *See also*
  individual careers
  common themes among professions,
    3–4
  range of jobs available, 2–3
  tenured positions versus number of
    PhD graduates, 1, 2*f*
Biomedical foundations
  career progression, 112–113
  dos and don'ts of jobs in, 118
  job search strategies, 115
  online resources, 111–112, 119
  a personal experience, 116–117
  positions overview, 109, 112–113
  proactive model of foundations,
    110–111
  related job options, 115
  skills and qualifications, 113–115
  types of foundations, 110
bioRxiv, 199, 212
Bioscience ClubhouseCT, 142
BioSupplyNet.com, 212
Biotechnology companies, 160, 161

Biotech start-ups and entrepreneurship
  career preparation, 141–142
  career progression, 137*f*, 142
  climate of opportunities for, 136
  dos and don'ts of jobs in, 144–145
  founder of a start-up, 138–139
  online resources, 145
  a personal experience, 143–144
  positions overview, 135–136
  skills and qualifications, 140
  small biotech companies, 137–138
Blank, Steve, 141
Blogs, science, 183–184, 189–190
Book editors, 205–206
Bower, Marvin, 148
Brain Awareness Week, 102
British Science Association Media
  Fellowship, 190

C

Center for Scientific Review (CSR),
  NIH, 60
Centers for Disease Control and
  Prevention (CDC), 79, 81
CESSE (Council of Engineering and
  Scientific Society Executives),
  93–94
CHDI Foundation, 111
Christine Mirzayan Science &
  Technology Policy Graduate
  Fellowship, 85, 101
Chronicle of Higher Education, 11
Claims (patent), 122
Clinical research organizations (CROs),
  160, 161, 162–164
Cold Spring Harbor Laboratory Press,
  212
*Cold Spring Harbor Perspectives in
  Biology*, 212
*Cold Spring Harbor Perspectives in
  Medicine*, 212

Cold Spring Harbor Protocols, 212
College rankings and school research
    emphasis, 9–10
Communications
    careers in medical companies (*see*
        Medical communications)
    careers in scientific societies, 96–97
    writing about science (*see* Science
        journalism and writing; Science
        publishing)
Confocal microscopy listing service, 25
Connecticut Innovations, 142
Connecticut United for Research
    Excellence (CURE), 142, 143
Core facility management
    about, 24–25
    advanced technician specialist, 28, 32
    associate dean of shared resources, 30
    career preparation, 34–35
    career progression, 35–36
    dean of shared resources, 33–34
    dos and don'ts of the jobs, 39–40
    entry level positions, 27–28, 31–32
    equipment maintenance, 25
    hierarchy of staff, 26*f*
    information technology, 27–28, 32
    institutions' move toward shared
        facilities, 24
    managing director, 28–29, 32–33,
        50–51
    mid-level positions, 28–29, 32–33
    need for qualified staff, 23
    online resources, 34–35, 40–41
    a personal experience, 38–39
    positions overview, 23–24
    range of jobs available, 26, 26*f*
    related job options, 36–37
    scientific director, 29–30, 33
    skills and qualifications, 30–34
    technician specialist, 27, 31–32
    training and education role, 25
    upper-level positions, 29–30, 33–34

Core Facility Marketplace, 34
Council of Engineering and Scientific
    Society Executives (CESSE), 93–94
Creative Arts Workshop, 144
Crick, Francis, 211
CSR (Center for Scientific Review),
    NIH, 60
CURE (Connecticut United for
    Research Excellence), 142, 143

D

Dean
    academic administration, 8, 49
    associate, of shared resources, 30
    of shared resources, 33–34
Department chair, 8, 48
Developmental editors, 205
Digital media and science journalism,
    181
Director, core
    academic administration, 48, 50–51
    facility management, 28–29, 32–33,
        50–51
Directory of Open Access Journals,
    199
Diversity positions, 52
Double Helix, The (Watson), 212

E

Edanz, 208
Editors
    book, 205–206
    editorial careers in research, 162–164
    in science journalism, 182
    in science journal publishing,
        116–117, 201–204
Education jobs. *See also* Academic
    administration; Small liberal arts
    colleges

Education jobs. (*Continued*)
medical communications and, 161–162
in scientific societies, 97–98, 102
Entrepreneurship. *See* Biotech start-ups and entrepreneurship
Equipment maintenance, 25
European Medical Writers Association (EMWA), 169–170
European Medicines Agency (EMA), 161
Executive careers
in academic administration, 45–48, 47*f*, 49–50
core facility management, 33–34
in medical communications, 165–166
publisher of a journal, 206
in scientific societies, 98–99

F

Fagin, Dan, 186, 187, 188
Fellowships
in science journalism, 190
in science policy, 85
in a scientific society, 101, 102
at small liberal arts colleges, 10–11
Finkbeiner, Ann, 179, 188, 194
Food and Drug Administration (FDA), 51, 80, 81, 161
Forbes, 9
Foundation careers. *See* Biomedical foundation careers
Fox, Jay, 35
Freelancers and science journalism, 182
Full professor, small liberal arts colleges, 15
Fundamentals of Finance and Accounting for Non-Financial Managers, 54
Funding at small liberal arts colleges, 16

G

Gender-based income inequality, 19
Genes & Development, 212
Genome Research, 212
Good Publication Practice 2, 167
Grants management
academic administration, 51
program officer at a foundation, 112
scientific review officer (*see* Scientist administrators at NIH)
The Grid, 143
The Grove, 141
GuideStar, 112

H

Health Research Alliance, 111–112
Health scientist administrator (HSA). *See* Scientist administrators at NIH
Howard Hughes Medical Institute (HHMI), 10
Huntington's disease, 111
Hybrid media, 181–182

I

I-Corps program, NSF, 141
Immortal Life of Henrietta Lacks, The (Sklott), 184
Immunology Today, 211
Information technology careers, 27–28, 32
Instructor positions, 8. *See also* Small liberal arts colleges
Intellectual property (IP)
management in academic administration, 51
patent process and, 121–123
International Conference on Harmonization of Technical Requirements, 167

International Society for Medical Publication Professionals, 167
Internships
in a biotech start-up, 141
in management consulting, 153
in medical communications, 169
in science journalism, 185–186, 190, 193
in a scientific society, 101, 102, 106
Interview process
demonstrating knowledge during, 169, 170
for a facility management position, 39, 40
informational interviews, 86, 130, 169, 175
in medical communications, 170–171
preparing for, 170
at small liberal arts colleges, 12–14, 21
Irion, Robert, 188, 189, 191

J

Job applications
at small liberal arts colleges, 11–14
strategies for entering medical communications, 170–171
strategies for entering patent law, 129–130
Journal des Scavons, 198
Journal editor, 116–117
Journalism. *See* Science journalism and writing
Journal of Experimental Biology (JEB), 174
Journal publishing. *See* Science publishing

L

Laboratory manager, 50
Lancet, The, 211

Lean Launchpad, 141
Learning & Memory, 212
Lecturer positions, 8
Liberal arts colleges. *See* Small liberal arts colleges
LinkedIn, 169

M

Management consulting
broadening of recruiting strategies, 149
career preparation, 153
frequently asked questions about the work, 156–158
growth in the field, 149
history of, 147–148
jobs and career progression, 150–151, 151f
a personal experience, 154–155
positions overview, 147
related job options, 153–154
skills and qualifications, 151–153
Managing director of a core facility, 28–29, 32–33
Mass Media Science and Engineering Fellows Program, AAAS, 102, 190
McKinsey, James O., 147–148
McKinsey & Company, 147–148, 149
Medical communications
account management careers, 164–165, 165f
applying for a job, 170
career preparation, 169–170
career progression, 171–172
dos and don'ts of jobs in, 175
editorial careers, communications and research, 162–164, 163f
editorial careers, pharmaceutical companies, 164, 168
education-based jobs, 161–162
executive careers, 165–166

Medical communications (*Continued*)
  interview process, 170–171
  main employer types, 160
  marketing materials preparation,
    160–161
  medical and scientific publishing,
    161–162
  need for qualified staff, 160
  a personal experience, 173–175
  positions overview, 159–160
  related job options, 172–173
  skills and qualifications, 166–168
Medical communications agencies,
  160–161, 162–164
Melinta Therapeutics, 143
Molecular Cloning, 212

N

National Academies, 80, 101
National Association for Science Writers
  (NASW), 181, 193
National Geographic, 183
National Institute of General Medical
  Sciences (NIGMS), 63
National Institutes of Health (NIH)
  fellowships offered by, 10
  grants budget, 59
  Office of Science Policy, 78, 89
  organization chart, 62*f*
  program officer, 62–64, 72–73
  R21 grant, 16
  science administration at (*see* Scientist
    administrators at NIH)
  science policy jobs, 79, 87
  scientific review officer, 65–68,
    73–74
  shared instrumentation grants, 24
National Science Foundation (NSF), 16,
  141
Nature, 117, 201, 202
Nature Neuroscience, 116–117

New Venture Creation Program,
  University of Massachusetts, 141
Nonexecutive positions, academic
  administration, 50–52, 55*f*
Notice of Allowance, 123

O

Office of Biotechnology Activities
  (OBA), 89
Office of Science Policy, NIH (OSP),
  78, 89
Open access journals, 199

P

Parasitology Today, 211
Patent and Trademark Office (PTO),
  123
Patent law
  biotech/pharmaceutical companies
    jobs, 125
  career preparation, 129–130
  dos and don'ts of jobs in, 133
  intellectual property and the patent
    process, 121–123
  law firms jobs, 124–125
  patent offices jobs, 125–126
  a personal experience, 131–132
  positions overview, 121
  related job options, 130
  skills and qualifications, 126–129
  tech-transfer offices jobs, 126
Patent process, 121–123
Patent prosecution, 123
Peer review in journal publishing, 199
Pfizer, 143
Pharmaceutical companies
  clinical research jobs and, 160, 161
  communications careers in, 164, 168
  patent law careers, 125

Philosophical Transactions of the Royal Society, 198
PhUn (Physiology Understanding) Week, 102
Presidential Management Fellows Program, 85
President of an academic institution, 9, 50
Prior art, 122
Professorships, 8, 14, 15
Program officer (PO) at NIH
  advice-giving role, 63
  facilitation of scientific opportunities, 64
  funding decisions and, 63–64
  job overview, 62–63
  oversight role, 64
  a personal experience, 72–73
Provost at an academic institution, 8, 49–50
PTO (Patent and Trademark Office), 123
Publisher, 206
Publishing. *See* Science journalism and writing; Science publishing
PubMed Commons, 209

R

Reappointment at colleges, 14–15
Reporters and science journalism, 182
Research
  career progression in small liberal arts colleges, 16–17
  clinical research organizations, 160, 161, 162–164
  college rankings as an indicator of research emphasis, 9–10
  editorial careers involving, 162–164, 163*f*
  expectations of research activity in colleges, 9

  research subjects protection in academic institutions, 51
  science policy careers in non-federal research organizations, 80–81
  senior research officer in academic institutions, 49
Research at Undergraduate Institution (RUI) grants, 16
Research journal editors, 201–204
Research subjects protection, 51
Review journal editors, 204
Rib-X Pharmaceuticals, Inc., 143
RNA, 212

S

Safety office in academic institutions, 52
Sales positions, 36–37
Science, 201, 202
Science, Health, and Environmental Reporting Program (SHERP), NYU, 186
Science, technical, and medical (STM) journal publishing. *See* Science publishing
Science and Technology Policy Fellowships, 85
Science journalism and writing
  about the field, 178
  blogging and social media and, 183–184, 189–190
  career preparation, 188–190
  career progression, 191, 193, 194
  digital media and, 181
  dos and don'ts of jobs in, 193
  hybrid media and, 181–182
  impact of media changes on, 180–181
  medical and scientific publishing, 161–162
  multimedia nature of, 184
  nature of the work, 184–185
  online resources, 195

Science journalism and writing
(*Continued*)
 a personal experience, 191–192
 positions overview, 177
 range of jobs available, 178–180,
  182–183
 skills and qualifications, 185–188
 specialized courses in, 186
 types of publications, 180
Science online, 11
ScienceOnline, 183
Science policy careers
 biomedical context, 78
 career preparation, 84–86
 career progression, 86–87
 degree requirements, 82
 dos and don'ts of jobs in, 92
 in the federal government, 79–80
 government relations and, 94, 96
 informing policy development and,
  81–82
 job search strategies, 85
 in non-federal research organizations,
  80–81
 online resources, 92
 personal experiences, 88–91
 policy process, 78–79
 positions overview, 8, 80
 related job options, 87, 88
 in scientific societies or professional
  organizations, 81
 skills and qualifications, 82–84
Science policy fellowships, 85
Science publicists, 179–180
Science publishing
 about STM journal publishing,
  197–199
 book editors, 205–206
 career paths, 200*f*
 career preparation, 208–209
 career progression, 209–210
 dos and don'ts of jobs in, 212–213

foreign language opportunities, 210
 hierarchy of positions, 202
 online resources, 213–214
 a personal experience, 211–212
 positions overview, 197, 199–201
 potential changes in peer review
  process, 199
 publisher, 206
 publishing cycle, 202*f*
 related job options, 210–211
 research journal editors, 201–204
 review journal editors, 204
 shift to web delivery of journal
  content, 199, 208
 skills and qualifications, 206–208
 web editors, 204–205
Scientific American, 183
Scientific director of a core facility,
  29–30, 33
Scientific review officer (SRO) at NIH
 contributing to new NIH policies by,
  66–67
 design and testing of new technologies,
  67–68
 job overview, 65
 organizing and overseeing peer review,
  65–66
 participation in and organization of
  workshops, 67
 participation in training opportunities,
  68
 a personal experience, 73–74
 work on congressional inquiries, 68
 work with other government agencies,
  67
Scientific societies, 81
Scientific society careers
 career preparation, 101–102
 career progression, 103
 communications jobs, 96–97
 dos and don'ts of jobs in, 106
 education jobs, 97–98, 102

executive office, 98–99
history of the APS, 106–107
online resources, 101, 102, 107
a personal experience, 104–105
policy and government relations, 94, 96
policy careers in, 81
positions and opportunities, 93–94
publications, 99–100
related job options, 103–104
sample organization chart, 95*f*
skills and qualifications, 100
Scientist administrators at NIH
about the NIH, 59–61, 60*f*
career preparation, 69–70
career progression, 70, 71*f*
dos and don'ts of jobs in, 75
online resources, 76
organization chart, 62*f*
personal experience of an SRO, 73–74
personal experience of a PO, 72–73
positions at NIH, 59–61
program officer, 62–64
related job options, 70, 74–76
scientific review officer, 65–68
scientific review process, 61
skills and qualifications, 68–69
types of, 60–61
SEB (Society for Experimental Biology), 174
Senior research officer (SRO), 49
Service industry careers, 167–168
Shared instrumentation grants, 24
SHERP (Science, Health, and Environmental Reporting Program), NYU, 186
Simons Foundation Autism Research Initiative (SFARI), 111, 117
Sklott, Rebecca, 184
Small liberal arts colleges
about, 5–6
academic positions available, 7*f*

administration jobs, 8–9
appeal of careers at, 5
applying for a job, 11–14
balancing work and family, 18
being realistic about the resources available, 11
career preparation, 10
career progression, 14–17
college rankings and, 9–10
dos and don'ts of jobs in, 20–21
educational philosophies, 6
expectations of research activity, 9
nontenure track jobs, 8
online resources, 21
a personal experience, 18–20
related job options, 18
skills and qualifications, 9–11
teaching fellowships and, 10–11
tenure track jobs, 7–8
typical career path, 14–15
Society for Experimental Biology (SEB), 174
Society for Neuroscience, 102
Society for Scholarly Publishing, 208
Society of Environmental Journalists, 193
SRO. *See* Scientific review officer, NIH; Senior research officer
Starr, Douglas, 186, 189
STM (science, technical, and medical) journal publishing. *See* Science publishing

T

Teaching. *See also* Small liberal arts colleges
challenges of, 15
fellowships at small liberal arts colleges, 10–11
nontenure track jobs, 8
tenure track jobs, 7–8

Technical specialists, 27, 28, 31–32, 37
Technology Exchange Portal, 143
Technology Incubator Program, University of Connecticut, 141
Technology transfer jobs, 51
Tenure track jobs, 6–8
"The Scholarly Kitchen," 208
Trends in Immunology, 211
Trends in Parasitology , 211
Twitter, 183

U

UCONN Ventures, 144
Usajobs.gov, 69
U.S. Department of Agriculture (USDA), 51
U.S. News and World Report, 9

V

Visiting professorships, 8

W

Washington Monthly, The, 9
Watson, Jim, 211, 212
Web editors for journals, 204–205
Williams, Andrew, 185
Wired, 183
WordPress, 183
Writing careers. *See* Medical communications; Science journalism and writing; Science publishing

Y

Yale Entrepreneurial Institute, 141, 143
Yale Journal of Biology and Medicine, 209
Yong, Ed, 185

Z

Zimmer, Carl, 184